T0326448

# Capital Without Borders

# Capital Without Borders

## Challenges to Development

Edited by

Ashwini Deshpande

ANTHEM PRESS
LONDON · NEW YORK · DELHI

Anthem Press
An imprint of Wimbledon Publishing Company
*www.anthempress.com*

This edition first published in UK and USA 2010
by ANTHEM PRESS
75-76 Blackfriars Road, London SE1 8HA, UK
or PO Box 9779, London SW19 7ZG, UK
and
244 Madison Ave. #116, New York, NY 10016, USA

© 2010 Ashwini Deshpande editorial matter and selection;
individual chapters © individual contributors

*British Library Cataloguing in Publication Data*
A catalogue record for this book is available from the British Library.

*Library of Congress Cataloging in Publication Data*
A catalog record for this book has been requested.

ISBN-13: 978 1 84331 838 5 (Hbk)
ISBN-10: 1 84331 838 5 (Hbk)

ISBN-13: 978 0 85728 957 5 (eBook)
ISBN-10: 0 85728 957 8 (eBook)

# TABLE OF CONTENTS

*Acknowledgements*                                                                                    vii

*List of Contributors*                                                                                 ix

1. Introduction                                                                                        1
   *Ashwini Deshpande*

2. How Financial Liberalization Led in the 1990s to Three
   Different Cycles of 'Manias, Panics and Crashes' in Middle-
   Income Countries                                                                                    11
   *José Gabriel Palma*

3. Timing the Mexican 1994–95 Financial Crisis using
   a Markov Switching Approach                                                                         39
   *Moritz Cruz and Edmund Amann*

4. Exchange Rates, Growth and Inflation: What If the Income
   Elasticities of Trade Flows Respond to Relative Prices?                                             53
   *Nelson H. Barbosa-Filho*

5. Alternative Measures of Currency and Asset Substitution:
   The Case of Turkey                                                                                  71
   *A. Özden Birkan*

6. Competitive Diversification in Resource Abundant Countries:
   Argentina after the Collapse of the Convertibility Regime                                           89
   *Leandro Serino*

7. Foreign Portfolio Investment, Stock Market and Economic
   Development: A Case Study in India                                                                  121
   *Parthapratim Pal*

8. Transnational Corporations and the Internationalization of
   Research and Development Activities in Developing Countries:
   The Relative Importance of Affiliates in Asia and Latin America    147
   *Célio Hiratuka*

9. External Debt Nationalization as a Major Tendency on Brazilian
   External Debt in the Twentieth Century: The Shifting Character
   of the State during Debt Crisis                                   165
   *Luiz M. Niemeyer*

10. Prudential Regulation and Safety Net:
    Recent Transformations in Brazil                                 187
    *Ana Rosa Ribeiro de Mendonça*

11. Re-crafting Bilateral Investment Treaties in a Development
    Framework: A Comparative Regional Perspective                    209
    *Biplove Choudhary and Parashar Kulkarni*

# ACKNOWLEDGEMENTS

The Annual Conference on Development and Change (ACDC) started in 2005 as a three year initiative with a grant from the Ford Foundation, New York, and was housed at the Carnegie Council of Ethics and International Affairs, New York. The ACDC, with the mission statement of 'promoting development in a globalized world', was formed with the belief that it was necessary to go beyond critiques of the current globalization process and offer concrete alternatives, grounded in the specific realities of developing countries. With this understanding, the mandate of the ACDC was to consolidate the group of *young* scholars and practitioners associated with different heterodox networks and organizations across the globe and to showcase their policy oriented research through annual conferences. The pool of applicants to the first conference in India was mainly from the alumni of the Cambridge Advanced Program on Rethinking Development Economics (CAPORDE), but by the time of the second conference, the ACDC had active involvement and participation of alumni of several different networks, the chief amongst which were the GEM (Gender and Macroeconomics) and ACE (Association of Caribbean Economists). The second conference was held at Campos do Jordao in Brazil in November 2006. This volume is a collection of selected papers, addressing the broad theme of international capital flows, from the second ACDC. While the majority of the participants were young, relatively unknown scholars, the discussion at the conference benefited immensely from the presence of several voices of wisdom and experience: Jose Antonio Ocampo of the UN, Manuel Montes (who during his years at the Ford Foundation was the chief progenitor of the ACDC), then at the UNDP, Marcio Pochman and Mariano Laplane, both from Campinas University, Brazil and Gabriel Palma from the University of Cambridge. I would also like to thank the Anthem Press for their interest in our work. Members of the steering committee: Keith Nurse, Codrina Rada, Peter Jacobs, Emel Memis and especially Luiz Niemeyer (being the local organizer) worked very hard to make the second ACDC exciting and intellectually stimulating. Thus, the conference and this volume would not have been possible without the teamwork of the ACDC steering committee and the tremendous enthusiasm of the presenters, discussants, panelists and participants.

Ashwini Deshpande
Chairperson, ACDC

# LIST OF CONTRIBUTORS

**Ashwini Deshpande** is a professor of economics at the Department of Economics, Delhi School of Economics, University of Delhi, India. She was a part of the first Cambridge Advanced Programme On Rethinking Development Economics in 2001 and returned the next year as a deputy director. She is interested in issues related to globalization and development and her specific research areas are: the economics of discrimination; inequality and inter-group disparities, with a focus on caste and gender in India; international debt; and aspects of the Chinese economy. She has published several papers in leading economics journals and is the editor of "Boundaries of Clan and Color: Transnational comparisons of inter-group disparity" (with William Darity, Jr.), Routledge, London, 2003, and "Globalisation and Development: A handbook of new perspectives", Oxford University Press, 2007.

**Edmund Amann** is a reader in development economics at the University of Manchester, Visiting Professorial Lecturer at The Paul H. Nitze School for Advanced International Studies, Johns Hopkins University and Lemann Visiting Professor at the Department of Economics at the University of Illinois. His research centres on the study of the economies of Latin America, especially Brazil. His work focuses on themes of industrial competitiveness, technological change and export dynamism. He is also interested in regulation and competition policy.

**Nelson Barbosa-Filho** received his PhD in economics from The New School for Social Research. He is currently a professor at the Federal University of Rio de Janeiro (UFRJ) and Secretary of Economic Policy at the Brazilian Ministry of Finance.

**A. Özden Birkan** was awarded her PhD in economics at the University of Utah in 2008. Previously she had received a MSc in economics in 1998 at the Middle East Technical University, Turkey. She is currently a lecturer at the Department of Economics, Yasar University, Izmir, Turkey. Her research interests include political economy of industrialization, Post Keynesian monetary theory, Marxian monetary theory, monetary policy, open economy macroeconomics and international economics. Her current research is on inflation targeting in developing economies and alternative monetary policy frameworks.

**Biplove Choudhary** is a development economist working as Officer-in-Charge and Programme Specialist with the UNDP Regional Centre for Asia and Pacific based in Colombo. He has a doctorate in foreign trade policy from the Jawaharlal Nehru University, New Delhi, India. At the UNDP, he works on regional cooperation and integration related programmes including promotion of inclusive and human development friendly South-South regional trade and investment agreements. His current research interests include work on services sector and on south-south trade cooperation arrangements.

**Moritz Cruz** was awarded his PhD in economics at the University of Manchester in 2005. Previously he received an MSc in economics at Mexico's National University (UNAM). Since 2005 he has been with the Institute for Economic Research (UNAM) as a Researcher, and he also supports the faculty of economics as Lecturer in its master and doctoral programmes. Moritz's main fields of interest are macroeconomics and development economics. His recent work has focused on the impact of trade and financial liberalisation on growth and development. He has also developed some studies on the impact of private remittances on growth and the role of international reserves accumulation as a source of financial stability.

**Célio Hiratuka** received his PhD in economics from the State University of Campinas (UNICAMP), Brazil. His main fields of interest are international economics, technological change, industrial policy and development economics. He is currently Assistant Professor at the Institute of Economics of State University of Campinas and researcher at the Center of Industrial and Technology Economics (NEIT) in the same University. His most recent works focuses on the impacts of transnational corporations and foreign direct investment in the Brazilian economy. He is also member of the Mercosur Economic Research Network, a research institution that links twelve research centres with broad experience in the analysis of the MERCOSUR integration process.

**Ana Rosa Ribeiro de Mendonça** received her PhD in economics from the Economics Institute at Campinas State University in 2002. She now works at Campinas State University as lecturer and research fellow at CERI (Center of International Economics Studies) and NEIT (Center of Industrial and

Technology Studies). Her main fields of interest are Keynesian Macroeconomics, Financial and Monetary Economics. Her most recent work focuses on bank regulation, public banks in Brazil and Employee Guarantee Fund.

**Luiz M. Niemeyer** is currently Associate Professor at the economics department of the Catholic University of Sao Paulo (PUC-SP). He holds an MA in economics from PUC-SP and a PhD in economics from the New School University (2000). In 2005, he was a Visiting Professor at Denver University's Graduate School of International Studies. In 2003, he was Deputy Director of the third Cambridge Advanced Program on Rethinking Development Economics. He has also taught at St. John's University, New York, and the State University of New York. Luiz has published several articles in Brazil and a book, *Brazil's External Debt in the 1990s in a Historical Perspective: The Role of Short-Term Portfolio Investment and the Shifting Character of the Brazilian State during Debt Crises*, which is available in English through University Microfilm, Ann Arbor, MI. His research areas are international finance, economic development, and monetary economics.

**Parthapratim Pal** is Assistant Professor at the Indian Institute of Management (IIM), Calcutta. He has a PhD from Jawaharlal Nehru University in New Delhi. He has worked in the areas of macroeconomics, development, financial markets and international economy. Before joining IIM, he worked with the Indian Council for Research in International Economic Relations, the Economic Research Foundation, and the Indian Institute of Foreign Trade. Partha was a fellow at the first Cambridge Advanced Programme on Rethinking Development Economics in 2001 and a fellow at the International Working Group on Gender and Macroeconomics in Utah in 2003.

**José Gabriel Palma** is a University Senior Lecturer at the Faculty of Economics, University of Cambridge. His research interests include the economic development of Latin America and East Asia, their integration within the global economy, and the study of these economies from the point of view of their economic history, macroeconomics, international trade and international finance.

**Leandro Serino** obtained a PHD in Development Studies from the International Institute of Social Studies (ISS) of Erasmus University Rotterdam, The Netherlands, for an investigation entitled "Productive Diversification in Natural Resource Abundant Countries: Limitations, Policies and the Experience of Argentina in the 2000s". He is at present working as a lecturer at the National University of General Sarmiento (UNGS) and is collaborating with the Ministry of Economy and Finances of the Argentine Economy (MECON) to update Argentina's Social Accounting Matrix and develop a Computable General Equilibrium model. Leandro was working at MECON as an adviser to the Secretary of Economic Policy and coordinating a research unit in 2008 and 2009. In recent years he has been working on topics related to the 2007 international financial and economic crisis, applied macroeconomics and development economics. Leandro was a consultant for ECLAC Argentina, where he developed the demo of an encyclopedia on development economics (www.cepalnacionesunidas.com.ar). He was also involved in teaching and research at *the* University of General Sarmiento and the University of Buenos Aires (UBA) in Argentina. He graduated as an economist at UBA, and completed a Master in Science in Development Economics in 2003 (jointly dictated by the ISS, Free University Amsterdam and Wageningen University).

# Chapter 1

# INTRODUCTION

## Ashwini Deshpande
Department of Economics, Delhi School of Economics

The introduction to this volume was first written in August 2008 with this opening paragraph: 'The global economy is reeling under one of the severest crises since the Great Depression of the 1930s, with record high oil prices, the global food crisis and a financial crisis, reverberating across the globe. As the US economy slides deeper towards a full-fledged recession, precipitated by the sub-prime mortgage crisis, the ability of financial markets to play havoc with the "real" economy could not have been more apparent. While some commentators, especially those associated with the mainstream media, are still debating the extent of the downturn in the US economy and defending the innovative aspects of financial markets, inside the US, the grim reality seems to have hit home. The implications of the collapse of the housing boom, the associated collapse of major banks with high exposure in the housing markets, coupled with the financial burden of the Iraq war has meant rising unemployment, cut back in consumer spending and overall economic downturn, with no signs of reversal in sight. These events bring to the fore the myriad connections between the "real" and the "financial" – and point to the urgency of understanding these connections, especially in the present era of globalization and financial deregulation.'

Exactly a year later, with a series of bank collapses, as the developed economies grapple with stimulus/rescue packages and bail-out measures to counter the cascading impact of lay-offs and closures, the debate is not whether this is a recession but on how bad it will get before it starts to get better. The terms of the discussion have shifted decisively: kudos to financial innovation have given way to demands for prudential regulation that ensure safety of investors' savings; an active role of the government in the economy is no longer seen as anathema as creation of new jobs to counter the increasing unemployment takes utmost priority; indeed, a wider role of the state in ensuring a welfare safety net is seen as inescapable. This enormous shift in the terms of the debate, several aspects of which validate the concerns of the ACDC, would not have been possible without this deep crisis.

While the spread and depth of the current events was not foreseen at the conference, all the participants, as is evident in the selection of studies that follow, were concerned about the implications of under-regulated financial flows and were very aware of the possible adverse consequences of a financial crisis on the real economy. At the time, some of these commentaries could have been dismissed as the usual anti—globalization rhetoric. However, given the turn of events in the real economy, when several of the pro-globalizers too are now raising questions about the implications of unbridled globalization and deregulation and are especially concerned about governance issues, the concerns raised by the collection in this volume not only stands up to scrutiny, but in fact, highly relevant.

The title of Gabriel Palma's chapter sums up the central concern of the volume: *How Financial Liberalization Led in the 1990s to Three Different Cycles of 'Manias, Panic and Crashes' in Middle Income Countries*. He focuses on four major financial crises that hit middle income countries since the 1982 debt crisis: Mexico 1994, East and South East Asia 1997, Brazil 1999 and Argentina 2001. The common characteristic of these crises was that all these countries had recently opened up their capital accounts at a time when international liquidity was high and the investment options in the OECD countries were limited. Palma identifies three different routes that these countries followed to absorb the sudden and large increase in inflows and shows that each of these routes ended up in a financial crisis in the recipient country. We can call this the crisis of absorption. He contrasts these crises with the better experience of India, China and Taiwan: countries that avoided financial crises due to their cautious and selective approach to opening up their capital accounts and integration with international financial markets.

Under Route 1, characterized by Mexico (1988–1994), the surge in inflows led to a pro-cyclical revaluation of the real exchange rate, explosion of credit to the private sector, consumption boom, asset bubbles and a massive deterioration in the current account. Route 2, characterized by Brazil (1994–1999), resulted in high interest rates and an aggressive sterilization of inflows led to fragilities in the banking system and public sector finance. Route 3, seen in Korea (1988–1997), led to very high corporate debt-equity ratios and made the balance sheets of banks vulnerable to currency depreciation. As was the case during the 1970s surge of international lending, Palma discusses how these high volumes of inflows (in Brazil, for example, as high as 129 percent of its exports in 1998) were a result of a combination of push and pull factors.

What needs to be noted and understood, especially in retrospect, is that during the time that a surge in lending/capital inflows is taking place, mainstream contemporary commentaries see it as yet another indicator of global integration, of soundness of markets and of 'good fundamentals' in the recipient countries. In this phase of mania, those who advocate a more cautious and/or a regulatory approach to financial inflows are branded as doomsayers and Cassandras. The other point worth noting is that despite the different end uses to which the inflows are directed, any 'excessive' volume of inflows is bound to create absorption problems and therefore is bound to be unsustainable. For example, under Palma's Route 1, the inflows were largely directed towards consumption whereas under Route 3, they were used to increase corporate investments.

How does one determine whether financial inflows are 'excessive' or not? Again, one of the big lessons from the 1970s debt explosion and the subsequent crisis is that international financial and regulatory bodies have a big role to play in determining warning signals and critical threshold levels and ranges of sustainability, so that both national governments as well as private agents have benchmark values of key indicators that serve as warning signals indicating how vulnerable, if at all, they are to a financial crisis. Indeed, the work of many scholars, such as Ilene Grabel, has shown that such warning systems can easily be put in place, provided the international investor community is willing to be supervised.

Palma's point is that given the sheer volume of inflows that the four countries in his study experienced, a crisis is inevitable. However, when a financial crisis erupts, many other explanations are offered. One of the most common and popular explanations offered is that investors start withdrawing their capital out of the recipient country as soon as they feel that the economic fundamentals are diverging from conditions that are considered 'sound' and of course, especially in emerging economies, the impact of ebbing investor confidence can be devastating.

Edmund Amman and Moritz Cruz's chapter *Timing the Mexican 1994–5 Crisis Using the Markov Switching Approach* attempts to examine the validity of this very common explanation. They find that there is superficial support to this explanation but raise the important point about the need to make a distinction between an objective phenomenon (change in fundamentals) and the subjective perception of agents. They argue that a change in the subjective perception is not always backed by changes in the objective fundamentals. Their basic point reinforces Palma's analysis: that the Mexican crisis was not accompanied by a deterioration of external or internal balance (the two key fundamentals), but rather, was the result of the growing exposure of private agents to risk because of their high accumulated debt levels.

They propose an alternative approach, strongly influenced by Minsky, to quantify changes in investor confidence by looking at the broad-money-to-international – reserves ratio as the key variable. The larger this ratio, the lower is the ability of the country to weather a speculative currency attack. In the case of the Mexican crisis, they identify which events contributed to the start and end of a financial crisis.

The events that eventually ended the financial crisis in Mexico merit special mention. The first one was an announcement by the government to further reinforce the liberalization agenda, especially the plan for trade and financial deregulation. Second, the government decided to honor the outstanding debts. Thus, in order to regain investor confidence, it had to reinforce the precise measures that had led to the crisis in the first place! This highlights very accurately how, for developing countries, the path of non-selective and unregulated opening up of the capital account constrains policy options both ex-ante and ex-post. The only way to regain investor confidence following a financial crisis (that follows opening up) is to open up even more.

Does all this suggest that developing countries have very few, if any at all, policy options left? Undoubtedly, policy autonomy is constrained in a globalized world. However, the purpose of this volume, in addition to highlighting the constraints, is also to suggest policy options. The beauty of the next chapter is that it manages to do both tasks elegantly. Since developing countries cannot issue international currency, they typically have to adjust their current account to the availability of foreign finance. Thus, their GDP targets, as well as their ability to intervene in the determination of the exchange rate, is thus constrained by the availability of external finance. Nelson Barbosa-Filho's contribution examines this very crucial constraint rigorously. The chapter argues that rather than being an inevitable constraint, the BOP determinants of economic growth can be shaped by economic policy and thus can become endogenous in the long run, as the examples of China and some of the East Asian economies demonstrate.

Barbosa-Filho extends Thirlwall's model of BOP constraint (in the long run, an open economy must have balanced growth of imports and exports) to include debt and financial variables, thus making a direct link with financial fragility, i.e. the idea that changes in international financial conditions can lead to currency crises and thus have an impact on growth, independently of trade movements. The implication of this adjustment, in the short run with constant trade elasticities, is that the trade surplus of the home country has to adjust to maintain liquidity ratios that would put it beyond the risk of currency crises. However, in the long run, there is no reason to assume that trade elasticities will be constant, and thus, the very elements that constitute the BOP constraint are likely to change. Thus, the chapter shows, in line with other heterodox research, that macroeconomic policy can influence growth in the long run.

The chapter then discusses how the *level* of the real exchange rate, (as opposed to its rate of change), via its effect on the prices of tradables versus non-tradables sector, can influence both the BOP constraint as well as growth. Thus the real exchange rate, in this scenario, is potentially a key policy variable. Mainstream economists are skeptical about the use of the real exchange rate, as it is supposed to be stationary in the long run. However, Barbosa-Filho argues that in the short run, effective management of the exchange rate can produce structural changes (e.g. growth of the tradable sector) to affect the BOP constraint in the desired direction. Additionally, especially for Latin American economies, the issue of inflation targeting is as crucial as that of growth, but the author cautions against a policy of inflation reduction that produces an appreciation of the currency, as it could be detrimental to growth.

Ozden Birkan's contribution on currency and asset substitution in Turkey discusses the complications introduced by the existence of multiple currencies in Turkey since 1989 when all controls on international capital movements were lifted. This policy brought in its wake huge challenges to government in its attempt to control its balance sheet, made more complicated by international events like the First Gulf War but mainly because of the unsustainable nature of government finance. This created a fragile financial environment and eventually led to a crisis in 1994, with a heavily depreciated Turkish Lira, loss of reserves by the Central Bank, soaring interest rates, bankruptcies in the banking sector and reduced growth. This was followed by another crisis in 1998 when external financial flows slowed down due to the East Asian and Russian crises.

Her econometric investigation points towards substantial irreversibility in currency substitution (use of multiple currencies as media of exchange), which does not mean that most transactions are carried out in foreign currencies, but that the liquidity of Turkish Lira denominated assets has been declining and those of foreign exchange denominated assets has been rising.

Confirming the conclusions of Barobsa-Filho, Birkan discusses how the policy of inflation targeting has involved a real appreciation of the exchange rate, which has successfully lowered inflation, but at the cost of increasing the vulnerability of the economy to foreign shocks, and additionally causing problems such as persistent current account deficits, fragile banking structures and no reduction in unemployment.

Several of the developing countries are abundant in natural resources and potentially their comparative advantage in this sector should enable them to take advantage of gains from trade and thus enable a diversification of their economic structures. Leandro Serino's contribution highlights the structural limitations to diversification in resource abundant countries like Argentina. Serino's model shows how the presence of a high productivity natural resource sector (like the agricultural sector in Argentina) constrains the development of other tradables sector and thus prevents competitive diversification.

The main results of his chapter show the following: an increase in productivity in the natural resource sector will lead to an increase in nominal and real wages: an increase that is positively associated with the size of the natural resource sector, but with ambiguous effects on employment. There is a size effect: if the natural resource sector is as large as it is in oil exporting countries, then a positive shock can lead to an increase in employment.

Other than this, the other effects that favor an increase in employment are productivity differences between the tradable manufacturing sector and the natural resource sector. Coming to external balance, the model points out conditions under which a positive shock will *not* lead to an improvement in the trade balance. Thus, resource abundance can hinder competitive diversification through a negative impact on the trade balance. However, the model also highlights why resource abundant countries need to diversify.

What could be the macroeconomic policies that would increase the productivity of the non-resource (manufacturing) sector? Serino discusses nominal devaluation as the main policy that enhances overall competitiveness, increasing employment and increasing the external balance. A traditional result in the literature shows that a devalued exchange rate increases the price of natural resource products, further reducing the real wages. What Serino shows is that since large decreases in real wages do not improve the competitiveness of the manufacturing sector, devaluation is more costly in economies with structural characteristics like Argentina that in economies with different structural characteristics. His analysis has another noteworthy result that is often omitted in other studies: creation of devaluation rents favoring the most productive natural resource sector. On balance, thus, in economies with abundant natural resources, devaluation has some clear benefits (e.g. increase in employment through tradable diversification), but with significant costs (e.g. decrease in real wages and a worsening of income distribution through the creation of devaluation rents. However, an export tax can transfer the rent to the government, which it can use to promote diversification policies, and presumably reverse the worsening of the income distribution.

Going a step further, the model endogenizes productivity growth that might come about indirectly (via expansion of output and scale economies) through devaluation. The model shows that Kaldor Verdoorn effects can reduce, or even reverse, the negative effects of devaluations on real wages. At this stage, the study draws our attention to the role of non-tradable productive linkages such as physical, technological and commercial infrastructure. Serino suggests that the export tax, discussed earlier, could actually be used to finance this infrastructure in order to reap full benefits of devaluation and to promote competitive diversification.

Whereas Palma's chapter focused on problems inherent in the absorption of a large volume of inflows, Parthapratim Pal's chapter, through the Indian case study, discusses how the presumed benefits of foreign portfolio investment (FPI) may not actually materialize because of the inadequate development of real sector linkages. India is more dependent on FPI than FDI and this is making India's private financial flows increasingly stock market dependent. Pal assesses the validity of mainstream arguments in favor of FPI (a source of non debt creating financial flows, improves allocative efficiency, creates various linkages via the domestic capital market, stimulates the development of the domestic stock market) and finds for instance, that the growth of the stock market need not always have a positive impact on the real economy, due to, say speculative trading. However, taking these claims at their face value, Pal finds that indeed, the large inflow of FPI in the second half of the 1990s via the FIIs has indeed stimulated the growth of the stock market, but the big spurt has been to the secondary component of the stock market, whereas the expected strengthening of the linkages with the real sector have not materialized.

The expectation was that the large volume of trading on the stock market would open up new sources of finance for Indian firms. However, capital raised (both the number of new issues as well as the money raised) through new issues by non-government firms after an initial increase, showed a continuous decline after 1995. Pal effectively demonstrates that this decline *does not* reflect a condition of stagnating or declining domestic demand. It is really the resource mobilization from the primary market as a proportion of gross capital formation that has been falling, such that in 2002–3, this ratio was a mere 1.6 percent. Pal shows that instead of the primary component of the stock market, it is the private placement market that has been a source of finance for private firms. Transactions in the private placement market are exempt from most of the rules that govern primary issues in the stock market and it is, thus, a largely unregulated market. As a result of this, FPI which is channeled through the stock market, has not been able to stimulate the expected linkages with the activities in the real sector.

This also brings the very critical and vexed question of governance of financial flows to the fore, which is almost a running thread in all the chapters. Essentially, private capital either gets legislation that is favorable to its interests or it finds ways of evading regulation wherever and whenever possible. This is an issue with no easy solutions, and we will return to it at the end of this introduction.

The discussion so far has been about financial flows and the bulk of this volume does indeed concern itself with different facets of this particular nature of international capital. Of course, international capital flows take different forms, perhaps the most important being foreign direct investment (FDI). Many would argue that FDI flows bring greater benefits to the host country than FPI. Literature on FDI, and its multi-faceted impact on the host countries, is too huge and contentious to be summarized. In this volume, Celio Hiratuka's study draws our attention to one particular aspect of FDI, that of transnationalization of research and development (R&D) activity. One of presumed benefits of FDI is diffusion of technology from developed to developing countries, via the R&D activities of MNC affiliates in developing countries. Hiratuka examines this claim by looking at the internationalization of R&D laboratories of large MNCs, comparing Latin America and Asia in this regard.

The argument against internationalization of R&D is that it is too costly to reproduce the research environment and other linkages that support high quality research in the home country to relatively underdeveloped host countries. As opposed to this, the argument supporting internationalization of R&D is that this would be a part of the larger phenomenon of transnationalization of production, sales and the search for new markets. A comparison of sales expenditures versus R&D expenditures of American MNCs reveals that the internationalization of sales far exceeds the internationalization of R&D. Not only that, comparing the developed country affiliates with developing country affiliates of American MNCs, Hiratuka finds that in 2003, for instance, as much as 87 percent of R&D expenditure was concentrated in *developed* country affiliates. Thus, the benefits of diffusion of technology largely accrue to other developed countries.

Comparing Asia and Latin America as destinations, he finds that the relative importance of the former has been rising, especially in the internationalization of R&D. Brazil is the country that performs the best in Latin America on this count. The country worth noting is China, the only country in the world where the share of its affiliates in R&D expenditures is actually greater than its share in sales! This again points to the importance of strong domestic policies in the host country that are imperative for the country to extract the maximum advantage for itself. Admittedly, China is more the exception than the rule among developing countries, but the point here is that with the right mix of hard bargaining and strong domestic policies, part of the gains from FDI can be diverted to the home country's advantage.

Governance issues (related to international capital) operate in two domains: national (within the host country) and international. At the moment, the bulk of regulation at both levels is designed to protect the interests of capital. Luiz Niemeyer's contribution suggests how, actually this is a tendency that runs through history. He shows through various debt crises in history, the Brazilian state, under pressure from international capital as well as domestic private debtors, has always taken over the debt risk as well as repayment obligations of the private sector. Thus, it has sought to nationalize the losses but privatized the gains from external debt. Niemeyer takes a long term, historical look at the various episodes of the debt crisis in Brazil since 1906 and finds that the state has a more or less consistent policy of "socialization of losses". The beginnings of this lie in the coffee valorization scheme, by which coffee producers managed to transfer the burden of volatility in coffee production to the rest of the society. The protection from the state came either in the form of nationalization of debt or management of the exchange rate, for instance, by keeping the exchange rate below par, the rest of the society ended up paying for the gains of coffee exporters.

Since the private sector operated with the implicit guarantee from the state that they will be bailed out in case of repayment difficulties, there would be no pressure on the private sector to utilize the lending efficiently and/or to create repayment capacity. Also, this guarantee would obliterate the distinction between risky and safe lending, since from the point of view of the lenders, all borrowers are safe. As it is, there is sufficient evidence in history to show that when lenders are awash with funds and are seeking profitable outlets, they throw routine caution to the winds. This tendency would only get exacerbated with state guaranteeing a bail-out. We see, through this fascinating historical account, how the state can, voluntarily, surrender its autonomy in the interests of private capital.

With Ana Rosa Ribeiro de Mendonça's chapter, the volume enters the policy and regulation arena. Her chapter examines the contributions of the original Basel Accord and the potential contributions of Basel II towards changing the banking sector regulation in Brazil. She finds that prudential regulation as developed in Brazil since the mid-1990s has indeed gone a long way towards making the banking system less vulnerable to shocks and successfully prevented a crisis. The belief is that the costs of this regulation are lower than the costs to the banking sector and the economy, should a banking crisis erupt.

Biplove Chaudhury and Parashar Kulkarni examine the impact of regulation on FDI by focusing on bilateral investment treaties (BITs). In principle, BITs are supposed to provide an enabling environment such that the rights and duties of investors as well as recipient countries are protected. This gives rise to the belief is that BITs are necessary to increase the flow of FDI. In practice, though, a treaty might not be as balanced as it is supposed to be. Given the global competition for investment, recipient countries are aggressively wooing foreign investors and offer all kinds of incentive in the form of bilateral agreements. The chapter examines the implications of these treaties and investment promotion efforts in the context of two case studies: the Dabhol power corporation in India and the Cochabamba water privatization in Bolivia.

It is believed that the treaties are supposed to favor development, but references to economic development are rare, if any at all. In fact, specific provisions in these treaties could be inhibiting to investors, as has been shown. The authors draw our attention to the dispute settlement clauses and mechanisms in the treaties that are becoming increasingly important. An important extension of investor rights has been the provision that grants investors the right to sue the state under the pretext of expropriation of the business of the firm. However, this is often misused, as investors try to pass off even the normal risks of running a business under the expropriation clause. The dispute resolution process, even though in its infancy, is already marred by controversies and questions about its legitimacy and transparency. The chapter then compares two models of BITs, one developed by India and the other by the International Investment for Sustainable development to demonstrate what kinds of improvements can be made to BITs in order to address the various concerns that have emerged over their content and thrust.

This study, as several others produced by ACDC scholars,[1] demonstrates that there are concrete, well worked out, alternatives that should be the basis of discussion and dialogue among the various stakeholders and should be the draft on the basis of which consensus is sought to be achieved. Of course, the compulsions of *realpolitik* imply that in order to achieve change, we might start with an alternative formulation but have to take it much beyond and place it, irreversibly, on the agenda of multilateral institutions and national governments. The current crisis has provided the much needed breakthrough in widening and expanding the terms of the debate. It remains to be seen whether the leadership of the industrialized world seizes the opportunities to actually implement a new paradigm of development or ends up succumbing to the deeply entrenched vested interests whose actions caused the crisis in the first place.

## Note

1. See, example, studies included in Deshpande, Ashwini (2007): "Globalisation and Development: A Handbook of New Perspectives" Oxford University Press, New Delhi.

# Chapter 2

# HOW FINANCIAL LIBERALIZATION LED IN THE 1990s TO THREE DIFFERENT CYCLES OF 'MANIAS, PANICS AND CRASHES' IN MIDDLE-INCOME COUNTRIES

## José Gabriel Palma[1]

Faculty of Economics, Cambridge University

'I can [understand and] calculate the motions of the heavenly bodies, but not the madness of [the South Sea Bubble] people.'

Isaac Newton

## Introduction

Four major financial crises have struck middle-income developing countries (DCs) since the 1982 debt-crisis: Mexico in 1994 (and the subsequent 'Tequila-effect' in Argentina); East and Southeast Asia in 1997; Brazil in 1999; and Argentina in 2001.

Two common characteristics of the these crises are that the countries involved had recently open up their capital accounts, and that they had done so at a time of high liquidity in international financial markets and slow growth in most OECD economies – i.e., at a time when an over-liquid, highly volatile and under-regulated international financial market was anxiously seeking new high-yield investment opportunities.[2]

The first part of this paper will attempt to show that no matter how diversely these financially liberalised DCs tried to deal with the absorption problem created by sudden surges in capital inflows, they inevitably ended up in financial crisis via a Kindlebergian cycle of 'mania, panic and crash'. However, there is a clear distinction between the Latin American and the East Asian crisis-building pattern; furthermore, within Latin America there is a further distinction between Brazil (where there was a major policy attempt to avoid the Kindlebergian cycle via an aggressive sterilisation of inflows) and the other crises countries of the region. Therefore, I have identified not two but three different ways in which DCs tried to deal (all unsuccessfully) with these inflow-surges, and have concluded that each of them led to financial crisis via a different 'route'; these are best illustrated by the Mexican (1988–1994), the Brazilian (1994–1999) and the Korean (1988–1997) experiences.

These three routes (from now on called 'route-1' for Mexico, 'route-2' for Brazil, and 'route-3' for Korea) will include the experiences of other crisis-countries, as for example the Chilean case leading to its 1982 crisis ('route-1'), those of Malaysia and Thailand leading to their 1997 crises ('route-3', but with some components of 'route-1'), and the Argentinian case leading to its 2001 crisis also following most of the crucial components of the Mexican 'route-1' – especially until its first 'Tequila' crisis in 1995.[3]

This paper further attempts to show that all three routes, but especially 'routes-1' and '2', led to financial crises in ways that have little to do with the financial processes described in second and third generation models of financial crises, in particularly (in Krugman's terminology) their supposed 'undeserved' and 'unpredictable' nature (Krugman, 2001). The key proposition of this paper is that the common feature of all 'routes' to financial crises are economies that opted to integrate into international capital markets with open capital accounts and then were unable to absorb the subsequent surge of inflows. The experiences of China, India and Taiwan during the same period show that a more selective path of participation in international capital markets is a far more effective way of avoiding both the pro-cyclical dynamics of unrestricted capital flows, and the huge costs associated to stampedes by restless fund managers (so prone to oscillating between manias and panics).

## The 'Three Routes' to Financial Crisis

Figure 1 shows the crucial issue at stake, common to *all* crisis-countries: the remarkable surge in inflows on the heels of financial liberalisation.

The turnaround is extraordinary: (in US$ of 2007 value) the difference in both periods amounts to $242 billion in Brazi, $173 billion in Argentina, $95 billion in Mexico, and $284 billion in the three East Asian countries.[5] These surges are even more impressive in relative terms. In Chile, they switched from a level equivalent to 45% of exports to 130%. In Argentina, net private inflows in 1993 (i.e., just before its first crisis following Mexico's 1994 one) were equivalent to 122% of exports, and net FDI inflows alone were on average equivalent to half the level of exports in the five-year period 1995–99

Figure 1 A: Latin America and East Asia: Aggregate Net Private Capital Flows before Financial Liberalisation and between Financial Liberalisation and Financial Crisis

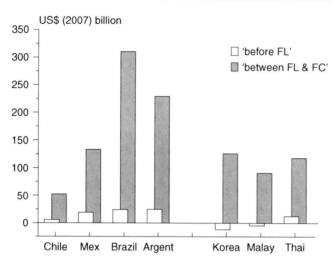

Figure 1 B: Latin America and East Asia: Aggregate Net Private Capital Flows before Financial Liberalisation and between Financial Liberalisation and Financial Crisis as % of Exports

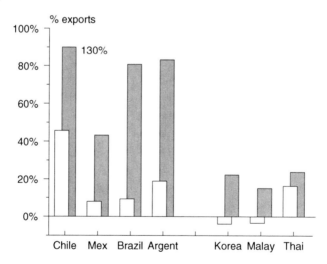

(and in 1999 equivalent to half the level of gross fixed capital formation). In Brazil, net private inflows in 1998 achieved a level equivalent to 129% of exports, and net FDI inflows peaked in 1998 at 56% the level of exports. In Chile and Malaysia, net private inflows reached 13% of GDP (1981 and 1993, respectively); in Chile during the second period (1975–82) they were

Figure 1 C: Latin America and East Asia: Aggregate Net Private Capital Flows
before Financial Liberalisation and between Financial Liberalisation and Financial Crisis
as % of GDP

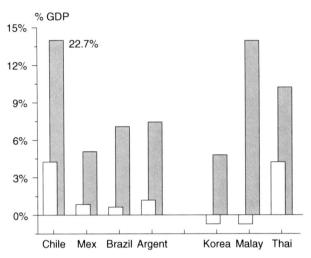

Figure 1 D: Latin America and East Asia: Aggregate Net Private Capital Flows
before Financial Liberalisation and between Financial Liberalisation and Financial
Crisis as % of Savings

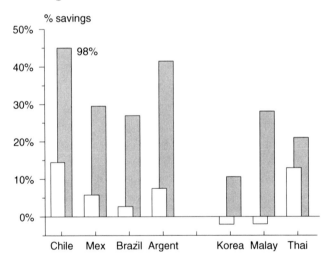

• **FL**=financial liberalisation; **FC**=financial crisis; **Mex**=Mexico; **Argent**=Argentina;
**Malay**=Malaysia; and **Thai**=Thailand.
• In each case the period '**between**' covers the years between financial liberalisation and financial
crisis – Chile, 1975–82; Mexico, 1990–94; Brazil, 1992–98; Argentina, 1991–2001; Korea,
1991–96; Malaysia, 1989–96; and Thailand, 1988–96. The period '**before**' covers a similar
number of years before financial liberalisation (in the case of East Asia and Argentina, however, as
the period 'before' would have included years preceding the previous 1982 debt crisis, only years
since 1982 have been included).
• *Source*: World Bank (2007a and b).[4]

also equivalent to gross domestic savings, and to $1,171 per capita (1981); and in Argentina they reached an average of $743 per capita in the four-year period between 1996–1999.[6]

In fact, some of these countries even began to be important players in the newly developed derivatives markets; for example, according to the IMF, in the 'Asia Pacific' market, the 'notional principal amount' outstanding for some selected derivatives grew (in current $) from just over $1 billion in 1986 to $2.4 trillion in 1996.

As mentioned above, the key proposition of this paper is that the common feature of all 'routes' to financial crises are economies that opted to integrate into international capital markets with open capital accounts and then were unable to absorb the subsequent surge of inflows. The experiences of China, India and Taiwan during the same period show both that unrestricted integration into international capital markets was not the only choice open to DCs, and that a more selective path of participation in international capital markets is a far more effective way of avoiding the pro-cyclical dynamics of unrestricted capital flows, and the huge costs associated to stampedes by restless fund managers (so prone to oscillating between manias and panics).

According to which of the three crises-routes was actually followed, the specific financial fragilities that began to emerge were, of course, varied: for example, in 'route-1' countries (e.g., Mexico) the surge in inflows led to (pro-cyclical) rapid revaluation of real-exchange rates, an explosion of credit to the private sector, consumption booms, asset bubbles and a massive deterioration in current accounts. In 'route-2' (Brazil), high interest rates and aggressive sterilisation of inflows, implemented to mitigate the pro-cyclical effects of massive inflows, helped instead to create other equally damaging financial fragilities (e.g., in the banking system and in the public-sector finance). And, in 'route-3' (Korea), the surge of inflows allowed corporate debt/equity ratios of remarkable heights and created balance-sheet structures of the banking sector ever more vulnerable to currency depreciation.

To the key question: "why did foreign capital swamp these countries so suddenly?", the answer is twofold: several 'push' and 'pull' factors. The main push factor consisted of 'excess' liquidity in international financial markets – DCs have historically played the role of 'financial market of last resort' (See Palma, 1998); in fact, this role is similar to the one played by the US 'sub-prime' mortgage market during the (highly liquid) financial cycle that followed 9/11. Other push factors included business cycles conditions, changes in interest rates, the rise of institutional investors (such as mutual funds, pension funds, hedge funds), and demographic forces in industrial countries. And among the 'pull' factors the combination of radical economic reforms (in particular privatisation) and the opening up of the capital account in a context of undervalued asset markets, high interest-rate spreads, and expectations of exchange-rate appreciation stood out. In particular, optimism regarding the success of economic reforms in DCs was in excess-supply, partly as a result of the massive 'spin' put on them by those to be found circling around the 'Washington Consensus'. A key characteristic of the 'pull' factors is that they fed into themselves: inflows were attracted by newly created domestic 'magnetism'; these inflows generated pro-cyclical dynamics, which attracted more inflows. Finally, a crucial 'pull' factor (at least until the last Argentinian crisis) was the 'moral hazard' created by the near-certainty in international financial markets that, as in every good old Western, the cavalry, in the form of a vast international rescue operation, could be counted upon to arrive in the nick of time, should the 'natives' threaten to default or close their capital account.

### The Latin American Story: To Sterilise or Not to Sterilise a Mainly 'Exogenous Push' of Foreign Capital – Route-1 vs. Route-2

Figure 2 shows the remarkable levels of two surges of capital inflows into Latin America and their (changing) composition.

Excluding FDI inflows into China, the two surges of inflows into Latin America are not only greater and with a more unstable composition than those into East and Southeast Asia but, as Figure 1 showed, they are especially large when looked at from the point of view of their respective exports, GDP and savings.

Figure 2 A: Latin America: Net Capital Inflows, 1950–2007

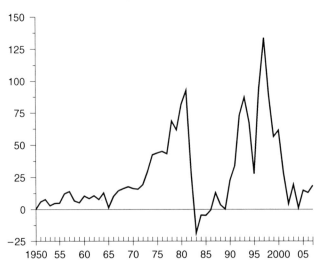

• US$ billions (2007 value).

Figure 2 B: Latin America: Net 'Other' Capital Inflows, 1950–2007

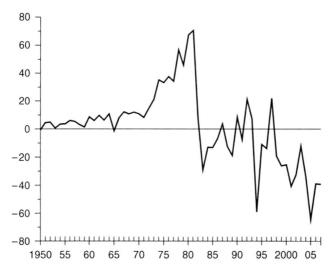

• US$ billions (2007 value).

Figure 2 C: Latin America: Net Inflows of Foreign Direct Investment, 1950–2007

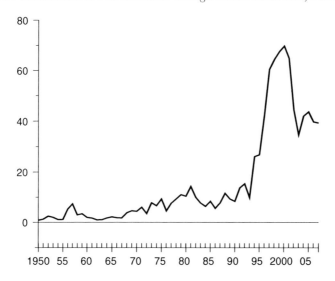

• US$ billions (2007 value).

Figure 3 shows the beginning of the major differences in Latin America between Brazil, which decided to make a massive sterilisation effort ('route-2'), and Chile, Mexico and Argentina, which did not ('route-1').

One response to the surge in private inflows in Latin America was (as in East Asia) to ride them out by unloading them into the economy via credit

Figure 2 D:  Latin America: Net Portfolio Inflows, 1950–2007

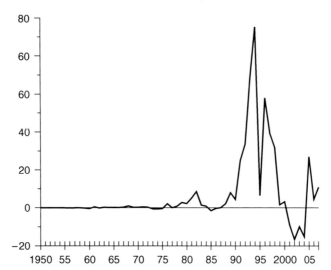

- US$ billions (2007 value).
- *Source*: 1950–1980, data provided by ECLAC Statistical Division; 1980–2007, IMF (2007)

Figure 3: East Asia and Latin America: Credit to the Private Sector between the Beginning of Financial Liberalisation and Respective Financial Crisis

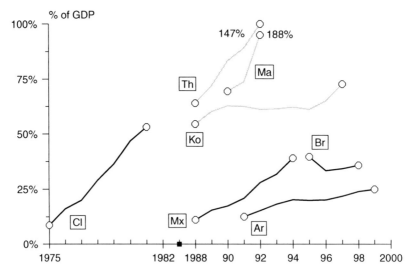

- **[Cl]**=Chile; **[Mx]**=Mexico; **[Ar]**=Argentina; **[Br]**=Brazil; **[Ko]**=Korea; **[Ma]**=Malaysia; and **[Th]**=Thailand. The same notation will be use in the graphs below. The figures for Thailand and Malaysia shown in the graph correspond to 1996 (those for 1997 are 166% and 210%, respectively).

expansion ('route-1');[7] the other (Brazil), was precisely the reverse: to try to stop the resulting pro-cyclical dynamics by placing an 'iron curtain' around them (via the usual mechanism of Central Bank sterilisation of the expansionary effect of inflow).

The crucial factor in understanding the different behaviour of Brazil is the timing of its financial liberalisation (second half of 1994); this practically coincided with the Mexican 1994 crisis. Therefore, high degrees of sterilisation and high interest rates were explicitly continued *after* the successes of the 'Real Plan' in conquering inflation in order to avoid following a Mexican 'route-1' crisis-path.

Even though there was a similarity in the speed of credit expansion between 'route-1' and 'route-3', there also was a crucial difference: the use made of this additional credit; while 'route-1' directed it towards increased consumption and asset speculation (Figures 4 and 5), 'route-3' (particularly the paradigmatic case of Korea) did so towards corporate investment (Figure 10). The difference between these two routes was also related to the 'magnetism' that first of all attracted these inflows: in 'route-3' it was an 'endogenous pull' – additional

Figure 4: Latin America and East Asia: Imports of Consumer Goods between the Beginning of Financial Liberalisation and Respective Financial Crisis

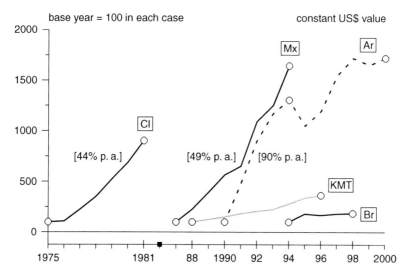

• **[KMT]**=average of Korea, Malaysia and Thailand. Percentages shown in the graph are average *annual* rates of growth. The percentage for Argentina corresponds to 1990–94 (i.e., between financial liberalisation and its first financial crisis).[8] Current US$ were transformed into constant US$ of 2000 value using price indices for imports (unit value) for each country (specific price indices for imports of consumer goods were not available).

Figure 5: Latin America and East Asia: Annual Stock Market Indices between the
Beginning of Financial Liberalisation and Respective Financial Crisis

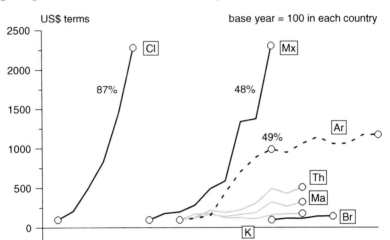

• For the clarity of the graph, the Argentinian data are shown as a 3-year moving average. The
percentages shown are average *annual* growth-rates; Argentina's rate refers to the 'pre-tequila'
period – i.e., up to the 1994 Mexican crisis.
• *Sources*: DataStream (the S&P/IFCG M index; see also IFC, 2004).

finance was actually needed to sustain high levels of investment in high-
technology activities at a time of rapidly falling profit-levels. In routes '1' and '2'
instead, it was rather an 'exogenous push' movement of foreign capital into these
countries, which then had to practically 'create' a domestic need for itself. The
age-old mechanism was then followed: additional inflows increase the amount,
reduce the price, ease the access and reduce the transaction costs of credit. A side
effect of easy credit was a surge in expectations and animal spirits. This process
reinforced itself, becoming (for a while) a self-fulfilling prophecy. Easy access to
cheap credit fuelled expectations regarding the performance of the economy, a
performance that was enhanced by the additional expenditure brought about by
extra borrowing and availability of foreign exchange. 'Over-lending' and 'overborrowing' were therefore not only the result of a closely interrelated process, but
also one that had a clear direction of causality: the propensity to 'over-lend' led
to the propensity to 'over-borrow'.

Finally, the cases of Malaysia and Thailand are characterised by having
one foot in each camp. Their surges in inflows were so large that they followed
Korea's 'route-3' using foreign finance to sustain their ambitious private
investment programmes – Malaysia actually *doubled* its share of private

investment in GDP (to 30.5%), while Thailand brought its own to 34.1%. But, contrary to Korea, there was plenty of spare credit to follow at least one element of 'route-1' too – the excess liquidity fuelled a Latin-style asset bubble in their stock markets and real estate.

However, remarkably, in these two East Asian countries massive credit expansion was associated with a *drop* in the share of consumption in GDP – in Thailand, it falls from 56.7% to 54.8%, and in Malaysia from 49.4% to 45.9%. No sign of a Latin 'route-1' here.

In sum, these seven DCs chose two different paths to inflow-absorption: one, following the credo of the classical 'efficient-market' theory and the first law of Welfare Economics, was inspired by two simple propositions: [i] keep public sector finance in balance; and [ii] allow markets to sort out the resulting private imbalances by themselves (routes '1' and '3'). Route-2 (Brazil), instead, tried to contain the expansionary effect of surges in capital inflows 'at source' via a high degree of sterilisation (see Figure 8 below).

In 'route-1' (Chile, Mexico and Argentina), although real interest rates started very high due to their simultaneous stabilisation policies, they soon fell to international levels (plus corresponding spreads). 'Route 3' countries in East Asia were characterised by a long-term Keynesian policy of low and stable rates. However, in the case of Brazil, real interest rates were not only set at a much higher level during the price-stabilisation programme, but due to the sterilisation policy (and other reasons discussed in detail elsewhere – see Palma, 2007), they were never allowed to fall anywhere near the values of 'route-1' (let alone 'route-3') countries.

The case of Brazil is also very important for the critique of 'moral-hazard-type' crisis-analysis. For example, according to McKinnon and Pill (1997), the main cause of borrowing agents losing their capacity to assess and price their risk properly is that internal and external moral hazards lead to 'artificially' low interest rates; these, in turn, gave a false incentive to agents to accumulate excessive amounts of private (let alone public) risk. However, in Brazil, although high interest rates did help to avoid a 'route-1' financial crisis, they did so by creating a different (but equally damaging) type of financial crisis ('route-2') – especially due to the negative effects of the resulting 'high-interest-rate-trap' in public finances and private banks (see Figure 8 below). So, the magical realism of Brazil's 'route-2' is that it created a financial crisis by trying to avoid one...

Probably no other macroeconomic variable reflects so transparently the different 'routes' to financial crises than the behaviour of private consumption and asset prices. Figure 4 shows the different impact of trade and financial liberalisation in one crucial component of consumption – imports of consumer goods.

In 'route-1', the expansion of imports of consumer goods (from relatively small initial levels) is really exceptional; this is not the case for the other two 'routes'. Figure 5 shows how easy access to credit in 'route-1' countries also led to an asset bubble in the stock market, 'tulip mania'-style.

What went on in 'route-1' countries was remarkable – and one should not forget that according to the 'efficient capital market theory', stock prices are supposed to be a 'random walk' – i.e., under risk neutrality, there should be no scope for profitable speculation. . .

The Summers were probably not very well acquainted with Latin America when they stated that '[In financial markets] prices will always reflect fundamental values [...]. The logic of efficient markets is compelling'. L and V Summers (1989).

As mentioned above, Malaysia and Thailand did have a 'route-1' component in this respect, but their bubbles are dwarfed in comparison to Chile or Mexico: even when comparing the increase between the lowest quarterly point vis-à-vis the highest one, in Malaysia the expansion is 6-fold and in Thailand is 5.4-fold.

Something similar took place in real estate (see Palma, 2003a). Again, the contrast between the three routes could not be more pronounced: another Kindlebergian 'mania' in 'route-1' – in Mexico, for example, the real estate price index jumps 16-fold between financial liberalisation and financial crisis; but there is little or no increase in the indices of Korea and Brazil. This time, Malaysia and Thailand are even closer to 'route-1'. In the case of Malaysia, the index between mid-1988 and mid-1997 grows (a more Latin-style) 12.3-fold, while in Thailand, if one takes the highest and lowest points of the index, it jumps by almost 8-fold. Particularly in countries of 'route-1', the surge of inflows also distorted 'fundamentals'; Figure 6 shows the case of the remarkable overvaluation of real exchange rates.

It is really difficult to fit this picture with the basic postulate of the neo-liberal creed regarding the need to 'liberalise', lift artificial market distortions, and stop governments' 'discretionary' policies so as to allow the economy to get 'its prices right'. Massive inflows into Latin America, particularly in relation to exports, and the use of exchange-rate based stabilisation policies – based on the oldest macroeconomic law of them all: one can only solve a macroeconomic imbalance by creating another one – brought this most crucial of prices to a level which it would be rather hard to brand as 'right';[9] particularly in view of the effect it was having in the current account.

As 'route-1' countries (with the partial exception of Argentina after 1995) did manage to keep their public-sector accounts in order, these current-account deficits obviously reflect private imbalances. Furthermore, DCs characterised by significant currency mismatches in their financial portfolios key adjustment mechanisms – such as the relative price (real exchange) adjustment – have failed

Figure 6: Latin America and East Asia: Real Effective Rate of Exchange between the Beginning of Financial Liberalisation and Respective Financial Crisis

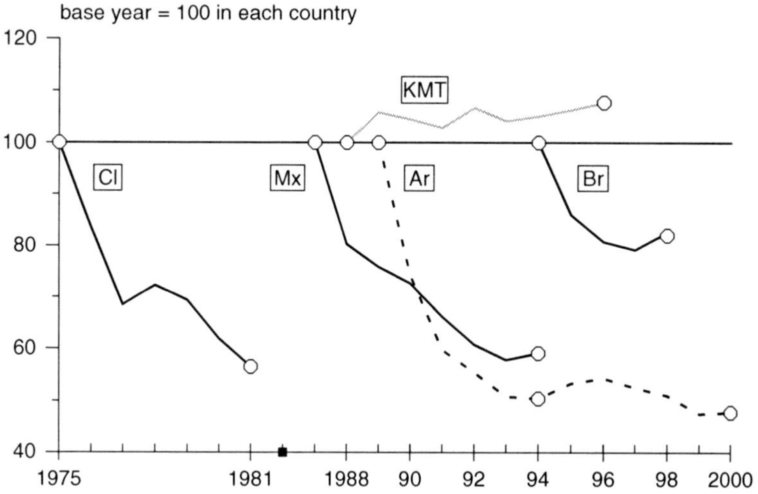

when faced with sharp changes in external liquidity; instead of helping to bring these economies back to equilibrium, these adjustment mechanisms have tended to augment the cycle through their pro-cyclical wealth effects.

Given this evidence, it is difficult to understand how, as late as 1996, the World Bank was still preaching to DCs to continue implementing *simultaneously* policies of exchange rate based stabilisation and of trade and financial liberalisation, even when admitting that 'second generation' reforms were totally lacking (see World Bank, 1996).

Moreover, the current account was not the only casualty of the exchange-rate overvaluation; (not surprisingly) it was also distorting the composition of what little investment there was towards the non-tradable sector. In Mexico, for example, whilst residential construction doubled between 1981 and 1994, investment in machinery fell by half and that in infrastructure even further (see Palma, 2005). Easy access to credit, the distortion in relative prices and the asset bubble in real estate set in motion a huge Kuznets' cycle – not surprisingly, the best performing sector in the Mexican Stock market was construction.

This is a rather odd picture: in fact, 'route-1' economies ended up switching the engine of growth away from their desired aim – domestically financed private investment in tradable production – towards a more 'post-modernist' one of externally financed private consumption, and private investment in non-tradable activities.

Finally, the collapse of savings in Latin America is definitely not the 'Promised Land' of McKinnon and Shaw's financial-liberalisation; in their

Figure 7: Brazil: How to Walk into a Public-Sector 'Ponzi' by Over-reacting to External Shocks, by the High Cost of Sterilization (i–r), and by the Violation of 'Golden Rule' (i >p)

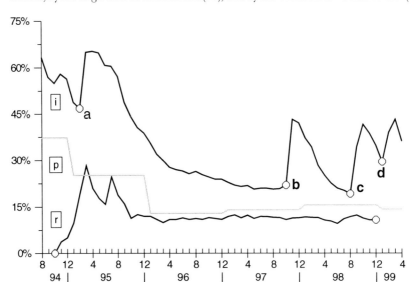

- **[i]** = annualised nominal monthly interest rate paid for public debt; **[p]** = annual growth-rates of public revenues; and **[r]** = income received for foreign-exchange reserves (assumed equivalent to returns on US Treasury Bills); domestic currency.[10]
- **[a]** = Mexican crisis; **[b]** = East Asian crisis; **[c]** = Russian default; and **[d]** = domestic default by the State of Minas Gerais.

respective periods between financial liberalisation and financial crises, gross domestic savings as a share of GDP fell in Argentina by 5.7 percentage points, in Brazil by 9, in Chile by 13.2 and in Mexico by 8.3 (see Palma, 2003b).

Turning to 'route-2', the crucial vulnerability of Brazil lies mainly in high interest rates leading straight into a public sector (Minskian) 'Ponzi'-finance (Figure 7).

First, the Brazilian Central Bank over-reacted to external shocks (an attitude I have called elsewhere 'macho-monetarism').[11] Second, the resulting high cost of sterilisation becomes evident in the difference between lines '**i**' and '**r**' – i.e., between what was paid for the paper sold to sterilise and what was recuperated from the return on their holding of foreign-exchange reserves.[12]

Finally, Brazil systematically violated the 'fiscal-golden-rule', by paying a much higher rate for its public debt than the rate at which it managed to increase public revenues (and, certainly, its income per capita). In part, this was the price paid for both the lack of (much needed) public sector reforms and political stalemate – in this sense, the financial crisis in Brazil was clearly more due to a weak public sector than it was in the other two 'routes'.

Figure 8:  East Asia and Latin America: Current Account between the Beginning of Financial Liberalisation and Respective Financial Crisis

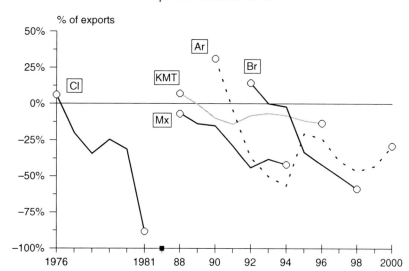

Furthermore, the levels of lending rates that followed were remarkable: the annualised real monthly interest rate paid for working capital peaked at 60% in October 1998, while that for consumer credit did so at 115%! With these rates, of course, hardly any private asset could perform; as discussed elsewhere, non-performing loans – as well as a remarkable lack of 'transparency' in the banking sector, weak regulatory public institutions and the end of 'inflation-income' by the banking system – led to a succession of banking crises, each adding a significant amount to the stock of the public-sector debt due to a populist policy of indiscriminate bail-outs.[13]

In fact, the ease with which the government could finance its domestic debt was due primarily to private banks falling over themselves to buy public paper, as this was just about the only financial asset that could perform at such rates. Regarding the rest of their portfolio (not having understood Stiglitz) private banks tried to increase profitability by the self-defeating policy of ever increasing spreads (see Palma, 2003a).

## The East Asia Story of an 'Endogenous Pull' of Foreign Capital: The Cost of Maintaining High Levels of Investment in the Face of Rapidly Falling Profits

In a sense, the East Asian story is less transparent than that of Latin America. Inflows were not so large and their composition was more stable; real effective

Figure 9: East Asia and Latin America: Private Investment between the Beginning of
Financial Liberalisation and Respective Financial Crisis

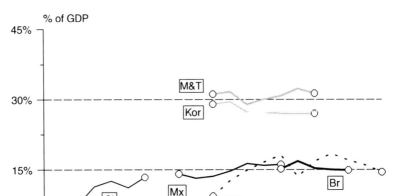

• **[M&T]**=average of Malaysia and Thailand.

exchange rates remained stable (Figure 6); current accounts deficits, when
looked at as share of exports, were small (Figure 8); interest rates were low and
stable, and there was no consumption boom (Figure 4); no collapse of savings;
and no deficits in the public sector. So, what about the often-mentioned
moral-hazard-led investment boom?

Figure 9 shows that, while in Latin America private investment seems to
find a 'natural' ceiling at around 15% of GDP, in 'Schumpeterian' East Asia
it seems to be twice as high. The graph also shows that in Korea, Malaysia
and Thailand private investment did not really increase in the period before
1997 – no much evidence here of an investment boom, moral-hazard led or
not! Therefore, even if it is obvious that countries in routes '3' used their
inflows in a different way than those in '1' and '2', the key question that still
needs to be answered is why the Korean corporate sector needed such large
capital inflows to finance an ambitious but relatively *stable* investment effort.
Figure 10 provides the answer.

As discussed in detail elsewhere (Palma 2003a), and mainly due to declining
profitability (a decline which had little to do with the Krugman-type critique of
Korea, and a lot to do with collapsing micro-electronic prices)[14] the corporate
sector had to finance its high, but relatively *stable*, levels of investment switching
from own-profits to external debt. As Figure 10 indicates, this process caused
the sectoral deficit of the corporate sector to increase from about 5% to nearly

Figure 10:  South Korea: Sectoral Surpluses of the Household, Government, Foreign and Corporate Sectors, 1987–96

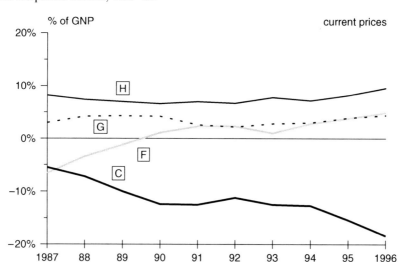

• **[H]**=households; **[G]**=government; **[F]**=balance of the financial account of the balance of payments; and **[C]**=corporate sector. Sectoral surpluses are the differences between sectoral savings and investment.

20% of GNP, absorbing in the process not only all the increase in the surplus of the 'foreign sector', but that of the household and government sectors as well.[15]

Consequently, was there 'over'-investment, as the IMF would like us to believe (see IMF, 1998)? The answer is (as is so often the case) more complicated than a typically simplistic 'Washington Consensus' one. The crucial issue that leads to misunderstandings in the East Asian crisis is to forget that once you have gone into the type of high-tech exports characteristics of the region, one can only be competitive if able to produce at the cutting-edge of (a rapidly changing) technology; and to be able to remain at that level, one has to invest at East-Asian heights. Therefore, when profitability collapsed, the choice for Korea was not that of 'blackboard economics' – of having the technological choice of being able to produce a given amount of output with different combinations of capital and labour. It was, however, either to stay in the micro-electronic business or to look for a new type of development pattern altogether (allowing a significant amount of its accumulated physical, human and institutional capital to depreciate). That is, export micro-chips 'warts and all', or switch to exporting potato-chips (or even return to silk, Korea's main export product before its massive industrialisation drive.)

In fact, what might have been an effective solution for East Asia would have been a Keynesian-style programme of regional investment co-ordination. For example, what triggered the collapse of the price of the D-Ram memory in 1995 was massive Taiwanese new investment coming into stream at the wrong time. However, the analysis of this issue falls outside the scope of this paper.

## The Day of Reckoning

Not surprisingly, macroeconomic imbalances and Minskian financial fragilities quickly began to emerge specific to each 'route'. In 'route-1', they included overvalued exchange rates, unsustainable deficits in the current account, asset bubbles threatening to burst, and growing non-performing bank-assets.[16] In 'route-2', Brazil, there was public-sector 'Ponzi-finance' and repeated private-banking crises; while in 'route-3' corporate debt/equity ratios reached unprecedented heights and balance-sheets structures became increasingly vulnerable to currency depreciation.

However, these countries also had to face at least three *common* problems: (i) constant changing composition of private inflows; (ii) progressive shortening of the term structure of their debt; and (iii) the constant danger that in a financially liberalised economy the attack could also come from 'within'.

Regarding the composition of inflows, Figure 2b to d showed that they were remarkably erratic in Latin America; this is also found in East Asia, but in a less extreme form. The changing composition made the already difficult matter of absorbing massive inflows even more complicated. Regarding the term-structure of inflows, these shortened significantly over the period (see Palma, 2003a).[17] Obviously, this added further fragility and heightened uncertainty in an already difficult situation. Figure 11 shows how increasing short-term debt added a further financial fragility.

In the case of Korea, its main weakness in 1997 – which made it so vulnerable to events in Thailand and Malaysia – was not just its high share of short-term debt, but the *combination* of such debt with exceptionally low levels of reserves. Figure 11 indicates that Korea's reserves could only cover half its short-term liabilities; in fact, they were not even enough to cover debt with 90 days maturity or less. The Korean authorities seemed to have had a sort of schizophrenia vis-à-vis economic planning and regulation: in matters relating to the real economy and in some aspects of domestic finance, they felt the need for strong, detailed and effective intervention, but in areas relating to the capital account and monetary policy, they only seem to have been concerned with long-term capital movement, exchange-rate stability and keeping interest rates as low as possible. This left unchecked what turned out to be two 'suicidal' tendencies: that of the corporate sector to accumulate short-term debt, and that of the Central Bank to keep low levels of reserves (as if international financial markets would never dare to attack).

Figure 11: Latin America and East Asia: Ration of Foreign-Exchange Reserves to Short-Term Debt between the Beginning of Financial Liberalisation and Respective Financial Crises

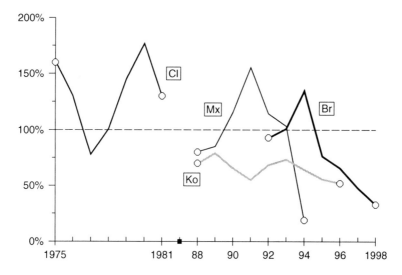

In Brazil, authorities had a mixed policy on these issues. First, as President Cardoso clearly stated, they were against intervening in the capital account to reduce the share of short-term debt – they were, for example, against Chilean-style capital controls.[18] Nevertheless, they did increase the level of reserves; but this seems to have lulled them into a false sense of security because short-term debt grew faster and, as the 'fundamentals' deteriorated rapidly, the economy was left extremely vulnerable to a sudden collapse of confidence and withdrawal of finance.

Finally, of course, in a financially liberalised economy, the 'attack' could also just as easily come from 'within'. Neither Mexico, Brazil nor Korea had significant defences against internal attacks on their exchange rates, as their 'reserves-M2' ratios were also particularly low (see Palma, 2003a). In Argentina, where the Currency Board was supposed to provide a self-regulating insurance against such an attack, the Finance Minister, facing in 2001 precisely this type of scenario, first increased interest rates on deposits from 9% to 16%, and then imposed a 'corralito' (i.e., a freeze on bank accounts).[19]

## Conclusions

In sum, 'route-1' countries (Chile, Mexico, and Argentina until its first financial crisis in 1994–95), after massive surges in capital inflows followed a path to financial crisis led by an explosion of credit to the private sector, low levels of interest rates (after stabilisation), and a rapid real-exchange revaluation. All these produced consumption booms, asset bubbles, collapse in savings, massive deterioration of current accounts, and distorted the already low levels of investment towards residential construction. Basically, the liberalisation of capital accounts, instead of creating 'automatic stabilisers' vis-à-vis surges in inflows, effectively created (in the words of Stiglitz, 2003) 'automatic *de*stabilisers'. In the meantime, foreign and domestic debt levels exploded, while both the term structure of the foreign debt deteriorated and the balance-sheet of the corporate and banking sector became ever more vulnerable to currency depreciation. This route generated so many financial fragilities that it did not take much for it to encounter a sudden collapse of confidence and an abrupt withdrawal of finance, leading to major financial crises. As events helping such collapses are usually in excess supply in Latin America, financial crises did follow. In 1994 Mexico, for example, in the twelve months before the December crisis there was a massive indigenous uprising in Chiapas in January; the assassination of the presidential candidate of the ruling party (PRI) in March; a not very transparent presidential election in August (delivering yet again a victory for the PRI); the assassination of the Secretary General of the PRI in September; the resignation of the Assistant Attorney General in November (who was in charge of investigating the assassination of his brother, the Secretary General of the PRI, complaining of a government cover-up); the widespread belief that the President had been involved in both assassinations; and the way in which the Central Bank released information on foreign reserves in November after four months of secrecy all provided plenty of political thrill. In fact, it only took a relatively small external shock (an increase in US interest rates in November, which produce a relatively minor bond crisis) for the debacle to take place.

In the case of Argentina, the crucial issue seems to be the difference between the two periods that make up the eleven years between financial liberalisation and its 2001 financial crisis: the period from trade and financial liberalisation to the Mexican crisis (1990–94), and the period between 1995–2001. During the first, Argentina followed mostly a 'route-1' path to financial crisis; that is, with the exception of the later deterioration of the public finances, most of the macroeconomic 'damage' in Argentina's 'fundamentals' brought about by the surge in inflows was done in the first period. In the second, (under both Menem and De la Rua) Argentina got into an endless 'crisis management' mode due to its refusal to devalue and to adjust properly to its first shock (as Mexico and Chile had done earlier after their respective financial crises).

The path to financial crisis for 'route-2'-Brazil in turn also started with a surge in inflows; but the scene was soon dominated by high interest rates (initially necessary for price-stabilisation, but later becoming permanent to avoid 'another Mexico', and to respond to continuous external shocks). These high interest rates were successful in avoiding a repeat of 'route-1', in consolidating price-stabilisation and in partially insulating Brazil from external shocks, but soon created massive domestic financial fragility in the banking sector and in state-government finances, leading to an increase in public debt through continuous (often indiscriminate and sometime politically corrupt) private banking and state-government rescue activities. And this public debt exploded due to high interest rates, which became systematically higher than both the growth in public revenues and the returns on reserves. In the meantime the real economy imploded because of these rates, which affected the growth of public revenues even further; but high interest rates became even more necessary as a (poor) substitute for missing public-sector reforms, and to defend the 'peg', so as to avoid both further domestic banking crises due to high foreign-exchange liabilities, and a stampede by restless international fund managers. The 'Ponzi' finance in the public sector ballooned out of control as a result of this (self-made) high interest rate 'trap'. Again, it did not take much (just one of many of Yeltsin's follies in 1998 and a minor internal political crisis) for this route to end up in a major financial crisis.

Finally, in 'route-3' countries, particularly Korea, again there was a massive surge in inflows leading to an increase of private credit at low interest rates. However, this did not lead to a consumption booms or asset bubbles. Rather, in the context of declining profitability, there were high (though *stable*) levels of investment (in a world, particularly the sphere of microelectronics, where there were both collapsing prices but competitiveness only at the cutting-edge of a very rapidly changing technology). This ended up producing corporate debt/equity ratios that even in this part of the world should have caused vertigo! Added to this, there were incomprehensive policy incentives to the corporate and financial sector to borrow abroad 'short', and a Central Bank that seemed to have enjoyed the thrill of living dangerously with low levels of reserves. Again – and despite the stunning growth record of Korea, its degree of competitiveness, and having fundamentals that although not perfect were the envy of most DCs – it did not take much (international financial markets turning their attention to Southeast Asia with some trepidation due to the return of Hong-Kong to Chinese rule),[20] for this route to also encounter a major financial crisis.

As far as Malaysia and Thailand are concerned, they followed a mix of routes '1' and '3'. After surges in inflows, they followed a path to financial crisis also led by an (even higher) explosion of credit to the private sector, but without the revaluation of exchange rates, consumption booms and declining savings of 'route-1'. However, they did have Latin-style asset bubbles and most of the problems of Korea as well. They also had the added problems that not only was further upgrading of exports becoming increasingly difficult (in particular to break away from a 'sub-contracting-type' industrialisation), but also of China becoming a formidable competitor (see Chang, Palma and Whittaker, 2001). Again – and also despite a strong growth record, a growing degree of competitiveness, and having fundamentals much better than those of Latin America – it was not long before voracious fund managers, eager to profit from long-standing but only precipitately acknowledged 'peccadilloes' (the precarious balance-sheet structure of the Thai banking system), had a sudden collapse of confidence that led to bank runs and a major financial crises.[21]

So, the moral of the story of the 'three routes' is that in whatever way DCs with open capital accounts facing sudden and massive surges in inflows have handled their absorption, they have ended up in major crises. Of course, with hindsight one can always think of hypothetical ways in which the worst excesses could have been avoided, but the fact is that the economic and political dynamic created by massive surges in inflows in economies with open capital accounts has proved extraordinarily difficult to manage.

All of the above make it difficult to understand the direction in which the mainstream literature on financial crises have trended, i.e., concentrating all the blame for these crises on very specific and supposedly avoidable issues: the relatively expansionary economic policy of an election year in Mexico; the lack of fiscal reform in Brazil; the ('crony' capitalism) moral-hazard-driven investment story in Korea; or the moral-hazard-driven bubble in Thailand creating a balance-sheet problem story.

As is well known, in financial literature 'first generation' crises are understood as deserve, predictable and harmless to the real economy. In turn, in 'second generation' models, crises, although equally harmless, are also supposed to be undeserved and unpredictable. Finally, 'third generation' crises are again supposed to be undeserved and unpredictable; however, this time they have a major negative impact on output and employment (see Krugman, 2001). So, the emphasis on the latter is on flight of capital from economies that (except from some avoidable moral hazards) are supposed to be fundamentally sound and moving in the 'right' direction (economic reform); i.e., they are about the possibility that something – almost anything – causing sudden large currency depreciation, which creates havoc with corporate balance sheets and the real economy. From this perspective, one of the main points of this paper is to show that all three routes, but especially 'routes-1' and '2', have little to do with this 'undeserved' and 'unpredictable' picture. Rather, and in particular in 'route-1' countries, among other problems, credit booms, asset bubbles, consumption booms, currency mismatches in financial portfolios, overvalued exchange rates, and current account deficit led to well deserve and fairly predictable crises.[22] The situation in 'route-3' countries is obviously more complex, but only

Malaysia could possibly argue that its crisis was, to a certain extent, 'undeserved' (see Ocampo and Palma, 2007).

In sum, how can one possible explain that for most of the economic profession, for financial markets, and for the financial press these crises were so unpredictable, and so 'undeserved'. Maybe the Wall Street Journal provides part of the answer; in an editorial after the (supposedly also unpredictable and undeserved) 'sub-prime' crisis of mid-2007 it stated that: "The recent market turmoil is rocking investors around the globe. But it is raising the stock of one person: a little-known economist whose views have suddenly become very popular [...] Hyman Minsky." (WSJ, "In Time of Tumult, Obscure Economist Gains Currency", August 18, 2007). Perhaps had the read and understood such obscure economists as Minsky, Kindleberger and so many others (including Stiglitz) they would have become more effective at predicting financial crises and at realising how 'deserved' they usually are...

What is remarkable in the mainstream crises-literature is how little attention is given to (what I believe are) the three main issues surrounding financial crises in DCs with open capital accounts: i) Why is it that during periods of surges of inflows the incentive mechanisms and resource allocation dynamics of domestic financial markets have failed under the pressures generated by the increased liquidity brought about by these surges by their own, *endogenous* reasons? As a result, borrowers and lenders have ended up accumulating more risk than was privately, let alone socially, efficient. This excessive amount of risk has become evident in the alternate phase of the cycle, that of the 'sudden stop' in external financing.[23] ii) Why is it that some typical adjustment mechanisms – e.g., relative price (real exchange) adjustment – have failed when faced with such sharp changes in external liquidity? Instead of helping to bring these economies back to equilibrium, these adjustment mechanisms have tended to augment the cycle. And iii) why is it that in financially-liberalised economies market forces have often pushed governments and central banks into pro-cyclical macroeconomic policies rather than into counter-cyclical ones?

Another common element in the genesis of all these crises is the way in which international financial markets and the financial press have interpreted economic news. In the first phase, which can be called the 'turning-a-blind-eye' stage (following economic reforms), good news has been exaggerated and bad news ignored. In the second, which can be called the 'omnipotent stage', when eventually bad news could not be ignored anymore, some has been acknowledged but assumed under control. In the final one, which can be called the 'panic-stricken stage', and sometimes following even relatively minor events, there has been a sudden turn towards panic, when bad news has been even exaggerated.

Of course, there is a series of other important issues that has not been possible to analyse here, particularly in relationship to Latin America – such as the peculiar politico-institutional framework and the degree of ideological fundamentalism in which financial liberalisation and economic reform were carried out.[24]

One of these issues is the extraordinary collection of 'first generation' Heads of State that initiated economic reform in Latin America. Although not unfamiliar to Latin American politics, the mélange of Pinochet, Salinas, Collor, Menem, Fujimori, Alemán, Bucaram (and many others), certainly deserves several entries in *The Guinness Book of Records*, particularly under the headings of human rights abuses, electoral fraud, petit-bourgeois parvenu-populism and corruption. After having initially got into power using an *anti*-neo-liberal discourse, their sudden eagerness to switch to the 'neo-liberal' camp was in part related to the opportunity to create a new structure of property rights from which massive new rents could be generated. And, of course, the more successful they were in selling the 'neo-liberal' programme, the more extravagant the predatory capitalism that followed could be.

With these 'first generation' individuals running the show to begin with, economic reforms (particularly privatisations) never stood a chance.[25] Also, in the face of all the evidence of links between these reforms and financial crises – particularly in their extremely corrupt and populistic 'first round' – how can so many economists still insist that these crises were simply the result of extraneous factors such as moral hazards and long standing forms of 'crony' capitalism?

Another explanation seems much more likely:

[Is financial liberalisation] being designed on the basis of the best available economic theory and evidence, or is there another agenda, perhaps a special interest agenda? (Stiglitz, 2000, p. 1085)

Perhaps the main lesson of these financial crises is that it is about time to think again about all the complex theoretical issues that led Minsky to conclude that finance was so fragile; that led Kindleberger to warn us of its propensity to oscillate between manias and panics; and, especially, that led Keynes to conclude that: "[…] above all, let finance be primarily national." (1933)

## Notes

1. This is a revised version of the paper published in Chang (2003). I would like to thank Edna Armendáriz, Stephanie Blankenburg, Ashwini Deshpande, Carlos Lopes, Richard Kozul-Wright, Jose Antonio Ocampo, Arturo O'Connell, Carlota Perez, Cornelia Staritz, Bob Sutcliffe, Lance Taylor, Fiona Tregenna, and participants at various seminars for helpful comments. The ideas of Kindleberger and Minsky strongly influence this paper. The usual caveats apply.

2. According to McKinsey's Global Financial Stock Databse, the value of global financial assets (equity securities, private debt securities, government debt securities and bank deposits) increased from US$12 trillion in 1980 to US$43 trillion in 1990, US$94 trillion in 2000 and US$167 in 2006. As a result, the value of financial assets as a share of

world's GDP practically doubled between 1980 and 2000 – from 109% of world's GDP (1980) to 201% (1990) and 294% (2000); by 2006 it had reached 346%! Between 1980 and 2000 the fastest growing components of global financial assets were private debt securities and equity securities (with average annual rates of 13.7% and 13%, respectively). See McKinsey Global Institute (2008).

3.  Perhaps the most important (and often forgotten) peculiarity of the Argentinian case is that it was the only country of those studied here that successfully managed to delay for several years its (fairly inevitable) crisis thanks to substantial help from the IMF and some skilful – but eventually self-defeating – 'financial engineering'. Therefore, events in the years preceding its 'Wagnerian' 2001 crisis are in a way unique and do not really fit in any of the 'routes' discussed here. However, for reason of space I cannot discuss in detail the intricacies of these events. For detailed analyses, see the papers collected in www.fund-cenit.org.ar

4.  Unless otherwise stated, this source, together with IMF (2007) and ECLAC (2007) will be the sources for all data in this paper.

5.  Unless otherwise stated, from now on all US-dollar figures throughout the paper are expressed in 2007 values.

6.  As the Argentinian Finance Minister once said, the overvaluation of the currency in real terms was not due to fixing the exchange rate; on the contrary, the fixed parity was actually preventing the nominal rate from revaluating!

7.  In Mexico, bank loan-portfolio grew (in current US$) from $55 billion (1989) to $200 billion (1994); see Palma (2005). However, one insider's 'conspiracy theory' was that higher portfolios also allowed Mexican groups to bid up the price at which these banks could be sold to 'gringos'.

8.  In the case of Argentina, this graph shows the difference between the two periods that make up the eleven years between financial liberalization and its 2001 crisis: the period up to the Mexican crisis (1990–94, corresponding also to the first administration of Menem), and the one between 1995–2001. During the first, Argentina followed a 'route-1' boom in imports of consumer goods (these grew at 90% per annum), while during the second period they grew at only 4.7%. As discussed below, a similar difference between these two periods is found in other variables. That is, with the significant exception of public finance, most of the macroeconomic 'damage' in Argentina's 'fundamentals' was brought about by the way in which it adjusted to trade and financial liberalization and fixed exchange rate regime in this first four-year period.

9.  Note that in the case of Argentina, yet again, most of the revaluation took place between 1990 and 1994.

10. Inflation between 1995–1998 was relatively low: the wholesale price index increased by 6.4%, 8.1%, 7.8% and 1.5%, respectively.

11. See Palma (2006). At times, and even when there was little fear of devaluation, the Brazilian Central Bank set deposit rates as much as 20 percentage-points above international rates plus country risk.

12. As in the case of the Mexican 'Tesobonos', Brazil also had a growing proportion of its bonds in a financial instrument indexed to the dollar (resulting in a huge increase of the domestic debt after devaluation.)

13. See Lopes (2003) and Palma (2006 and 2007).

14. The D-Ram price per megabyte, for example, fell (in current US$) from $26 (1995) to $10 (1996), $4 (1997), and less than $1 (1998). Memory-chips were one of Korea's main export-items.

15. Daewoo alone, for example, ended up with a (current US$) debt of 80 billion!

16. Non-performing loans in Mexico's banks reached nearly 10% of GDP in 1994 (see Kregel, 1998).

17. In Brazil, for example, the share of short-term debt in total debt grew from 19% in 1994 to 56% in 1998.

18. He once famously said: "We will never use capital controls: we want to be a First World nation"; see Palma (2006). Obviously, his knowledge of financial history was rather limited! For analyses of capital controls in Colombia, see Ocampo and Tovar (1999); and in Chile, Colombia and Malaysia, Ocampo and Palma (2007).

19. That is, instead of trying to stop the capital flight with Malaysian-style 1998-outflow-controls, his 'swan song' was to freeze bank accounts, provoking the collapse of banks (and of himself). In 2001, before the 'corralito', deposit accounts in domestic currency fell by 20% and those in dollar-accounts by 30% (Chudnovsky, 2002).

20. The Thai government was forced to float the baht on the $2^{nd}$ of July 1997, one day after the British transfer of Hong-Kong to China.

21. On bank-runs, see Chang and Velasco (1999).

22. See the Trade and Development Report of 1994 (published in mid-year) for a prediction of the Mexican crisis (TDR, 1994). Also, in a paper written at the beginning of 1998 and published in November of that year (i.e., before the January 1999 crisis), I conclude that "Brazil's growing financial vulnerability signals the probability of another major crisis in the not too distant future." (Palma, 1998). For a pre-July 1997 clear analysis of East Asia's financial fragilities, see the 1997 BIS Annual Report (BIS, 1997).

23. According to Kindleberger, international financial markets can do one thing that is more damaging for DCs than 'over-lending': to halt that lending abruptly! (see Kindleberger, 1978).

24. In terms of fundamentalism, a case in point is Gustavo Franco, President of the Brazilian Central Bank up to the 1999 financial crisis. According to him "[For Brazilians, the alternative] is to be neo-liberal or neo-idiotic [...]. [Our real task] is to undo forty years of stupidity (Veja 15/11/1996). The fact that Brazil's previous development strategy had delivered for most of those forty years one of the fastest growth-rates in the world, was, according to Franco, a mere detail of history.

25. However, as late as 1998, in the annual meeting of the IMF and the World Bank, Michel Camdessu, then Managing Director of the IMF, introduced Menem as "the President with the best economic polices in the world"! In fact, only two presidents gave a speech in the main session, Clinton and Menem.

# References

Allen R E (ed.) (2004) *The International Library of Writings on the New Global Economy: The Political Economy of Financial Crises*, Elgar.

BIS (1997) *67th Annual Report*.

Chang, H-J (2003) *Rethinking Development Economics*, Anthem Press.

Chang, H-J, J G Palma, and H Whittaker (2001) *Financial Liberalisation and the Asian Crisis*, Palgrave.

Chang, R and A. Velasco (1999) 'Illiquidity and Crises in Emerging Markets', NBER.

Chudnovsky, D (2002) 'La Gestación de la Crisis Argentina', CENIT.

ECLAC (2007) *Statistical Survey*.

IFC (2004) *Emerging Stock Markets Factbook*.

IMF (1998) *World Economic Outlook*.

———— (2007) *WEO database*.

Keynes, J M (1933) 'National Self-sufficiency', *The Yale Review*, Summer.

Kindleberger C P (1978) *Manias, Panics, and Crashes: a history of financial crises*, Basic Books.

Kregel, J (1998) 'East Asia is not Mexico: the difference between balance of payments crises and debt deflation', UNCTAD.

Krugman, P (2001) 'Crises: the next generation?', mimeo, Razin conference, Tel Aviv University, March 25–6.

Lopes, C (2003) 'Public debt and the Brazilian crisis', mimeo.

McKinnon, R and H Pill (1997) 'Credible economic liberalizations and overborrowing', *American Economic Review*, 87.

McKinsey Global Institute (2008) 'Mapping Global Capital Markets. Forth Annual Report', McKinsey&Company, January.

Michie, J (2003) *Handbook of Globalisation*, Elgar.

Ocampo, J A and C Tovar (1999) 'Price-Based Capital Account Regulations: The Colombian Experience', ECLAC.

Ocampo, J A and J G Palma (2007) 'Dealing with volatile external finances at source: the rôle of preventive capital account regulations', in J E Stiglitz and J A Ocampo (2007).

Palma, G. (1998) 'Three and a half cycles of "mania, panic and [asymmetric] crash": East Asia and Latin America Compared', *Cambridge Journal of Economics*, 22.

———— (2003a) 'The 'three routes' to financial crises', in Chang (2003). Reprinted in R E Allen (2004).

———— (2003b) 'Latin American during the second half of the 20th Century: from the 'age of extremes' to the age of 'end-of-history' uniformity', in Chang (2003).

———— (2005) 'The six main stylised facts of the Mexican economy since trade liberalisation and NAFTA', Industrial and Corporate Change, 14 (6), December.

———— (2006) 'The 1999 financial crisis in Brazil: "macho-monetarism" in action', *Economic and Political Weekly*, 41(9).

———— (2007) 'The 1999 Brazilian crisis: the cost of using monetary policy as the main defence against surges in capital inflows and external shocks', in Stiglitz et. al. (2007).

Summers, L and V Summers, (1989) 'When financial markets work too well', *Financial Services*, 3.

Stiglitz, J E (2000) 'Capital market liberalization, economic growth and instability', *World Development*, 28.

———— (2003) 'Whither reform? Toward a new agenda for Latin America', *CEPAL Review*, 80.

Stiglitz J E and J A Ocampo (eds.) (2007) *Capital Market Liberalization and Development*, OUP.

Stiglitz J E et. al. (eds.) (2007) *Stability with Growth*, OUP.

TDR (1994) Trade and Development Report, UNCTAD.

World Bank (1996) World Development Report.

———— (2007a) *World Development Indicators*.

———— (2007b) *Global Development Finance*.

# Chapter 3

# TIMING THE MEXICAN 1994–95 FINANCIAL CRISIS USING A MARKOV SWITCHING APPROACH

## Moritz Cruz
Universidad Nacional Autónoma de México (UNAM), Instituto de Investigaciones Económicas

## Edmund Amann
Economics, School of Social Sciences, University of Manchester, England

**Abstract**

It is increasingly asserted that recent financial crises have been driven by changes in market sentiment, the latter stemming from alterations in so-called fundamentals. There are, however, few studies aimed at identifying empirically whether this is true. Applying a Markov switching autoregressive model and using the broad money-to-international reserves ratio as the variable that captures market confidence, this chapter *times* the start and the end of Mexico's 1994–95 financial crisis. The estimated probabilities indicate that financial panic started since November 1993 and that it ended in May 1995. It is established that the beginning and end of the crisis is associated with a change in private agents' confidence and *not* to *ex post* events, such as the abandonment of the exchange rate or the recovery of the economy led by export growth. The results also indicate that in order to recover agents' confidence, the government had to reinforce its strategy of financial liberalisation. This placed strong limitations on the authorities' room for manoeuvre in setting macroeconomic policy.

*Keywords*: Markov switching autoregressive model; market confidence; financial crises; Mexico.
*JEL Classification*: E44, C22.

## Introduction

One of the most well-worn arguments within the vast and divergent literature concerning recent financial crises is that they stem from changes in market confidence. Such confidence is held to rest on so-called economic fundamentals and domestic political conditions. As soon as the fundamentals diverge from what may be considered *sound*, so it is argued, the confidence of investors ebbs away causing progressive withdrawals of capital overseas. In emerging economies, such withdrawals can have a devastating impact. Once private agents begin to withdraw capital abroad it consequently becomes increasingly difficult to maintain steady growth. When the scale of the withdrawals becomes sufficiently large, in the absence of capital controls, contractions in GDP indubitably follow.

Within this setting, it is conventionally asserted that the start of any financial crisis is associated with the decision to float the exchange rate freely. The end of crisis occurs once the ensuing currency depreciation triggers export growth recovery. On a superficial level, there is some evidence to suggest that such an explanation fits the facts of a range of emerging market financial crises experienced over the past two decades. In the case of Brazil, for example, the decision to allow a float of the *Real* at the start of 1999 became associated with a sharp reduction in foreign capital inflows (Amann & Baer, 2003). The scale of this reduction was so accentuated that only under the auspices of an IMF standby facility was Brazil able to continue to meet its debt servicing obligations. Nevertheless, short run growth performance was very badly affected. At the same time devaluation was associated with severe trauma in the financial system despite the fact that currency floatation had been widely anticipated. Some 2–3 years after the crisis, however, the economy had clearly entered a period of recovery, the most notable feature of which was a strong improvement in export performance. The rise in exports was closely tied to the now highly competitive valuation of the *Real*.

More recently, the case of Argentina appears to offer some support for the floatation → crisis → export-based recovery story. At the beginning of 2002, the Argentine Peso was allowed to float freely downwards following the abandonment of a decade-long convertibility plan. As in the Brazilian case, the floatation of the Peso was at first associated with an acute economic crisis with GDP contracting sharply in 2002. The financial sector was among the worst affected and, indeed, suffered far more than its Brazilian counterpart a couple of years earlier. Subsequently, however, the more competitive exchange rate valuation has helped to induce a sharp increase in Argentinean exports. This has in turn been associated with a healthy recovery in growth performance.

While explanations such as these appear superficially persuasive, the question arises as to whether meaningful conclusions can be drawn from an examination of the real objective facts of an event that has been associated with changes in market confidence, which itself a subjective rather than objective phenomenon.[1] In other words, it is important to draw a methodological distinction between variations in the fundamentals and agents' perceptions of them. One should not presume that alterations in the fundamentals always map in a direct and consistent manner into the evolution of market sentiment. Consequently we propose to adopt an alternative approach, strongly influenced by the seminal contributions of Minsky (1982, 1986). Minsky focuses his analysis on the relevance of expectations in the endogenous evolution of an economy. He argues that, in order to understand how and when financial crises start and end, we need to employ and analyse variables that allow us capture subjective changes in market confidence.

The Mexican financial crisis of 1994–95 provides an ideal setting for an exercise of this nature. The crisis, famously dubbed "the first of the 21st Century", has some similarity with those of Argentina and Brazil in that it eventually entailed floatation and substantial currency depreciation. However, in some regards the Mexican crisis stands apart from its counterparts elsewhere in Latin America or, indeed, Asia. This is to do with the fact that its emergence was linked not to sharp deteriorations of the internal or even the external balance (two key fundamentals), but rather, to the growing exposure of private agents to risk based on their rapid accumulation of debt. As these agents became increasingly overextended, the likelihood that sudden alterations in market perception could trigger crisis also rose (Cruz, Amann & Walters, 2006). In this context especially, we would argue that a proper understanding of the crisis requires a thorough understanding of the shifting pattern of agents' expectations.

The aims of this chapter are twofold. In first place the chapter sets out to identify *when* financial crises start and terminate. To this end, we propose, in the context of Minsky's financial instability hypothesis (FIH), the broad money-to-international reserves (M2/R) ratio as the variable that can best capture changes in agents' confidence as alterations in economic or political fundamentals occur and affect agents' capacity to service their debts. The second aim of this chapter is to identify *which events* contribute to the start and the end of a financial crisis. This enables us to reach some conclusion as to whether financial liberalisation compromised economic policy in the *ex post* sense (Grabel, 1996).

In order to shed light on these issues, we proceed in the following manner. Section 2, which follows this introduction, offers a brief explanation as to why the M2/R ratio is an appropriate means of capturing changes in private agents' confidence in the context of Minsky's FIH. Next, Section 3 briefly explains the MS-AR model and applies it to the Mexican experience. Specifically, we *time* the 1994–95 Mexican crisis, applying a two-regime Markov switching autoregressive (MS-AR) model and presenting the results. Following this, some general and policy-related conclusions are drawn.

## Minsky's Financial Instability Hypothesis and the M2/R Ratio

Minsky's (1982, 1986) approach stresses that we live in a world where investment decisions are formed on the basis of expectations and where expected cash flows to cope with the financial commitments incurred in the investment process can vary. Investment therefore determines the pace of the economy, and is dependent on cash flows and agents' financial requirements. Cash flows are based on expectations and they vary according to market conditions.[2] If cash flows are more than enough to satisfy current cash commitments[3] then "they are the source of dividends and retained earnings which positively affect long term expectations of banks, firms and shareholders" (Bellofiore & Ferri, 2001, p. 13). Accordingly, cash flow variations affect agents' balance sheets, leaving them either servicing their debts, embarking on new projects, or defaulting on their debts. Since the economy is an interlinked system characterised by a network of intertemporal, uncertain cash flows, non-payment of debts by one firm to another (especially banks) generates multiple defaults. This succession of defaults may, in certain circumstances, provoke the collapse of the economy.

In this sense, the cyclical nature of an economy is the result of fluctuations in private investment and the endogenous evolution of agents and institutions due to their profit-seeking nature, and to domestic and external conditions. Importantly, this endogenous tendency towards instability is exacerbated in a financially deregulated context, particularly when financial liberalisation is haphazardly implemented and capital controls are removed. This is because some agents are propelled to embark on projects with a long gestation period, issuing short-term debts denominated in foreign currency. This, in turn, increases the country's vulnerability to sudden and swift endogenous domestic changes or external disturbances (the economy is now more vulnerable to increases in the rate of interest or sudden movements of the exchange rate, see footnote 4).

Right after the Mexican crisis of 1994–95 ended there emerged a surge in interest concerning the causes of currency crises. This interest only increased in the wake of subsequent financial collapses all over the developing world. The literature which has issued forth has revealed the high importance of the M2/R ratio as an indicator of currency crises. As emphasised by Calvo & Mendoza

(1996) "the ratio M2/R is a very good indicator of crises and financial difficulties". And this is so because it "… captures the extent to which liabilities of the banking system are backed by international reserves…" (Bird & Rajan, 2003, fn. 10, p. 881). In this sense, the larger the ratio, the lower is the ability of a country to weather a speculative currency attack (Calvo & Mendoza, 1996).

What is important to note is that the ratio not only assesses the potential demand for foreign assets among domestic agents, but that in doing so, it also captures the extent to which agents' confidence shifts with respect to changes in the fundamentals. Therefore, to a large extent, this ratio is capable of disclosing the intentions of agents to withdraw capital from an economy. This is an intention that is likely to be fulfilled only when no capital controls are in existence. For example, when private agents opt to demand foreign exchange persistently and in large amounts, one likely explanation behind this behaviour is that agents' expectations are sceptical concerning the capacity of the government to maintain 'policy credibility'. Such scepticism has typically arisen surrounding the maintenance of a currency peg when no capital controls have been set aside, the recent experiences of Argentina and Brazil being cases in point (Amann & Baer, 2003).

Let us trace through, in the context of Minsky's FIH, the consequences of a swift change in domestic market conditions (e.g. a devaluation of the foreign exchange rate[4]). If a swift change of this type occurs, agents' preference to hold a higher proportion of domestic currency (cash) may alter essentially for two reasons. On the one hand, agents will need to exchange domestic currency in order to discharge foreign currency denominated debt. On the other hand, agents will maintain holdings of foreign denominated currency so as to hedge themselves against future downward movements in the external value of the domestic currency. This may translate into a decreasing level of domestic currency and an increasing demand for foreign currency.

In this sense, during periods of calm, a low M2/R ratio is expected. Meanwhile, prior to, and during a crisis, an increasing domestic currency to international reserves ratio might be expected to prevail. Figure 1 shows that Mexico's M2/R ratio follows the expected pattern prior to (and after) the crisis: from the early 90s to mid 1993 the ratio shows a decreasing and stable trend. This indicates that financial calm dominated. However, between the end of 1993 and 1995 the ratio soared and was very unstable with marked up and downs. This suggests, as expected, that agents' confidence was becoming progressively undermined, a process that led to the onset of financial panic.

Importantly, in the same way that the M2/R ratio allows one to identify *when* agents' financial panic started (in the form of withdraws of capital), it also allows to verify *why* and *when* agents returned to financial calm. In this sense, the use of the M2/R ratio enables us to capture the policy measures implemented by the

Figure 1: Monthly Evolution of the M2/R Ratio, 1990.1–2002.9

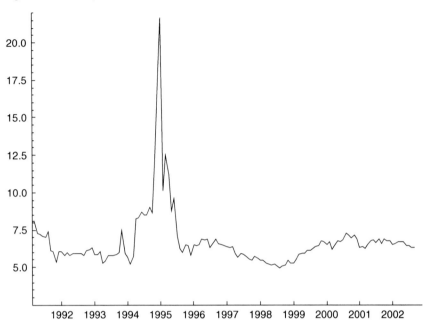

*Source*: IMF-*International Financial Statistics*, 2002, Cd-Rom.

government in the aftermath of the crisis aimed at regaining agents' confidence and stemming capital flight. The argument in this regard is that in order to regain market confidence, the government must implement policies that reinforce the financial liberalisation strategy. In other words, policy autonomy, according to Grabel (1996), as a result of the adoption of a financial liberalisation agenda, can be seen as compromised in an *ex ante* and *ex post* sense. On the one hand, a country's government (especially a developing one) that seeks to attract and maintain external investment inflows (direct and portfolio) as a strategy to boost growth may be from the beginning severely constrained in an *ex-ante* sense. For a government, to create an adequate climate to attract capital, it is necessary to adopt a set of policies aimed at securing investors' confidence and reward. These policies include restrictive monetary and fiscal policies aimed exclusively at price stabilization, maintaining interest and exchange rates higher than otherwise would be preferred and sound public finances, i.e. budgetary balance or surplus. In addition, privatisation programmes and measures to liberalise the economy would be necessities (Grabel, 1996).

On the other hand, in the event of a run of capital or a currency crisis the government could be compelled to adopt reinforcing measures aimed at reversing the outflow of capital. These measures would essentially involve an intensification of the policies initially adopted. Thus, the policy autonomy will be in a state of an *ex-post* constraint, a situation which may be aggravated once the country receives financial support from a multilateral institution (Grabel, 1996). Hence policymakers, once they have implemented a financial liberalisation strategy, may have little room to manoeuvre. Their ability to reduce or mitigate the risks introduced by the strategy, and therefore to avert a crisis may also be limited. This leaves little or no scope for growth-oriented policies.

## Timing the 1994–95 Mexican Financial Crisis

To shed light on whether the M2/R ratio is able to capture the changes that agents' confidence might undergo prior, during and after a crisis and to recognise the policy measures that are necessary to adopt to regain market confidence in this section we apply the MS-AR model (see Hamilton, 1989, 1994). So as to accomplish this we employ the rate of growth of Mexico's monthly seasonally adjusted M2/R ratio (IMF-International Financial Statistics, 2002, Cd-Rom) from 1990.1 to 2002.9.[5] The reason for choosing this period is that it reflects fully the adoption of the financial liberalisation strategy.[6] The latter, of course, has frequently been associated with the origin of the financial collapse (see, *inter alia*, Cruz, Amann & Walters, 2006).

Assuming (as Coe (2002) does) that the financial sector is at any point either in a regime of financial calm or in one of panic[7] (the former associated with increased uncertainty), we have established that an adequate two-regime model corresponds to an MSIH(2)-AR(13) schema.[8] The specification of this model has a shifting intercept and variance terms (MS *Intercept-Heteroskedastic*). Recall that "… for a MSI[*ntercept*] model smoothing and filtering probabilities are less computationally demanding (and therefore much faster) than the statistical analysis with a MSM[*ean*] model" (Krolzig, 1997, p. 126). The model representation is:

$$y_t = \delta_{s_t} + \sum_{k=1}^{13} \phi_k y_{t-k} + \varepsilon_t$$

where $\varepsilon_t \sim NID\left(\sigma^2_{S_t}\right)$ and $S_t \in \{1, 2\}$ are generated by a first-order Markov chain. For a first order Markov chain the probability the $S_t$ equals some particular value $j$ depends on the past only through the most recent value $S_{t-1}$:

$$P\{S_t = j \mid S_{t-1} = i\} = p_{ij}$$

Such a process is described as an N-state Markov chain with transition probabilities $\{p_{ij}\}_{ij=1,2\ldots N}$. The transition probabilities $p_{ij}$ give the probability that state $i$ will be followed by state $j$. Note also that:

$$\sum_{j=1}^{N} p_{ij} = 1$$

The maximum likelihood estimation of the model is based on an implementation of the expectation maximization two step algorithm proposed by Hamilton (1989). The estimations reported herein were carried with the MSVAR class for Ox (see Krolzig, 1998).

Figure 2 shows the estimated filtered and smoothed probabilities of the regime of financial panic. If the disruptions of the financial sector during the period under analysis can be thought of as a shift to a regime of financial crisis, this should be reflected in the smoothed and filtered probabilities. More specifically, one would expect to see a probability close to one assigned to the financial panic regime during periods in which agents' confidence changed (Coe, 2002).

As we can see, the probabilities suggest that there are three marked periods in which financial panic dominated. However, the first period, which spans during the last quarter of 1991 (see Table 1), is the result not of (negative) changes in the fundamentals (1991 was one of the most successful years in

Figure 2: Probabilities of Regime of Financial Panic

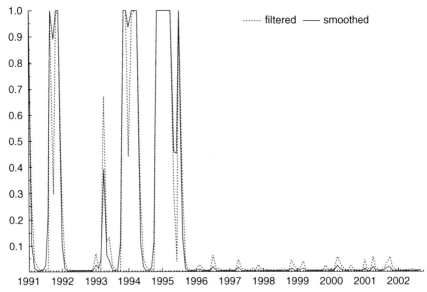

**Table 1: Financial Panic Regime Classification**

| Period | Probability |
|---|---|
| 1991:9–1991:12 | 0.9726 |
| 1994:11–1995:4 | 1.0000 |
| 1995:7–1995:7 | 1.0000 |

terms of economic growth since trade and financial liberalisation reforms were adopted[9]) but of an atypical increase in M2 due, as Mexico's Central Bank (1991, p. 9) points out, to the substantial rise (by 157.7 per cent) of M1. This was a consequence of the boom in checking account deposits.[10]

Regarding the second period, the probabilities are consistent with the assertion that the change in the domestic conditions (and the change in market sentiment) began in early 1994, due to the *Zapatista* army rebellion in January. However, as can be seen, from November 1993, the probabilities started to increase, reflecting the financial sector's initial uncertainty about domestic conditions. One of the events that kept the probability of panic high was the assassination of the Partido Revolucionario Institucional (PRI) presidential candidate, Luis Donaldo Colosio, in March. These events had two main negative reinforcing effects.

The first was a speculative currency attack in March. As a consequence, from March to April international reserves fell around US$6 billion. The exchange rate band then was loosened by around 4 per cent, driving the exchange rate from $3.11 pesos/dollar in January to $3.27 in April.[11] The second negative event was the continuous increase in the domestic rate of interest, putting pressure on the cost of agents' debts. According to the probabilities classification, the economy re-established itself in the calm regime in May, suggesting that the measures taken by the authorities were, to some extent, successful in restoring agents' confidence.

This calm, however, lasted only six months, as once again, political events – this time the assassination of the PRI Secretary General, Jose F. Ruiz Massieu in September – dented agents' confidence. Also, economic imbalances contributed to the undermining of agents' confidence: Mexico's level of current account deficit and short term external debt were high by international standards standing at 6.9 per cent and 9.2 per cent of GDP respectively. Taken together, these factors led to another speculative attack in November. International reserves fell by around US$5 billion in just one month, falling by another US$6 billion the following month. It is in November, precisely, when probabilities shifted once again from (still) low values to unity. And it was in this month when, we argue, the crisis started and not on December 20, when the exchange rate peg was abandoned.

**Table 2: Estimated Transition Probabilities of the MSIH(2)-AR(13)**

|  | $P_{iP}$ | $P_{iC}$ | Duration |
|---|---|---|---|
| Panic Regime | 0.7434 | 0.2566 | 3.90 |
| Calm Regime | 0.0383 | 0.9617 | 26.12 |

Table 2 supports the above evidence. It shows that the transition probabilities from the panic regime to the calm regime (and vice versa) are high. This indicates the fact that agents' confidence was likely to shift very rapidly and that, in the context of free mobility of capital, the final upshot was likely to be a financial crisis.

When and why did confidence return to the financial sector? The fact that the crisis lasted until May of 1995 (when probabilities of the financial panic regime became negligible again) seems to suggest that financial calm gained hold once more with the stabilisation of the exchange rate and the decline in the domestic rate of interest. These improvements stemmed from three main economic measures, all of which were announced during the beginning of 1995 and which were exclusively aimed at regaining investors' confidence. First, during the early days of January, and again in March, the government promised to reinforce the economic policies recommended by the liberalisation agenda, that is, to continue the process of financial and trade deregulation as well as the adoption of a tighter monetary policy and the reinforcement of fiscal retrenchment.

Second, the government guaranteed to honour outstanding debts. This was done thanks to the massive financial bailout (around US$50 billion) provided by the US government. In early January the US government announced an initial bailout for Mexico of around US$15 billion and the IMF offered an additional US$2 billion. Later, in mid-January, when the crisis was deepening, the US government increased the bailout to US$40 billion and in early February it offered US$50 billion. However, it was not until the 22nd of that month that the bailout was approved by the US President. Finally, a federal insurance savings fund was created (this instrument was known as the FOBAPROA). This measure was taken essentially to rescue from bankruptcy several banks that were unable to discharge their foreign currency denominated debts. In sum, the return of agents' confidence and the beginning of the end of the financial crisis began in May of 1995 and *not* when exports recovered. The restoration of agents' confidence took six months, though, as Figure 1 indicates, another short-lived panic was registered in July. All this evidence is further supported by Buira (1999) who notes that "the Mexican recession was deep, but it was also brief, thanks to the structural reforms undertaken in Mexico… and to the Mexican government's determination to pursue the IMF-supported economic recovery program" (p. 7).

The above facts suggest that the Mexican government was indeed policy compromised in the *ex-post* sense and that in order to control the crisis or regain investors' confidence in the aftermath of the collapse it had to reinforce the measures initially applied, when the financial liberalisation strategy was fully adopted in 1990. This did not leave scope for growth-oriented goals. It can be argued, therefore, that Mexico lost a unique opportunity to change its economic strategy and return to a pro-growth path.

## Conclusions

This chapter analysed the experience of Mexico in 1994–5 as it underwent what has often been termed "the first economic crisis of the 20th Century". The crisis was distinct in that its foundations rested more upon the accumulation of private sector liabilities than on "conventional" fiscal or current account disequilibria. Rather than modelling the crisis in terms of a link between the evolution of ex post fundamentals and changes in agents' behaviour, our analysis has followed an alternative, Minskyan path. Our analysis sought to ground itself on an examination of the impact of agents' subjective expectations. Applying a two-regime MS-AR model, we showed that the beginning and end of a financial crisis is associated with an alteration in private agents' confidence linked to economic and/or political changes that could *not* be characterised as *ex post* events. Thus, we find that the evolution of financial crisis was little affected by the key *ex-post* events of the Mexican Crisis. These were the abandonment of the exchange rate anchor and the eventual recovery of the economy led by export growth.

Our estimated probabilities suggest that the Mexican crisis started in November of 1994 with the second speculative attack of that year and not on December 20th 1994, when the exchange rate was allowed to float freely. The financial panic lasted six months, until May 1995, when financial calm was restored again. The return of calm was a direct consequence of the economic measures that the government took during the early months of the collapse. These measures were aimed explicitly at regaining investors' confidence and centred on reinforcing financial liberalisation. Ironically, it can be argued that it was the very presence of financial liberalisation which had predisposed the Mexican economy to crisis in the first place.

These findings have more general implications both in a policy sense and in terms of crisis modelling. Regarding the former, it is clear that once an economy adopts a strategy of financial liberalisation, policy autonomy is sacrificed in the interest of maintaining investors' confidence. This renders difficult or perhaps impossible the pursuit of a conventional growth-oriented strategy. The final result is that even when the economy is able to overcome the financial panic, its growth is likely to remain at low levels. This is particularly true where there has been a failure to implement systemic supply-side policies aimed at boosting non-financial sector competitiveness. In the same vein, our findings support the hypothesis that the presence or absence of capital controls might be fundamental in triggering or averting a financial crisis. Regarding crises modelling, the evidence presented in this chapter makes it clear that the effective analysis of crises requires that much more attention be paid to the measurement and examination of market expectations. Alterations in market fundamentals do not necessarily alter expectations in a smooth, consistent or predictable manner. We have argued, therefore, that the incorporation of a variable for expectations, in this case the M2/R ratio, is a vital part of the modelling exercise.

## Notes

1. For example, Obstfeld (1994) in describing his second generation-currency model argues that the reason for governments resisting speculative attacks depends on what he calls endogenous variables. These endogenous variables are basically the market expectations of depreciation, i.e. economic agents, in the past, expected the domestic currency would be depreciated at some time and/or they now expect it will be depreciated in the future (see Alves Jr., Ferrari & De Paula, 2000).
2. For example high or low levels of aggregate demand and the cost of credit.
3. Cash commitments are created at the same time that investment is made.
4. It is important to highlight that an increase in the interest rate has two singular effects on agents' balance sheets. First, it reduces the present value of the cash flows expected to be earned from operating leveraged financial projects. Second, it increases the cash flow commitments for financing charges when lending is primarily short term or set on an adjustable or roll-over basis. For firms with a large proportion of imported inputs, export sales or foreign borrowing, depreciation in the exchange rate has the same effect on cash flow commitments as an increase in interest rates (Kregel, 2001, p. 197).
5. The monthly growth rate is calculated as $100*\ln(y_t/y_{t-1})$. The ADF statistic test for the test of the null hypothesis that a series is I(1) against the alternative that it is I(0) around a constant is $-13.08$ This implies a rejection of the hypothesis that the growth rate of the seasonally adjusted M2/R follows a random walk at the 1 percent level.
6. Mexico initiated a financial deregulation strategy from 1977 which was intensified in 1988. However, it can be argued that only in 1990 that the strategy of financial openness was fully launched. In March 1989 the Brady Plan to refinance the external debt was announced and in July it was signed. There followed a succession of measures to relax or abolish bank reserve requirements, credit quotas to high priority sectors and control over interest rates were implemented. The elimination of restrictions governing foreign investment in domestic bonds, most government bonds, and the stock market took place in 1989 and 1990. In order to give security to investors, the Financial Group Law was announced and passed in July 1990. The Law allowed private-sector majority ownership of Mexican banks and initiated the privatisation process. Also, foreign investment in banks was permitted at a level of up to 30% of total equity (Ros, 2001).
7. Coe (2002) proceeds in a different way by applying a Markov switching model in its multivariate form (MS-VAR) to make inferences about the timing of the 1930 US financial crisis. He employs monthly data from 1919 to 1941 concerning the rate of

growth of the deposit-currency ratio and a proxy for the cost of credit intermediation (defined as the yield spread of corporate bonds rated Baa by Moody's, and the yield of long-term government bonds). The former is expected to be low during the years of the crisis due to the withdrawal of money; the latter is expected to increase during the crisis as a consequence of the rise in the cost of credit intermediation.

8. The Akaike Information Criteria (AIC) was used to select the lag order.
9. In 1991, for example, Mexico's GDP grew 4.1 per cent and other macroeconomic indicators (like inflation, the fiscal deficit and the nominal rate of interest) also exhibited an improving trend. The optimism that had prevailed since 1990 was enhanced by the announcement of the forthcoming NAFTA agreement with the United States and Canada. During this period, Mexico received large amounts of capital inflows (by 1992 it was the world's second largest emerging market).
10. It is worth noting that using quarterly data, the MS-AR does not capture this substantial increase.
11. Since 1988, as a part of a stabilisation programme, Mexican authorities had implemented a crawling peg exchange rate system.

## References

Alves Jr., Ferrari, A. and De Paula, L. "The Post Keynesian critique of conventional currency crisis models and Davidson's proposal to reform the international monetary system." *Journal of Post Keynesian Economics*, 2000, 22, 207–225.

Amann, E. and Baer, W. "Anchors away: the costs and benefits of Brazil's devaluation". *World Development*, 2003, 31, 1033–1046.

Banco de México. *Resumen del Informe Anual*. México, 1991.

Bellofiore, R. and Ferri, P., eds. *Financial fragility and the investment in the capitalist economy. The legacy of Hyman Minsky*. Vol. I, UK: Edward Elgar, 2001.

Bird, G. and Rajan, R. "Too much of a good thing? The adequacy of international reserves in the aftermath of crises." *World Economy*, 2003, 26, 873–891.

Buira, A. "An alternative approach to financial crises". *Essays in International Finance*, Princenton University, 1999, 212.

Calvo, A. and Mendoza, E. "Mexico's balance-of-payments: a chronicle of a death foretold". *Journal of International Economics*, 1996, 41, 236–264.

Coe, P. "Financial crisis and the great depression: a regime switching approach". *Journal of Money, Credit, and Banking*, 2002, 34, 76–93.

Cruz, M., Amann, E. & Walters, B. "Expectations, the business cycle and the Mexican peso crisis". *Cambridge Journal of Economics*, 2006, 30, 701–723.

Grabel, I. "Marketing the third world: the contradictions of portfolio investment in the global economy". *World Development*, 1996, 24, 11, 1761–1776.

Hamilton, J. "A new approach to the economic analysis of nonstationary time series and the business cycle". *Econometrica*,1989, 57, 357–384.

Hamilton, J. *Time Series Analysis*. USA: Princeton University Press, 1994.

Kregel, J. "Yes 'it' did happen again. The Minsky crisis in Asia" in R. Bellofiore and P. Ferri, eds., *Financial fragility and the investment in the capitalist economy. The legacy of Hyman Minsky*. Vol. II, UK: Edward Elgar, 195–212, 2001.

Krolzig, H-M. "Econometric modelling of Markov-Switching Vector Autoregressions using MSVAR for Ox". Institute of Economics and Statistics and Nuffield College, Oxford University, 1998.

Krolzig, H-M. *Markov-switching Vector Autoregressions. Modeling Statistical Inference, an application to the business cycle analysis. Lecture Notes in Economics and Mathematical Systems 454.* Berlin: Springer-Verlag, 1997.

Minsky, H. *Inflation, recession and economy policy.* Great Britain: Wheatsheaf Books, 1982.

Minsky, H. *Stabilizing an unstable economy.* USA: Columbia University Press, 1986.

Obstfeld, M. "The logic of currency crises." *Cahiers économiques et monétaries*, 1994, 43, 189–213.

Ros, J. "From the capital surge to the financial crisis and beyond: the Mexican economy in the 1990's" in *Financial crises in "successful" emerging economies*, R. Ffrench-Davis, ed. USA: ECLAC-Brookings Institutions Press, 107–140, 2001.

# Chapter 4

# EXCHANGE RATES, GROWTH AND INFLATION: WHAT IF THE INCOME ELASTICITIES OF TRADE FLOWS RESPOND TO RELATIVE PRICES?

## Nelson H. Barbosa-Filho

Professor of Economics, Instituto de Economia, Universidade Federal do Rio de Janeiro

## Abstract

This chapter analyzes the operation of the balance-of-payments (BoP) constraint on developing economies, with a special emphasis to the link between inflation targets, real-exchange-rate dynamics and growth in the short and in the long run. The analysis starts with a brief survey of the main models of the BoP constraint. Using a "canonical" BoP-constraint model, the chapter investigates how inflation targets can influence growth in the long run through the impact of real exchange rates on the income elasticities of exports and imports. Based on Woo (2005) and Frenkel and Taylor (2006), the basic theoretical argument is that short-run inflation management may imply substantial and prolonged changes in real exchange rates, which in their turn may not only increase financial fragility, but also change the very own BoP constraint on growth in the long run. The main conclusion of the chapter is that the real exchange rate can be an important instrument to foster growth and development through temporary but sufficiently long changes in the relative price between tradable and non-tradable goods.

## Introduction

The Balance-of-Payments (BoP) constraint is one of the most important determinants of growth in developing economies. More specifically, since developing countries cannot issue the international currency and usually face liquidity constraints in international financial markets, they tend to adjust their current account to the availability of foreign finance. In such a process, both the exchange rate and the GDP growth rate are constrained to produce the adjustment of the current account to the international financial conditions.

Most models of the balance-of-payments (BoP) constraint on growth assume that the income elasticities of exports and imports are given in the long run, so that the growth rate of the GDP of the constrained economy is determined by the growth rate of the world income. In gap models the income elasticity is set equal to one, whereas in Thirlwall's Law and its extensions such a parameter is assumed to be constant but not necessarily equal to one.

The long-run determination of GDP growth by the growth rate of world income does not exclude the possibility of deviations between these two variables in the short run, since capital flows can raise or lower the BoP independently of trade flows. In fact, the most recent versions of the BoP constraint are focused on the link between current-account imbalances, foreign-debt accumulation, international reserves and financial fragility.

The role of real exchange rates is obviously crucial in the operation of the BoP constraint, but in most studies of the topic this is not usually stressed on the assumption that some sort of purchasing-power parity holds in the long-run. In contrast, in short-run models of financial fragility, the real exchange rate plays a central role in the determination of growth and inflation.

One of the main problems of the constant-elasticity assumption implicit in most models of the BoP is that such a parameter is bound to experience structural breaks in the long run. In other words, the very own constraint imposed by international financial conditions lead to changes in relative prices and in economic policy, which in their turn generate changes in the income and price elasticities of exports and imports.

In should be noted that recognizing the sensibility of elasticity parameters to relative prices does not necessarily imply accepting the neoclassical view that flexible prices solve any problem. Quite the contrary. The history of economic development shows that the adjustment of the "technology of production" to changes in relative prices is usually slow, characterized by wide income fluctuations and, most importantly, marked by multiple equilibria (for instance, the persistence of "underdevelopment" and "dependency".)

If we add to the above picture the fact that prolonged changes in relative prices can be used to promote structural change (Woo 2005), the "parameters" of the BoP constraint become endogenous in the long-run. In other words, rather than an inevitable constraint, the BoP determinants of the GDP growth rate can be shaped by economic policy, as indicated by the successful catching-up strategy of many East Asian countries in the 20th century, and of China and India today.

Finally, given the importance of inflation reduction in the macroeconomic agenda of many developing countries today, especially in Latin America, there is another important issue to be investigated, namely: the implication of a quick reduction in inflation for growth and development. From the previous considerations the main argument is clear and intuitive: a quick reduction of inflation that comes together with a prolonged period of exchange-rate appreciation can be detrimental for growth in the long run, because it may induce a change in the structural determinants of the BoP constraint.

This chapter aims to present a brief analytical survey of the BoP constraint, and then to use a "canonical" BoP-constraint model to investigate what would happen if one allows the structural determinants of the trade flows to depend on the level of the real exchange rate. The main result is that temporary but prolonged changes in the real-exchange-rate can have permanent impact on the structure of the economy and, through this, determine growth and development in the long run (Frenkel and Taylor 2006). The chapter concludes with an analysis of the implications of such a finding for inflation management in the short run, and the obvious conclusion is that inflation targeting should be done with moderation to avoid producing a "slow-growth" equilibrium position.

## Two Views on the Balance-of-Payments Constraint

In general terms the BoP constraint means that an open economy must have a balanced growth of exports and imports in the long run, otherwise either it or the rest of the world will run into a financial crisis. The basic idea is that no economy can have an explosive current account deficit with the rest of the world indefinitely, that is, Ponzi finance is not viable in the long run. Whether or not the balanced growth of exports and imports happens with a trade deficit or surplus is an open question, since the export-import ratio of the economy under analysis may be stable at values different than one.[1]

The first model of the BoP constraint proposed by Thirlwall (1979) assumed that the trade balance should be zero in the long run, on the grounds that trade surpluses and deficits tend to balance out during a sufficient long period of time. The subsequent of extensions of Thirlwall's model allowed for temporary deficits or surpluses, introducing the possibility that foreign finance could raise or lower the BoP constraint (Thirlwall and Hussain 1982, McCombie and McCombie 1997, Moreno Brid 1998, Barbosa-Filho 2001a). Most importantly, since the introduction of trade imbalances brings the dynamics of foreign debt explicitly into the analysis, the extensions of Thirlwall's (1979) model also tended to reformulate the the BoP problem in terms of the stability of some key flow-flow ratios, as the ratio of the current-account deficit to GDP

(Moreno-Brid 1998), or stock-flow ratios, as the ratio of foreign-debt to GDP (Barbosa-Filho 2001a).

The extension of the BoP constraint to include debt and financial considerations naturally leads to the concept financial fragility, that is, to the idea that changes in international financial conditions can lead to currency crises and, through this, cause changes in growth and exchange rates independently of trade considerations. In other words, the operation of the BoP constraint may come through the capital account instead of through the current account, especially after the financial liberalization and increase in capital mobility that took place in the world economy since the 1970s. In fact, the introduction of stock-flow considerations in the analysis makes it necessary to link the determinants of international trade with financial considerations in the operation of the BoP constraint as, for instance, the level of reserves considered safe to avoid currency crises and the export growth rate compatible with the interest rate paid on foreign debt.

Despite the many existing models of the BoP constraint,[2] its basic idea and the natural evolution of the analysis from trade to financial fragility can be represented in a very simple way. To do this without cluttering the exposition with technical details of the vast literature on the subject, let us jus restrict our analysis to two models, the original long-run model proposed by Thirlwall (1979) and the more recent short-run model proposed by Barbosa-Filho (2001b). These two models capture most of the issues under discussion and, as we will discuss in the next section, they both suffer from the same limitations: the assumption of constant elasticities in their trade functions.

The starting point is a set of four simple assumptions: (i) the world economy is divided in a small "home" country and a large "foreign" country; (ii) the two countries are one-sector economies; (iii) there is imperfect substitution between the home and foreign goods; and (iv) the foreign country issues the world currency. In this situation the home country has to export goods, sell assets or issue debt to finance its purchases from the rest of the world.

The next and crucial assumption is that exports and imports should grow at the same rate in the long run, as specified by Thirlwall (1979), to rule out Ponzi finance. Formally this means that

$$p_h + q_x = e + p_f + q_m \tag{2.1}$$

where $p_h$ is the growth rate of the price of the home good, in home currency; $p_f$ is the growth rate of the price of the foreign good, in foreign currency; $e$ is the growth rate of the nominal exchange rate, the home currency per unit of foreign currency; and $q_x$ and $q_m$ are the real growth rates of home exports and imports, respectively.

Following Thirlwall's model, let the growth rates of real exports and imports be a function of the change in relative prices and the growth rates of the home and foreign economies, that is:

$$q_x = \gamma(e + p_f - p_h) + \delta q_f \qquad (2.2)$$

and

$$q_m = -\alpha(e + p_f - p_h) + \beta q_h \qquad (2.3)$$

where $q_f$ and $q_h$ are the growth rates of the foreign and home incomes, respectively, and $\alpha$, $\beta$, $\gamma$ and $\delta$ are positive parameters that represent the price and income elasticities of the trade flows.

Substituting (2.2) and (2.3) in (2.1) and rearranging the terms we have:

$$q_h = \left(\frac{\delta}{\beta}\right) q_f - \left(\frac{1 - \alpha - \gamma}{\beta}\right)(e + p_f - p_h) \qquad (2.4)$$

Following Thirlwall's (1979) model and assuming that the real exchange rate is constant in the long run,[3] the second term on the right-hand-side of (2.4) is zero and, therefore, the BoP constraint becomes simply

$$q_h = \left(\frac{\delta}{\beta}\right) q_f \qquad (2.5)$$

The intuitive meaning of (5) is that, in order to keep its export-import ratio constant in a context of fixed real exchange rates, the growth rate of the home country is constrained by the income elasticity of its exports ($\delta$) and imports ($\beta$), and by the growth rate of the foreign country ($q_f$).

As we mentioned earlier, the BoP constraint specifies that exports and imports must grow at the same rate in the long run, but not necessarily that the home country must have a trade surplus or deficit. To close this important question is necessary to bring the stock-flow dynamics of the whole balance of payments into the analysis, as done, for instance, by Barbosa-Filho's (2001b) model of international liquidity and growth.

The starting point of the Barbosa-Filho's stock-flow analysis is to assume that the home country must not only keep its trade balance stable, but that it should also keep its foreign reserves above the minimum level that is considered "safe" to cope with the usual fluctuations in international financial conditions without suffering a currency crisis. To simplify the analysis, such a safe level of a foreign reserves is defined as a fixed ratio of the home country's foreign debt, that is, a "liquidity ratio" determined by market expectations and the institutional development of the world financial markets.

More formally, let $l$ be the observed liquidity ratio the home country, that is, the ratio of its foreign reserves ($R$) to its foreign debt ($D$).

$$l = \frac{R}{D} \tag{2.6}$$

The dynamics of the liquidity ratio can be analyzed through the dynamics of the foreign reserves-income and the foreign debt-income ratios, that is

$$r = \frac{ER}{P_h Q_h} \tag{2.7}$$

and

$$d = \frac{ED}{P_h Q_h} \tag{2.8}$$

where $E$ is the nominal exchange rate and $P_h$ and $Q_h$ represent the home price and income levels.

As shown by Barbosa-Filho (2001b), the dynamics of $r$ and $d$ can be represented as

$$\frac{dr}{dt} = x - m - (i_f + \sigma)d - n + u + f_d + f_i - (p_f + q_h - z)r \tag{2.9}$$

and

$$\frac{dd}{dt} = f_d - (p_f + q_h - z)d \tag{2.10}$$

where $x$ and $m$ are the export-income and import-income ratios of the home country, respectively; $i_f$ and $\sigma$ are the foreign interest rate and the risk premium paid by home borrowers on their foreign debt, respectively; $u$ and $n$ are the ratios of net unilateral transfers received and net profits and dividends paid by the home country to foreign agents, also normalized by the home income, respectively; $f_d$ and $f_i$ are the net inflow of capital received by the home country through interest-bearing bonds and through foreign direct investment, divided by the home income, respectively; and $z$ is the growth rate of the home-foreign real exchange rate, that is:

$$z = e + p_f - p_h \tag{2.11}$$

Now, as we mentioned earlier, the BoP constraint implies that exports and imports should growth at the same rate. In the stock-flow model given by (9) and (10) this means that the export-income and import-income ratios should be constant, which according the import and export functions specified earlier imply that the growth rates of home income and the real exchange rate should satisfy the following conditions:

$$q_h = \left( \frac{1-\alpha}{1-\alpha-\gamma+\beta\gamma} \right) \delta q_f \qquad (2.12)$$

and

$$z_h = \left( \frac{1-\beta}{1-\alpha-\gamma+\beta\gamma} \right) \delta q_f \qquad (2.13)$$

The economic intuition behind (2.12) and (2.13) is that the BoP constraint determines both the income growth and real-exchange-rate variation of the home country. In fact, in contrast to Thirlwall's original model, Barbosa-Filho's (2001b) version of the BoP constraint implies not only a constraint on income growth, but also a constraint on real-exchange-rate growth. Moreover, it is straightforward to see that (2.12) and (2.13) include Thirlwall's Law as a special case when the income elasticity of imports ($\beta$) is equal to one.

Given $x$ and $m$ and assuming that the other variables in (2.9) and (2.10) are also fixed, we have a $2 \times 2$ dynamical system for the debt-income and reserve income ratios. As also shown by Barbosa-Filho (2001b), this dynamical system is stable under very reasonable assumptions about the value of the price and income elasticities of home exports and imports. Assuming for simplicity that this is the case, we can concentrate our analysis on the value of the liquidity ratio at the steady state, that is

$$l = \left( \frac{x - m - n + u + f_i}{f_d} \right) - \left( \frac{i_f + \sigma + z - p_f - q_h}{p_f + q_h - z} \right) \qquad (2.14)$$

The final step of the analysis is to introduce the liquidity constraint in the model to determine the trade balance of the home country. More formally, since the liquidity constraint implies that the liquidity ratio $l$ should be greater that a critical value $l^*$, we can solve (2.14) for $x$-$m$ in order to find the ratio of net exports to home income consistent with the BoP constraint. From (2.14) this means that:

$$x - m \geq n - u - f_i + f_d \left( \frac{i_f + \sigma + z - p_f - q_h}{p_f + q_h - z} + l^* \right) \qquad (2.15)$$

In words, the right-hand-side of (15) gives us the minimum ratio of net-exports to income necessary to avoid currency crises.

Translating Barbosa-Filho's (2001b) version of the BoP constraint in terms of Tinbergen's (1955) classic analysis of economic policy, the home country has three instruments ($q_h$, z, and x-m) to achieve three targets (stable x, stable m, and $1 \geq l^*$). Moreover, given the foreign financial conditions, the adjustment of net exports to the liquidity constraint involves two analytically distinct phases. First, an once-off change in the real exchange rate to put the home net-export ratio at the level consistent with the liquidity constraint and, second, a continuous control of income and real-exchange-rate growth to keep the home net-export ratio at such level. In practice these two phases overlap and (2.15) allows us to identify the five types of shocks that can tighten the liquidity constraint on the home country:

- First, assuming that the home country receives a net inflow of foreign capital through interest-bearing bonds ($f_i$), an increase in its critical liquidity ratio ($l^*$) increases its minimum net-export ratio. The economic intuition is that an increase in the perceived risk of a currency crisis forces the home country to increase its net exports.
- Second, also assuming that the home country receives a net inflow of foreign capital through interest bearing bonds, an increase in the real cost of foreign debt in home currency ($i_f + \sigma + z - p_f$) increases its minimum net-export ratio. The economic intuition is that an increase in the interest payments to foreigners forces the home country to increase its net exports.
- Third, assuming that the real cost of foreign debt in home currency is greater than the home growth rate ($i_f + \sigma + z - p_f > q_h$), an increase in the capital inflows through interest-bearing bonds ($f_d$) increases the minimum net export ratio. The economic intuition is that foreign loans force the home country to increase its net exports when the corresponding real interest rate is "high". In contrast, if the real cost of foreign debt in home currency is smaller than the home growth rate, a reduction in the capital inflows through interest-bearing bonds increases the minimum net export ratio.
- Fourth, a reduction in the net foreign direct investment in the home country ($f_i$) or an increase in the net dividends and profits paid to the foreign country ($n$) leads to an increase in the minimum net-export ratio. The economic intuition is that, once foreign direct investment falls below its corresponding capital income, the home country has to increase its net exports.
- Fifth, a reduction in the net unilateral transfers received from the foreign country ($u$) forces the home country to increase its net exports. The economic intuition is that the home country has to compensate for less unilateral transfers with higher net exports.

In comparison to Thirlwall's (1979) original model, the stock-flow version of the BoP constraint presented by Barbosa-Filho (2001b) combines trade and financial issues in the same framework. The growth rate of home income is still determined by the growth rate of foreign income and the trade elasticities, as in Thirlwall's original model. However, differently than in Thirlwall's model, the change in the real exchange rate is specified to attend to the BoP constraint, and the trade surplus of the home country has to adjust to maintain the liquidity ratio above the minimum level considered safe to avoid currency crises.

## Exchange Rates and Growth in the Long Run

In the two models presented in the previous section the elasticities of the trade flows are assumed to be constant during the period under analysis, so that just the income and the real exchange rate of the home country adjust to the international conditions. This assumption is not too strong for a short-run analysis as proposed by Barbosa-Filho (2001b), but it is problematic for long-run considerations as implied by Thirlwall's (1979) Law. The reason is simple and intuitive, the longer the period under analysis, the higher the probability that the trade structure of the home country changes, especially if the operation of the BoP constraint occurs through exchange-rate crises and wide income fluctuations.

One of the main limitations of the literature on the BoP constraint is that it is mostly focused on the conditions necessary for an economy to avoid currency crises. Exactly how the economy meets these conditions is usually left open because of the complexity of modeling dynamical systems of more than two variables. Leaving the mathematical difficulties aside, the qualitative argument for the possibility of structural changes in the operation of the BoP constraint is not difficult to grasp. For instance, suppose that the home country is initially growing faster than what it should to keep is foreign finance stable. Sooner or later there will be a financial crisis and the combination of real-exchange-rate devaluation and growth deceleration may affect the structure of the economy. In fact, if the crisis is followed by a policy of export promotion and/or import substitution, the very own parameters of the BoP constraint are likely to change.

In a paper not related with the BoP constraint, the possible change in the trade elasticities as way to solve the differences between the growth rates of exports and imports was proposed by Krugman (1989). Adapting Krugman's mainstream interpretation to the terminology of the BoP constraint, we have the following logical sequence. First, the income growth rates of the home and foreign countries are determined by the supply side along Solow's growth theory. Second, the purchasing power parity holds and the real exchange rate is constant in the long run. Third, since exports and imports should grow at the same rate in the long run, the income elasticities of these two variables become the adjusting variables. In other words, whereas Thirlwall argues that the home income growth rate adjust to the elasticities for a given foreign income growth rate, Krugman argues that the trade elasticities adjust to match any possible difference between the home and foreign income growth rates.

One does not need to share Krugman's faith in the power of relative prices in changing the structural determinants of exports and imports to admit that the trade elasticities implicit in the BoP constraint may change. In a short-run analysis it is reasonable to think that the elasticity parameters are constant, so that the adjustment has to come through changes in income and real exchange rate, as proposed by Thirlwall (1979) and Barbosa-Filho (2001b). However, in a long-run analysis it is also reasonable to think that the elasticity parameters may change, not necessarily for the reasons pointed by Krugman. In fact, Thirlwall's and Krugman's views represent the two extremes poles of the possible adjustments of an open economy to the BoP constraint. As usual in economics, most of the relevant cases lie between the two extremes and, most importantly, the possibility of changes in the elasticity parameters opens the door for macroeconomic policy to influence growth and development in the long run.

The possibility that macroeconomic policy can influence growth and development in the long run is a common feature of heterodox models that build on the analysis of Keynes and Kalecki. For the specific case of the BoP constraint, a recent argument proposed by Woo (2001) gives an important insight into why this can happen. The basic idea proposed by Woo is that the relevant relative price to understand the structural change associated with export growth is not the one between exports and imports, but the one between the tradable and non-tradable goods produced domestically.

To understand Woo's point and usefulness for the BoP constraint, it is worthy to reconstruct the logical sequence of his analysis. First, according to most mainstream interpretations of the successful catching-up strategy of some East Asian economies, the reason that industrial policy worked in those economies was that it gave equal protection to exports and imports and, in this way, it did not make the domestic terms of trade deviate too much from what prevailed internationally. More formally, the basic idea is that, in the successful East Asian economies, the domestic price of imports and exports were given by

$$P_m = E\,(1 + t)P_m^* \tag{3.1}$$

and

$$P_x = \frac{EP_x^*}{(1 - s)} \tag{3.2}$$

respectively, where $P_m^*$ and $P_x^*$ are the international prices of imports and exports, $t$ is the import tariff, and $s$ the export subsidy rate.

The mainstream argument is that, if there were no industrial policy, $t$ and $s$ would be zero and the domestic and international terms of trade would coincide. In the same vein, even in the presence of industrial policy, the two relative prices can be made to coincide as long as $(1+t)(1-s) = 1$. In the later case industrial policy would be redundant since it would not alter the comparative advantages of the home country, it would just create the administrative costs of managing tariffs and subsidies. According to the mainstream interpretation, the reason some East Asian economies managed to catch up successfully was that they set their industrial policy close to the rule that $(1+t)(1-s) = 1$.

The second point of Woo's argument is that the mainstream interpretation is wrong because it fails to see the relevant relative price that was changed. In other words, by subsidizing exports and taxing imports in a balance way, the East Asian developing strategy manage to keep the domestic and international terms of trade close to each other, while introducing an important incentive to the production of tradable goods. In other words, the effectiveness of the East Asian industrial policy came from the fact that it subsidized the production of tradable goods.

The final point of Woo's argument is that technical progress and productivity growth are usually higher in the production of tradable goods than of non-tradable goods, so that by stimulating the former, industrial policy ended up promoting a structural change in the East Asian economies, a shift of production and employment, from backward low-productivity sectors, to advanced high-productivity sectors. The basic idea here is that the incentives to the tradable sector ended up pulling up the productivity and competitiveness of the whole economy in a virtuous cycle along the lines proposed by the Kaldor-Verdoorn laws of productivity growth.[1]

Moving back to the BoP constraint, it should be noted that even though Woo's argument was made in terms of import tariffs and export subsidies, the same logic can be applied to exchange rates. As pointed out by Frenkel and Taylor (2006), exchange-rate policy can also be made to promote the production of the tradable sector without creating a big difference between the domestic and international terms of trade of the home country. To see this, let $\rho$ be the relative price of the tradable goods in terms of the non-tradable goods. Frenkel and Taylor define

$$\rho = \frac{\mu P_m + (1-\mu)P_x}{P_n}, \tag{3.3}$$

where $P_n$ is the price of the non-tradable good and $\mu$ is the weight of the import price in the price index of tradable goods.

After substituting (3.1) and (3.2) in (3.3) it is straightforward that changes in the exchange rate can be used to alter the relative price between the tradable and non-tradable sectors of the home economy. In other words, exchange-rate policy can also have the same effect of import tariffs and export subsidies, and this was also an important element of the successful development strategy by some East Asian economies.

In both models presented in the previous section, the exchange rate entered in the analysis only through its variations. In Thirlwall's (1979) model the real exchange rate was assumed to be constant in the long run and, therefore, it did not have any effect on the determinants of the BoP constraint. In Barbosa-Filho's (2001b) stock-flow model, the changes in the real exchange rate were constrained to stabilize the export-income and import-income ratios, with no effect beyond that. From the points raised by Woo (2001) and Frenkel and Taylor (2006), there is an important point missing from both models of the BoP constraint, namely: the level of the real exchange rate may be an important determinant of the price and income elasticities of the trade flows.

In other words, even if we assume that the growth rate of the real exchange rate is zero in the long run, its level may still be important because it affects the relative price between the domestic production of tradable and non-tradable goods and, in this way, it can affect the structure and the growth rate of the economy. The models of the BoP constraint presented in section two did not capture this because they did not separate domestic production in two goods, and because they assumed the trade parameters to be constant. However, for the reasons pointed by Woo (2001), it is reasonable to assume that the level of the real exchange rate can and probably does alter the elasticity parameters of the exports and imports.

Assuming that the trade elasticities can be altered by the real exchange rate, the BoP constraint is no longer immutable as in Thilwall's and Barbosa-Filho's models. For instance, through the proper management of exchange rates, it is possible to alleviate the BoP constraint by increasing the income-elastictity of home exports, or reducing the income elasticity of home imports. As usual the logic runs both ways, that is, an improper management of exchange rate can worsen the BoP constraint and reduce the long-run growth rate of the economy, as we will analyze in the next section.

Before we move to the implications of inflation targeting for exchange rates and growth, it is worth to discuss the implications of Woo's propositions for exchange-rate policy a little further. According to most mainstream models of international finance, the real exchange rate cannot be a policy variable in the long run, so that any attempt to use it as an instrument for growth and development tends be ineffective. Using the jargon of modern econometrics, the real exchange rate tends to be a stationary variable for most economies and, as such, it cannot be manipulated by the Government authorities indefinitely.

In contrast to the skepticism of mainstream macroeconomic theory regarding exchange-rate management, it should be noted that even though the real exchange rate may indeed be stationary in the long run, the short run may be long enough to promote the structural changes pointed out by Woo. In other words, a temporary management of exchange rates to promote the development of the tradable sector may be sufficient to alter the BoP constraint permanently in a favorable or unfavorable manner.

On a more practical level, it should also be noted that there is a fundamental asymmetry in exchange-rate management. The home country cannot impose an appreciated ceiling for its exchange rate indefinitely because it does not issue the foreign currency. Sooner or later the stock of foreign reserve dries up and the home country is forced to devalue. The story is different in the other direction. The home country can sustain a depreciated floor for its exchange rate because it can issue the home currency necessary to buy the domestic currency. Moreover, since increase in money generated by the purchases of foreign currency can be sterilized by open market operations, the cost of sustaining a floor to the exchange rate is the difference between the interest rate earned on the foreign assets and the interest rate paid on domestic debt. If this spread is not large, the home country is in a much better position to sustain an exchange-rate floor than an exchange-rate ceiling, as indicated by the recent example of China.

## Inflation Targeting and Exchange Rates

In the previous section we analyzed how the real exchange rate can be an important instrument to promote growth and development. Since the real exchange rate is also an important instrument to control inflation, we conclude our analysis with the implications of inflation targeting for the balance of payments and growth.

Many countries today adopt inflation targeting as a guide for monetary policy. Since the exchange rate is one of the main determinants of inflation in developing countries, inflation targeting necessarily implies some sort of exchange-rate targeting, a dirty floating, which in its turn depends on the evolution of the balance of payments. In other words, the stability of the inflation rate depends on the stability of the real exchange rate, which depends on the BoP constraint on the economy.

Following the approach of the previous sections, it is useful to frame the analysis in terms of a simple and intuitive model. From the analysis of the previous sections, the main lesson is that inflation targeting must be compatible with a stable competitive real exchange rate in order to be sustainable in the long run. If inflation targeting is based on an appreciated real exchange rate, the vulnerability of the economy to foreign shocks tends to increase as export growth decelerates and import growth booms. On the other hand, if the real exchange rate is stabilized at a level consistent with high export growth, the external solvency of the economy improves and the structural change induced by the development of the tradable sector creates a virtuous circle of productivity and output growth.

Moving to the model, let us define the change in the growth rate of the nominal exchange rate as function of the interest-rate arbitrage. The basic idea here is that devaluation accelerates when the home interest rate is too low in relation to the foreign interest rate and the home country risk premium, and decelerates when the opposite happens. The simplest way to represent such an idea is to define

$$\frac{de}{dt} = \phi\left(i_f + \sigma + e - i_h\right), \qquad (4.1)$$

where $i_h$ is nominal interest rate in the home country and $\phi$ is a positive parameter that measures the sensitivity of devaluation to the interest-rate arbitrage condition. To simplify the exposition, we assume that the expected devaluation coincides with the effective devaluation, so that the latter enters in the right-hand-side of (4.1).[5]

Next, to introduce inflation targeting in the model, assume that the home interest rate is adjusted according to the deviations of the home inflation rate, $p_h$, from the inflation target, $p_h$, that is:

$$\frac{di_h}{dt} = \chi\left(p_h - p_h^*\right), \qquad (4.2)$$

where naturally $\chi$ is also a positive parameter that measures the velocity of the adjustment of the home interest rate.

Given that home inflation depends on the price of tradable and non-tradable goods, let us now assume that the home country produces these two goods, so that the home inflation rate can be described as a weighted average of the tradable and non-tradable inflation rates, that is

$$p_h = \theta p_{hn} + (1-\theta)p_{ht}, \qquad (4.3)$$

where $p_{hn}$ and $p_{ht}$ are the growth rates of the prices non-tradable and tradable goods, respectively, and $\theta$ is a positive parameter, between zero and one, that represents the share of non-tradable goods in the home inflation rate.

To simplify the analysis, assume that the tradable inflation rate is simply equal to the growth rate of the foreign price in home currency, that is

$$p_{ht} = e + p_f \tag{4.4}$$

Finally, assume that monetary policy has some influence on the growth rate on the price of non-tradable goods, that is:

$$p_{hn} = \pi - \lambda(i_h - p_h), \tag{4.5}$$

where $\lambda$ is a positive parameter and $\pi$ controls for any possible fixed effects.

After some algebraic substitutions we obtain the following differential equation for the change in the home interest rate:

$$\frac{di_h}{dt} = \chi \left[ \frac{\theta(\pi - \lambda i_h) + (1 - \theta)(e + p_f)}{1 - \theta\lambda} - p_h^* \right] \tag{4.6}$$

From (4.1) and (4.6) the equilibrium lines for the interest rate and the devaluation rate are given by:

$$i_h = \frac{\pi}{\lambda} + \left( \frac{1-\theta}{\theta\lambda} \right)(e + p_f) - \left( \frac{1 - \theta\lambda}{\theta\lambda} \right) p_h^* \tag{4.7}$$

and

$$e = i_h - i_f - \sigma. \tag{4.8}$$

respectively.

Assuming as we did before that the home risk premium $\sigma$ is exogenous, the Jacobian of the dynamical system formed by (4.1) and (4.6) is

$$\begin{bmatrix} \dfrac{-\chi\theta\lambda}{(1-\theta\lambda)} & \dfrac{\chi(1-\theta)}{(1-\theta\lambda)} \\ -\phi & \phi \end{bmatrix},$$

and the two stability conditions are:

$$-\chi\theta\lambda + (1 - \theta\lambda)\phi < 0 \tag{4.9}$$

and

$$\chi\phi\left[\frac{(1-\theta)-\theta\lambda}{1-\theta\lambda}\right]>0 \tag{4.10}$$

Note that from the assumptions made so far, the two stability conditions above are satisfied, provided that the velocity of the adjustment of the interest rate is fast (a "high" $\chi$), and the impact of the real interest rate on the non-tradable inflation is small (a "low" $\lambda$). Since the response velocity of the interest rate is a policy parameter, it can be set at the value necessary to stabilize the system. As for the impact of the real interest rate, it is reasonable to assume that $\lambda$ is smaller than one, that is, that non-tradable inflation does not fall one-to-one in face of an increase in the real interest rate. Altogether these two assumptions mean that the system is stable and we will concentrate the rest of our analysis on its steady state.[6]

From (4.7) and (4.8) the steady-state value of the domestic interest rate is:

$$i_h = \frac{\theta\pi - (1-\theta)(i_f + \sigma - p_f) - (1-\theta\lambda)p_h^*}{\theta\lambda - (1-\theta)}, \tag{4.11}$$

from which the steady sytate value of $e$ can be directly obtained from (4.8).

Now, to check the implications of inflation targeting for the BoP constraint and growth, we have to find the steady-state solution for the growth rate of the real exchange rate. On the one hand, the intuitive meaning of this is clear, if inflation targeting implies a continuing appreciation of the home currency, sooner or later the home country will face a currency crisis. On the other hand, it should also be pointed that even if inflation targeting is made consistent with a stable real exchange rate, it can still be detrimental to growth if the level of the real exchange rate is set too low that makes it impossible to foster the growth and development of the tradable sector.

Going back to the $2\times2$ dynamical system, we just have to substitute the solution for $e$ in the definition of $z$ to know whether inflation targeting is consistent with a stable real exchange rate. More formally, since $z = e + p_f - p_h$, from (4.7) and (4.8) we have:

$$z = \theta\left[\frac{\pi - p_h^* - \lambda(i_f - p_f + \sigma)}{\theta\lambda - (1-\theta)}\right]. \tag{4.12}$$

In words, the real exchange rate is not necessarily stable at the steady state of the inflation targeting regime, and this may lead to BoP problems.

It should be noted that since we have been working only with linear functions, there is one and only one inflation target that is consistent with $z = 0$ in (4.12).

A change away from such an equilibrium target leads to changes in the real exchange and, most importantly, the lower the target, the faster the appreciation of the real exchange rate. To see why this happens, note that from the previous assumption that $\lambda < 1$, the denominator of (4.12) is negative and, therefore, $dz/dp_h^* < 0$. In words, a reduction in the inflation target reduces the growth rate of the real exchange-rate). If the inflation target is set too low, it may even induce a continuing appreciation of the real exchange rate ($z < 0$).

The main conclusion from the above analysis is that inflation targeting should be done with care, not to create BoP problems in the short run and reduce the growth prospects of the economy in the long run. When inflation targeting is too ambitious, it may induce a continuing appreciation of the real exchange rate and, through this, generate a currency crisis. Moreover, if inflation targeting is handled in a way consistent with the stability of the real exchange rate, it still can be problematic for growth and development when the real exchange rate is stabilized at a level too low. For the reasons pointed out by Woo (2001), in such a case the incentives for the tradable sector are wrong and the economy may become locked in a slow-growth path.

## Notes

1. The intuition here is that a country may have a stable trade deficit as long as its export revenues are sufficient to pay its imports and debt service without causing a further increase in its debt-export ratio.
2. For a recent survey of the main contributions on the topic, see McCombie and Thirlwall (2004).
3. I will discuss this assumption in the next section.
4. In general terms, according to the Kaldor-Verdoorn Laws, the faster the growth rate of production in manufacturing, the faster the growth rate of labor productivity in the economy because of economies of scale, learning-by-doing and changes in the composition of employment. For a survey of the Kaldor-Verdoorn Laws, see Thirlwall (1983).
5. The alternative would be to introduce the expected devaluation as a separate state variable in the inflation-targeting dynamical system, which would result in 3-variable system. The mathematics would become more complex, but the insight would not grow in the same proportion.
6. Moreover, note that if the dynamical system is unstable or has a saddle path, inflation targeting would be problematic independently of its effects on the BoP constraint. By focusing on the stable case we are analyzing the best-case scenario.

## References

Barbosa Filho, N.H. (2001b), International Liquidity and Growth in Brazil, The Schwartz Center Working Paper 2001–04, New York: New School University.

Barbosa-Filho, N.H. (2001a), "The balance-of-payments constraint: from balanced trade to sustainable debt," Banca Nazionale Del Lavoro Quarterly Review, n. 219, p. 381–399.

Frenkel, R. and L. Taylor (2006), "Real Exchange Rate, Monetary Policy and Employment", DESA Working Paper No. 19, United Nations.

Krugman, P. (1989), "Differences in Income Elasticities and trends in real exchange rates," European Economic Review, 1989, 33, 1031–1034.

McCombie, J.S.L. and Thirlwall, A.P. (1997). "Economic Growth and the Balance of Payments Constraint Revisited," in: P. Arestis, G. Palma, and M. Sawyer (eds.) Markets, Unemployment and Economic Policy: Essays in Honour of Geoffrey Harcourt, Vol. 2. London: Routledge, 1997, 498–511.

McCombie, J.S.L. and Thirlwall, A.P. (2004), Essays on Balance of Payments Constrained Growth – Theory and Evidence, London: Routledge, 2004.

Moreno-Brid, J.C. (1998), "On capital flows and the balance-of-payments constrained growth model", Journal of Post Keynesian Economics, 21, pp. 283–98.

Thirlwall, A.P. (1979), 'The Balance of Payments Constraint as an Explanation of International Growth Rate Differences', Banca Nazionale del Lavoro Quarterly Review, 128, pp. 45–53.

Thirlwall, A.P. (1983), "A plain man's guide to Kaldor's growth laws", Journal of Post-Keynesian Economics, Vol. 5 No. 3, pp.345–58.

Thirlwall, A.P. and Hussain (1982), "The Balance of Payments Constraint, Capital Flows and Growth Rate Differences between Developing Countries," Oxford Economic Papers, Oxford University Press, vol. 34(3), pages 498–510, November.

Tinbergen, Jan (1955), On the Theory of Economic Policy, Amsterdam: North-Holland.

Woo, Wing Thye (2005). Some Fundamental Inadequacies in the Washington Consensus: Misunderstanding the Poor by the Brightest. In Jan Joost Teunissen (ed.). Stability, Growth, and the Search for a New Development Agenda: Reconsidering the Washington Consensus. FONDAD (Forum on Debt and Development), The Hague.

# Chapter 5

# ALTERNATIVE MEASURES OF CURRENCY AND ASSET SUBSTITUTION: THE CASE OF TURKEY

## A. Özden Birkan

Department of Economics, Yaşar University, Izmir, Turkey

**Abstract**

Like many developing countries that liberalized their capital account, Turkey has been at the mercy of short term capital inflows accompanied by a continuous real appreciation of the domestic currency since 1989. Open foreign exchange positions and increasing foreign exchange related assets in residents' portfolios have been the inevitable side affect. The recent inflation targeting policy is claimed to have reversed this trend. However the currency substitution measure developed in this study suggests an alternative interpretation of the situation. Although the share of TL denominated assets in total monetary assets has been increasing relative to the share of foreign currency related assets, the liquidity services of TL denominated assets is in fact not increasing. In this study distinct measures of asset substitution and currency substitution, as opposed to the generic FCD/M2Y, are developed and the different degrees of liquidity provided by alternative monetary assets are distinctly measured. These AS and CS measures follow the conventional intuition as to their driving factors and suggest the existence of hysteresis in currency substitution in Turkey. From a policy standpoint, this provides evidence that targeting and decreasing the inflation rate alone may not be sufficient to overcome the structural problems of the economy that have been in the making for decades.

*Keywords*: currency substitution; asset substitution; Turkey; Divisia aggregates.
*JEL Classification*: E5, E6, F3.

## Introduction

The widespread experience in most developing countries of the use of foreign currencies and foreign currency denominated assets has been an issue of vast academic interest since the 1970s. The literature points to a theoretical and empirical distinction between *currency substitution* (CS) and *asset substitution* (AS). CS refers to the use of multiple currencies as media of exchange while AS refers to the existence of foreign currency denominated financial assets in addition to domestic ones in domestic residents' portfolios as a store of value. The former is a result of inflation and the latter of international capital mobility.

Different theoretical frameworks are used to analyze the implications of the two phenomena for exchange rate and interest rate determination and to measure their extent. Problems common to most of the research are the difficulty of modeling the different  degrees of liquidity services different assets provide and the difficulty of formally distinguishing between the store of value and medium of exchange functions of money in the models. Moreover, when it comes to empirical tests of proposed policy implications, the convention is to use the ratio of foreign currency denominated assets to some monetary aggregate like M2 or M3 as the measure of currency substitution. This is an *ad hoc* measure, which does not differentiate between CS and AS.

In this study a model based on the Divisia monetary aggregates literature is considered. The model is based on the Barnett critique and produces theoretically consistent distinct measures for CS and AS, as well as addressing deliberately the issue of differing degrees of liquidity of different assets.

This chapter investigates how these alternative measures can contribute to the analysis of the Turkish experience. First a brief outline of the developments in the Turkish economy is provided; then the theoretical model, on which distinct measures of CS and AS are founded, is presented. The relevant measures of substitution are developed and tests of the CS and AS hypotheses are carried out in a cointegrated VAR framework. The question of whether either AS or CS or both exhibit irreversibility is addressed with an attempt to identify the source of the irreversibility. Finally the theoretical and empirical conclusions of the study are presented.

## Turkish Economy 1989–2007

The existence of multiple currencies became an issue for Turkey following a series of legislative acts that brought current account convertibility and allowed residents to hold foreign currency deposits in domestic banks and carry out foreign exchange transactions in 1984, and one that finally lifted the restrictions on international capital flows in 1989.

At a time of increasing necessity for public sector borrowing, exposing the newly developing market for government securities to international capital did not turn out to be a viable policy. The result was high interest rates on government securities which had to compete internationally, accompanied by high and unstable inflation rates. Foreign exchange under the circumstances became the safe haven for residents. Attempts by the central bank to control its balance sheet, especially the foreign exchange related items, and contain exchange rate volatility in the following years proved impossible, not only because of external factors like the first Gulf War and political elections and the consequent coalition government, but mainly because of the unsustainable Ponzi pattern of government domestic debt finance. In fact the central bank was trying to pursue monetary targeting whereby money would not be created except for foreign exchange purchases of the Turkish central bank and accordingly the TL would be strong. Strong TL coupled with high interest rates offered in treasury auctions encouraged banks to hold open foreign exchange positions. While foreign exchange denominated assets held by residents were increasing, banks were investing the acquired foreign reserves in TL denominated assets, mainly securities issued by the treasury. The fragile financial environment brought about by currency and asset substitution, open positions and Ponzi debt finance collapsed in early 1994, bringing a major crisis with a heavy depreciation of the TL, loss of reserves by the central bank, soaring interest rates, bankruptcies in the banking sector and reduced growth. The April 5th Economic Measures Implementation Plan and a stand-by agreement with the IMF followed the crisis. They were, however, short-lived. Monetary policy thereafter has been directed towards increasing foreign assets of the central bank in order to establish the credibility of the exchange rate as the nominal anchor. Policy has been one of controlling the nominal devaluation of the TL.

The next major disturbance came in 1998 when capital inflows slowed down due to the East Asian and Russian crises. The major earthquake in northwest Turkey contributed to the recession. Eight banks were taken over by the Saving Deposit Insurance Fund, the public agency responsible for fulfilling the full deposit insurance guarantee. Fortunately there was no further disturbance to the banking system, but the burden on the public debt was unavoidable. A stabilization program and another stand-by agreement with the IMF followed the crisis.[1]

The December 1999 exchange rate based stabilization program involved a crawling peg with a preannounced exit date. The program had a quasi currency board arrangement, which prohibited money issue unless it was backed by increases in the net foreign assets of the central bank. The crawling peg proposed a path for exchange rates in line with the targeted inflation rate and the preannounced exit clause was meant to overcome the uncertainty about the timing and eventual extent of the depreciation. However the preannounced exit ended up accelerating the speculation around the performance of the program when inflation targets turned out difficult to achieve. The pace of the depreciation still allowed room for profits through open positions. In fact TL was appreciating in real terms. When inflation turned out to be too rigid, fear of a sharp depreciation at the exit date on top of other factors brought about a sudden exit from the TL in November 2000. This early attack left behind soaring interest rates, inability for the treasury to borrow long term and depleted international reserves. Although reserves were replenished by an agreement with the IMF in December, after a second wave of financial turmoil in February 2001 the peg was finally abandoned.

Since February 2001, for the first time in two decades the TL has been left to float freely. Monetary policy in the 2001–2007 period has been inflation targeting. While the short term interest rate is the policy instrument, base money was considered as an anchor, but it had to be abandoned due to the large margin of error stemming from currency and asset substitution. Eventually the nominal exchange rate rather than base money came to be used as the indicator in setting the interest rate. The central bank started conducting pre-determined foreign exchange auctions to increase its reserves and made a point of its commitment to the free float. The auctions were not intended to use the exchange rate as a policy tool. Nor was an exchange rate target maintained. The informal practice of inflation targeting became a formal commitment in December 2005 when the report on the framework of inflation targeting and the program for 2006 was issued.[2] The program had an end-of-year target inflation rate of 5%, while the actual rate turned out 9.2%. The central bank attributed this to supply side shocks. The 2007 inflation targeting program announced an end-of-year target inflation rate of 4%[3] and emphasized once again that inflation is the sole target and short term interest rate the sole monetary policy tool. The exchange rate, growth or the current account were not themselves targets.

The seemingly successful policy of inflation targeting has, however, been ineffective in inducing much change on the open FX positions of the banks and on the almost three decades long trend of real appreciation of the TL, as seen in Figure 1. Interestingly the conventional measure of currency substitution, FCD/M2Y, suggests a reversal of substitution. This is puzzling since FCD and open positions are, after all, parts of the same bank balance sheet phenomenon. An alternative way to measure asset substitution and currency substitution may provide more consistent insights and that is the basic motivation behind the following exercise.

Figure 1:

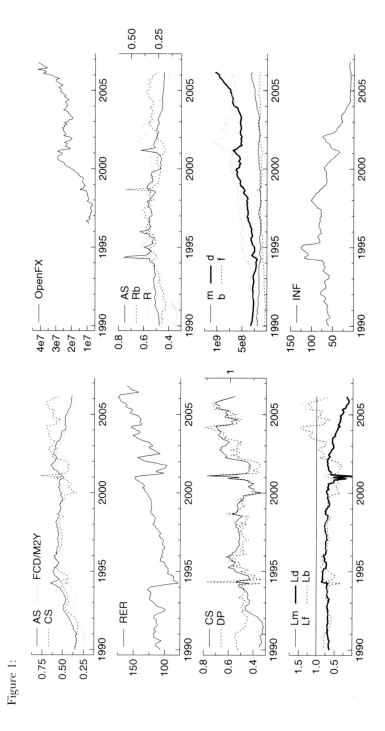

## The Model

Morón (2002) provides a model for money demand based in the Divisia literature, where the representative agent solves an infinite horizon utility maximization problem to decide on her portfolio over consumption and monetary assets.[4] The constraints are the *transaction costs technology* as a function of aggregate liquidity and consumption and the *wealth* as a function of her portfolio of domestic and foreign currency, domestic and foreign interest bearing assets, current consumption and savings.

Using the Euler equations of the problem, it is possible to write the aggregate liquidity as the sum of liquidity provided by assets denominated in domestic currency and those denominated in the foreign currency.[5] Then measures of AS and CS are constructed. AS ratio is the ratio of the sum of foreign currency and foreign currency denominated interest bearing assets to the sum of all four asset groups. CS ratio is the ratio of the liquidity provided by assets denominated in foreign currency to aggregate liquidity. Relative liquidity of an asset is represented by the difference between the gross rate of return on the asset and the gross rate of return on a benchmark asset that does not provide any liquidity services. If the liquidity services of all assets were equal AS and CS measures would coincide.

The model has been slightly modified for the case of Turkey. Purchasing power parity assumption has been dropped and confiscation risk for foreign currency denominated assets ignored. Overall the resulting expressions are consistent with the conventional approach to testing for currency and asset substitution.[6] The point here is this model provides a testing procedure where relative demands for domestic and foreign currency denominated interest bearing assets can be estimated as distinct from the relative demand for domestic and foreign money with the respective relevant variables. As such the hypotheses proposed by Thomas (1985) can be separately tested.

## The Empirical Investigation

The AS and CS ratios implied by the model, the conventional measure FCD/M2Y and the data used in the estimation are in Table 1. The empirical investigation consists of establishing the time series properties of the variables, testing for cointegration between AS and the domestic-foreign interest rate differential and between CS and domestic-foreign inflation differential. This is done to verify that measures that come from a utility maximizing framework still follow the conventional macroeconomic intuition. We then test for irreversibility in AS and CS using inflation, the interest rate, depreciation and AS/CS ratchet variables.

**Table 1:  Data and Variable Definitions**

| | |
|---|---|
| **AS** | Asset Substitution Ratio (Estimated) $(f+b)/(m+f+d+b)$ |
| **B** | FCD+FDA |
| **b** | B/CPI |
| **c** | Consumption |
| **CPI** | Domestic Consumer Price Index (2003=100) (Turkstat, CBRT) |
| **CS** | Currency Substitution Ratio (Estimated) $[(Rf-R)f+(Rb-R)(1-\theta)b]/[(Rm-R)m+(Rd-R)d+(Rf-R)f+(Rb-R)(1-\theta)b]$ |
| **D** | Domestic Currency Time Deposits in the Turkish Banking System (CBRT) |
| **d** | D/CPI |
| **DP** | Inflation Rate Differential (Estimated) $[(Rf-R)/(Rm-R)]$ |
| **e** | Rate of Annual Depreciation of TL against USD |
| **F** | Foreign Currency Sight Deposits (CBRT) |
| **f** | F/CPI |
| **FCD** | Foreign Currency Denominated Time Deposits in the Banking System (CBRT) |
| **FDA** | Foreign Currency Deposits Abroad (BIS) |
| **INF** | Inflation, change in CPI relative to same month previous year |
| **Lb** | Relative Liquidity of Foreign Currency Deposits $[(Rb-R))/(Rm-R)]$ |
| **Ld** | Relative Liquidity of Domestic Currency Deposits $[(Rd-R))/(Rm-R)]$ |
| **Lf** | Relative Liquidity of Foreign Currency $[(Rf-R)/(Rm-R)]$ |
| **Lm** | Relative Liquidity of Domestic Currency (=1 since it is the basis of comparison) |
| **M** | Domestic Currency Bills and Sight Deposits (M1) (CBRT) |
| **m** | M/CPI |
| **OpenFX** | Open Foreign Exchange Positions of the Banking System (FX Liabilities-FX Assets) |
| **r** | Interest Rate on the Benchmark Asset (UTT) *Annual compounded interest rates of T-Bill auctions weighted by quantity* |
| **R** | Gross return of the Benchmark Asset (Estimated) $Max\{Ri\}=(1+r)$ |
| **Rb** | Gross return of the Foreign Currency Deposits (Estimated) $(1+rb)(1+\varepsilon)/(1+p)$ |
| **rb** | Interest Rate of Foreign Currency-Denominated Deposits (CBRT) *Weighted average of 1, 3, 6, 12+ month deposits* |
| **Rd** | Gross return of the Domestic Currency Deposits (CBRT) $(1+rd)/(1+p)$ |
| **rd** | Interest Rate of Domestic Currency-Denominated Deposits (CBRT) *Weighted average of 1, 3, 6, 12+ mo. deposits* |
| **RER** | Real Effective Exchange Rate Index (CPI based, 1995=100) |
| **Rf** | Gross return on Foreign Currency Bills (Estimated) $(1+\varepsilon)/(1+p)$ |
| **Rm** | Gross return on Domestic Currency Bills (Estimated) $[1/(1+p)]$ |

The variables used for modeling are AS, CS, Rb, R, DP, and the ratchet variables: pmax, emax, rmax, ASmax, and CSmax. The results of the augmented Dickey-Fuller tests for the variables are presented in Table 2. All variables are I(1).

**Table 2: Unit Root Tests**

| Variable | AS | CS | Rb | R | DP | Pmax | Emax | Rmax | ASmax | Csmax |
|---|---|---|---|---|---|---|---|---|---|---|
| **ADF** | –1.92 | –2.45 | –3.56 | –2.25 | –3.46 | –2.11 | –2.23 | –2.00 | –2.87 | –0.66 |
| **C.V.** | –3.47 | –3.47 | –4.01 | –3.47 | –3.47 | –3.47 | –3.47 | –3.47 | –3.47 | –3.47 |
| **Order** | 1.00 | 1.00 | 1.00 | 1.00 | 1.00 | 1.00 | 1.00 | 1.00 | 1.00 | 1.00 |

## Testing for the AS Hypothesis

In order to check the AS hypothesis, we test for cointegration between the AS ratio and Rb and R, using Johansen's maximum likelihood procedure. The lag order for the VAR was established based a series of system lag reduction tests as three.[7] A constant term is included in the model to allow for a linear deterministic trend and it is not restricted to the cointegrating space. The resulting VAR is acceptable from an econometric standpoint.[8] Results of the trace test are given in Table 3. The asset substitution ratio and the gross return on foreign currency denominated deposits follow a stable long run relationship, where increases in the yield of foreign currency denominated interest-bearing assets are associated with higher asset substitution ratios. Interestingly, higher asset substitution ratios are also associated with higher gross rates of return on the benchmark asset. This can be explained by the particular asset chosen to be the benchmark. R represents the gross rate of return on T-Bills as determined by treasury borrowing auctions. As such it also represents the cost of borrowing for the treasury which is central to debt sustainability and the likelihood of a financial crisis. Higher borrowing costs for the treasury imply less confidence and certainty about the future of the TL denominated assets, implying a higher AS ratio.

## Testing for the CS Hypothesis

The same procedure is followed to test for a long run relationship between the currency substitution ratio (CS) and the inflation differential proxy (DP). The VAR is of order three. Again the constant is not restricted to the cointegrating space. Results of the cointegration tests are given in Table 5 and Table 6. The higher relative liquidity of foreign currency brought about by higher domestic inflation rates is associated with higher CS ratios in the long run.

## Irreversibility in CS/AS?

Irreversibility in CS/AS is usually conceptualized in terms of a temporarily high inflation leading to permanently high CS/AS ratios. The most commonly mentioned explanations for this are learning and switching costs and network

**Table 3:  Testing for Cointegration (AS Model)**

| Rank< = | λ | loglik | λtrace | prob |
|---------|------|--------|--------|------|
| 0** |  | 884.07 | 37.24 | 0.01 |
| 1* | 0.10 | 894.18 | 17.01 | 0.03 |
| 2.00 | 0.07 | 901.51 | 2.35 | 0.13 |
| 3.00 | 0.01 | 902.68 | n/a | n/a |

**Table 4:  Reduced form Beta (AS Model)**

|  | AS | Rb | R |
|------|-------|------|------|
| β' | −1.00 | 0.93 | 0.11 |
| s.e. | 0.00 | 0.25 | 0.10 |

**Table 5:  Testing for Cointegration (CS Model)**

| Rank<= | λ | loglik | λtrace | Prob. |
|--------|------|--------|--------|-------|
| 0** |  | 520.32 | 23.25 | 0.00 |
| 1* | 0.08 | 528.69 | 6.50 | 0.01 |
| 2.00 | 0.03 | 531.94 | n/a | n/a |

**Table 6:  Reduced Form Beta (CS Model)**

|  | CS | DP |
|------|-------|------|
| β' | −1.00 | 1.89 |
| s.e. | 0.00 | 0.39 |

externalities. In an empirical model, a network externalities type of argument can be represented by a variable that approximates the previous highest value of the asset substitution or currency substitution proxy. If this variable is significant in the long run equation for AS or CS with a positive coefficient, this is evidence for irreversible behavior, in the sense of higher previous levels of AS or CS being associated with high levels currently. Similarly the highest value to date of the inflation rate, depreciation rate or the interest rate can be used as the ratchet variable. These ratchet variables are introduced into the VAR system as deterministic variables restricted to the cointegration space, i.e. they are not modeled and lagged values are not included in the estimation but the level variable is forced in the long run relation. Then the existence of a cointegrating vector is investigated, and if there is one, the significance of the ratchet variable in that vector is tested.[9] Summary results are presented in Tables 7 and 8.

**Table 7: Ratchet Variables (AS Model)**

| Variable | ASmax | Rmax | emax | pmax |
|---|---|---|---|---|
| rank | 1 | 1 | 1 | 1 |
| β' | (−1, −0.41,0.13, 0.26,0.73) | (−1,1.64,0.11, −1.20, −0.06) | (−1, −1.19, 0.15, 1.12,0.17) | (−1, −18.52, 0.50, 12.57,5.29) |
| LR $\chi^2$(1) | 3.8046 | 0.34896 | 2.5528 | 0.80513 |
| Prob | 0.0511 | 0.5547 | 0.1101 | 0.3696 |

**Note:** In each case a VAR of order three is estimated, then cointegration between AS, Rb, R and the ratchet variable is tested, followed by the LR test for the significance of the ratchet variable in the long run relation. Reduced form beta is reported as β' = (AS, Rb, R, c, ratchet).

**Table 8: Ratchet Variables (CS Model)**

| Variable | CSmax | Rmax | emax | pmax |
|---|---|---|---|---|
| rank | 1 | 1 | 1 | 1 |
| β' | (−1, 1.22, −0.42, −0.07) | (−1, 0.72, −0.17, 0.04) | (−1, 0.58, −0.09, 0.07) | (−1, 0.88, −0.45, 0.22) |
| LR $\chi^2$(1) | 0.0097058 | 1.2164 | 4.0834 | 0.67148 |
| Prob | 0.9215 | 0.2701 | *0.0433** | 0.4125 |

**Note:** In each case a VAR of order three is estimated, then cointegration between CS, DP and the ratchet variable is tested, followed by the LR test for the significance of the ratchet variable in the long run relation. Reduced form beta is reported as β' = (CS, DP, c, ratchet).

None of the ratchets seem relevant for AS. For CS only emax is plausible as a ratchet variable in the long run indicating that temporarily high rates of nominal depreciation lead to a permanently high CS ratio.

## Conclusion

Given the widely accepted policy implications of the macro theoretical work on currency and asset substitution, it is of significant relevance for policy design to detect if a particular economy should be concerned about them and to what extend. For the case of Turkey, both asset and currency substitution have been important issues in policy design. There is considerable econometric evidence supporting the existence of irreversibility for currency substitution. In the context of Turkey, this does not imply that most transactions are carried out using foreign currency. What our measure of CS and the irreversibility result imply is that given the structure of returns to different assets in the economy and the path of the rate of nominal depreciation of the TL, although the share of TL related assets in total monetary assets has been rising, the liquidity of TL denominated assets has been drastically declining and most of the liquidity in the system is acquired from foreign exchange and related assets.

Like many other developing countries, the Turkish economy is subject to a serious balance of payments constraint, making the exchange rate central to any policy design. In their practice of inflation targeting, the CBRT seems to have acknowledged this. The CBRT is using the nominal exchange rate as an indicator in setting the interest rate. However acknowledging the situation addresses only half of the problem. As research on inflation targeting and exchange rates suggests, the stability of the inflation rate depends on the stability of the real exchange rate and if inflation targeting is based on an appreciated real exchange rate, the vulnerability of the economy to foreign shocks increases.

Inflation in Turkey has declined drastically since the start of inflation targeting in February 2001. This however is accompanied by continuous real appreciation of the TL since 1989. Current account deficits are more the rule than the exception and are only offset by short term capital inflows. After the 2001 crisis, GDP growth recovered quickly from a negative rate. In the meantime the unemployment rate has not fallen. Moreover, real appreciation and high-return T-Bills have induced a fragile structure in bank balance sheets in the form of persistent open foreign exchange positions. Under the circumstances, the reduction of the inflation rate *alone* does not seem to have been sufficient to address the structural problems of the economy.

Some technical reservations should also be made about the econometric findings. Needless to say the results are ultimately conditional upon the nature and extent of available data. Turkish economy has experienced at least two major crises, several minor disturbances and at least two major policy regime changes over the last 25 years. The power of the econometric tests is bound to be affected by this. An extension of this work would be to incorporate structural changes in the econometric methods involved.

## Appendix

### The Model

The model presented in the body of the article is based on Morón (2002). In this model there are four groups of assets: domestic and foreign currency notes, interest bearing assets denominated in domestic and foreign currency. All assets are demanded for their transactions services. Demand for each asset depends on three considerations: the liquidity services they provide, the return they offer, the risk associated with them. Liquidity services obtained from the assets are combined by a liquidity aggregator function:

$$L_t = \Lambda \left( m_t, f_t, b_t, \alpha_t \right) \tag{a1}$$

where $m$ and $f$ are domestic and foreign currency notes respectively, $d$ and $b$ are interest bearing assets denominated in domestic and foreign currency respectively. $\alpha_t$ captures technical change that effects $\Lambda(.)$. There is also a pure bond $h_t$ with a return of $r$. All assets are measured in real terms, preferably deflated by a true cost of living index.[10] $\Lambda(.)$ is assumed to be linearly homogenous in all its monetary arguments and additively separable in domestic currency against other monetary assets.[11]

The assumptions on $\Lambda(.)$ mean $L_t$ can be written as:

$$L_t = m_t + \psi\ (f_t,\ d_t,\ b_t,\ \alpha_t) \tag{a2}$$

Moreover $L_t$ satisfies:

$$L_t = m_t + \Lambda_{f,t}f_t + \Lambda_{d,t}d_t + \Lambda_{b,t}b_t \tag{a3}$$

where $\Lambda_{i,t}$ are the derivatives of the liquidity aggregator function with respect to the $i^{th}$ asset. This is the Currrency Equivalent Monetary Aggregate referred to in Rotemberg, J., J. Driscoll, and J. Porteba (1995), as applied to this simplified model. They claim *"the CE aggregate can be interpreted as the stock of currency that yields the same transactions services as the entire constellation of monetary assets".*[12]

Agents' utility in this model is constrained by transaction costs and a series of budget constraints in relation to their wealth at time t. Wealth, also measured in real terms, is given by:

$$w_t = m_t + f_t + d_t + (1-\theta)b_t + h_t \tag{a4}$$

where $\theta$ represents a risk tax on foreign currency denominated interest bearing assets. It can also be interpreted as a measure of the confiscation risk, as in Morón (2002).

The budget constraints are as such:

$$c_t + \frac{M_t}{P_t} + \frac{F_t}{P_t^*} + \frac{D_t}{P_t} + (1-\theta)\frac{B_t}{P_t^*} + h_t$$
$$= \frac{M_{t-1}}{P_t} + \frac{F_{t-1}}{P_t^*} + (1+r_d)\frac{D_{t-1}}{P_t} + (1+r_b)(1-\theta)\frac{B_{t-1}}{P_t^*}$$
$$+(1+r)h_{t-1} + y_t + s_t \tag{a5}$$

where $c_t$ is real consumption, $s_t$ is the transaction cost and $y_t$ the real income. $P$ is the domestic true cost of living index and $P^*$ is its foreign counterpart. $P_t = P_t^*E_t$ is also assumed, that is the purchasing power parity relation holds. $E_t$ is the nominal exchange rate expressed as domestic currency over foreign currency. The $r_i$ are respective nominal rates of return on the assets. Domestic and foreign currency notes do not earn any interest. The budget constraint in domestic currency then is:

$$c_t + \frac{M_t}{P_t} + \frac{F_t E_t}{P_t} + \frac{D_t}{P_t} + (1-\theta)\frac{B_t E_t}{P_t} + h_t$$
$$= \frac{M_{t-1}}{P_t} + \frac{F_{t-1} E_t}{P_t} + (1+r_d)\frac{D_{t-1}}{P_t} + (1+r_b)(1-\theta)\frac{B_{t-1} E_t}{P_t}$$
$$+ (1+r)h_{t-1} + y_t + s_t \tag{a6}$$

dividing and multiplying the right hand side by $P_t/P_{t-1}$ we get:

$$c_t + m_t + ff_t E_t + d_t + (1-\theta)bb_t E_t + h_t$$
$$= \frac{m_{t-1}}{1+p_t} + \frac{ff_{t-1} E_t}{1+p_t} + \frac{(1+r_d)}{1+p_t}d_{t-1} + \frac{(1+r_b)(1-\theta)}{1+p_t}bb_{t-1} E_t$$
$$+ (1+r)h_{t-1} + y_t + s_t \tag{a7}$$

dividing and multiplying the right hand side by $E_t/E_{t-1}$ we get:

$$c_t + m_t + ff_t E_t + d_t + (1-\theta)bb_t E_t + h_t$$
$$= \frac{m_{t-1}}{1+p_t} + \frac{(1+e_t)}{1+p_t}ff_{t-1} E_{t-1} + \frac{(1+r_d)}{1+p_t}d_{t-1}$$
$$+ \frac{(1+r_b)(1+e_t)(1-\theta)}{1+p_t}bb_{t-1} E_{t-1} + (1+r)h_{t-1} + y_t + s_t \tag{a8}$$

Now let's define the domestic currency value of foreign currency notes as $f_t = ff_t E_t$, and the domestic currency value of interest bearing foreign currency assets as $b_t = bb_t E_t$. Using (a4) we can rearrange terms to see:

$$w_t = y_t - c_t - s_t + \frac{m_{t-1}}{1+p_t} + \frac{(1+e_t)}{1+p_t}f_{t-1} + \frac{(1+r_d)}{1+p_t}d_{t-1}$$
$$+ \frac{(1+r_b)(1+e_t)(1-\theta)}{1+p_t}b_{t-1} + (1+r)h_{t-1} \tag{a9}$$

Then if we add and subtract $(1+r)w_{t-1}$ to this expression we get the law of motion of wealth:

$$w_t = y_t - c_t - s + (1+r)w_{t-1} + \left[\frac{1}{1+p_t} - (1+r)\right]m_{t-1} + \left[\frac{1+e_t}{1+p_t} - (1+r)\right]f_{t-1}$$
$$+ \left[\frac{1+r_d}{1+p_t} - (1+r)\right]d_{t-1} + \left[\frac{(1+r_b)(1+e_t)(1-\theta)}{1+p_t} - (1+r)(1-\theta)\right]b_{t-1} \tag{a10}$$

In order to simplify notation, we define:

$R = (1+r)$   Gross rate of return on $h$

$R_m = \dfrac{1}{1+p_t}$   Gross rate of return on $m$

$R_f = \dfrac{1+e_t}{1+p_t}$   Gross rate of return on $f$ (a11)

$R_d = \dfrac{1+r_d}{1+p_t}$   Gross rate of return on $d$

$R_b = \dfrac{(1+r_b)(1+e_t)}{1+p_t}$   Gross rate of return on $b$

Thus the wealth constraint can be rewritten as:

$$w_t = Rw_{t-1} + (R_m - R)m_{t-1} + (R_f - R)f_{t-1} + (R_d - R)d_{t-1}$$
$$+ (R_b - R)(1-\theta)b_{t-1} + y_t - c_t - s_t$$
(a12)

We can now set up the representative agent's problem as follows:[13]

$$\text{Max } \sum_{t=0}^{\infty} \beta^t u(c_t)$$

s.t. $s_t = \Phi(L_t, c_t)$ (a13)

$$w_t = Rw_{t-1} + (R_m - R)m_{t-1} + (R_f - R)f_{t-1} + (R_d - R)d_{t-1}$$
$$+ (R_b - R)(1-\theta)b_{t-1} + y_t - c_t - s_t$$

where $\beta \in (0, 1)$ is the subjective discount factor, u(.) is the period utility function, and $\Phi(.)$ is the transactions production technology. $\Phi(.)$ is assumed to be continuously differentiable and $\Phi_L < 0$, $\Phi_c > 0$, $\Phi_{cc} > 0$, $\Phi_{LL} > 0$, $\Phi_{cL} < 0$. $L_t$ is given by (a2)

The first order conditions of the constrained maximization problem are:

$$\lambda_t = \lambda_{t-1}\beta R$$
(a14)

$$\frac{\partial u(c_t)}{\partial c_t} = \lambda_t \left[ 1 + \frac{\partial \Phi(L_t, c_t)}{\partial c_t} \right]$$
(a15)

$$\frac{(R_m - R)}{R} = \frac{\partial \Phi}{\partial L} \frac{\partial L}{\partial m} \tag{a16}$$

$$\frac{(R_f - R)}{R} = \frac{\partial \Phi}{\partial L} \frac{\partial L}{\partial f} \tag{a17}$$

$$\frac{(Rd - R)}{R} = \frac{\partial \Phi}{\partial L} \frac{\partial L}{\partial d} \tag{a18}$$

$$\frac{(R_b - R)(1 - \theta)}{R} = \frac{\partial \Phi}{\partial L} \frac{\partial L}{\partial b} \tag{a19}$$

Since $\dfrac{\partial L}{\partial m} = 1$ by (a2), we have in fact:

$$\frac{(R_f - R)}{(R_m - R)} = \frac{\partial L}{\partial f} \tag{a20}$$

$$\frac{(R_d - R)}{(R_m - R)} = \frac{\partial L}{\partial d} \tag{a21}$$

$$\frac{(R_b - R)(1 - \theta)}{(R_m - R)} = \frac{\partial L}{\partial b} \tag{a22}$$

We have now enough information to construct the Currency Equivalent Monetary Aggregate given by (a3):

$$L_t = m_t + \frac{(R_f - R)}{(R_m - R)} f_t + \frac{(R_d - R)}{(R_m - R)} d_t + \frac{(R_b - R)(1 - \theta)}{(R_m - R)} b_t \tag{a23}$$

This CE explicitly states the amount of liquidity acquired from foreign currency denominated monetary assets and the amount acquired from domestic currency denominated monetary assets. This information is the basis of a measure of currency substitution as distinct from asset substitution.

Using equations (a21) and (a22), in the optimum the following should hold;

$$\frac{\partial L \big/ \partial b}{\partial L \big/ \partial d} = \frac{(R_b - R)(1 - \theta)}{(R_d - R)} \tag{a24}$$

Since L is homogenous of degree one, the partial derivatives are homogenous of degree zero. So (a24) can be rewritten as a relative demand equation;

$$\frac{b_t}{d_t} = \Omega^{AS}\left[\frac{(R_b - R)(1 - \theta)}{(R_d - R)}\right], \text{ with } \frac{\partial \Omega^{AS}}{\partial R_b} > 0 \tag{a25}$$

By the same token relative demand for foreign and domestic money can be written as;

$$\frac{f_t}{m_t} = \Omega^{CS}\left[\frac{(R_f - R)}{(R_m - R)}\right] = \Omega^{CS}\left[\frac{\dfrac{1}{(1+p^*)} - R}{\dfrac{1}{(1+p)} - R}\right], \text{ with } \frac{\partial \Omega^{CS}(.)}{\partial p} > 0 \tag{a26}$$

The latter part of the equation is valid under the assumption that purchasing power parity condition holds, i.e. $P = P^*E$ and consequently $(1+p) = (1+p^*)(1+e)$.

The assumptions on the signs of the partial derivatives are what is minimally required to reflect the asset substitution and currency substitution hypotheses and are the basis of the empirical tests presented in the chapter.

## Notes

1. Akyuz et al. (2001).
2. CBRT (2005).
3. CBRT (2006).
4. The explicit set up and solution of the model is in the appendix.
5. This liquidity aggregator function is a variant of the Currency Equivalent Index discussed by Rotemberg et al. 1995.
6. For a brief treatment of liquidity services model, portfolio balance model and the "agnostic" model for money demand and the types of empirical money demand functions they propose, see Freitas (2003).
7. The conventional information criteria were also checked and were in agreement with the lag reduction tests.
8. Diagnostic tests and graphs are not included due to space considerations but are available upon request. This applies for all the following empirical models estimated.
9. Eight VAR models were estimated and evaluated. Due to space considerations only summary results are reported. Full estimation results and diagnostics are available upon request.
10. Throughout the model lowercase letters indicate real variables and uppercase variables nominal variables.
11. These assumptions are based on Rotemberg,J., J. Driscoll, and J. Pertoba (1995) and are necessary to obtain the Currency Equivalent Index from the model.
12. Rotemberg,J., J. Driscoll, and J. Pertoba (1995).
13. For a discussion of problems and the literature concensus on aggregation over individuals, see Anderson,R.G., B. Jones and T. Nesmith (1996a).

# References

Anderson, R.G., B.E. Jones, and T.D. Nesmith. 1997a. Monetary Aggregation Theory and Statistical Index Numbers. *Federal Reserve Bank of St. Louis Review* 79(1) January/February.

Anderson, R.G., B.E. Jones, and T.D. Nesmith. 1997b. Building New Monetary Services Indices: Concepts, Methodology and Data. *Federal Reserve Bank of St. Louis Review* 79(1) January/February.

Akyüz, Y., and K. Boratav. 2001. The Making of the Turkish Financial Crisis. Paper prepared for conference: Financialization of the Global Economy, December 7–8, 2001. http://www.umass.edu/peri/pdfs/fin_akyuz.pdf

Central Bank of the Republic of Turkey. 2005. General Framework of Inflation Targeting Regime and Monetary and Exchange Rate Policy for 2006. *Basic Policy Readings* 2005–45.

Central Bank of the Republic of Turkey. 2006. 2007 Yilinda Para ve Kur Politikasi. *Basic Policy Readings*. December 13th, 2006.

Doornik, J.A., and D.F. Hendry. 2001. *PcGive 10: An Interactive Econometric Modelling System.* London: Timberlake Consultants Ltd.

Freitas, M. 2003. Revisiting Dollarization Hysterisis: Evidence from Bolivia, Turkey, Indonesia. *NIPE Working Papers* 12. https://repositorium.sdum.uminho.pt/bitstream/1822/1304/1/doll.pdf

Moron, E. 2002. Currency Substitution and the Moneyness of Monetary Assets, in *Essays on Dollarized Economies*, PhD. Thesis submitted to Department of Economics UCLA.

Rotemberg, J.J., J.C. Driscoll, and J.M. Poterba. 1995. Money, Output and Prices: Evidence from a New Monetary Aggregate. *Journal of Business and Economic Statistics* 13(1): 67–83.

Thomas, L.R. 1985. Portfolio Theory and Currency Substitution. *Journal of Money Credit and Banking* 17:347–357.

## Chapter 6

# COMPETITIVE DIVERSIFICATION IN RESOURCE ABUNDANT COUNTRIES: ARGENTINA AFTER THE COLLAPSE OF THE CONVERTIBILITY REGIME[Ψ]

## Leandro Serino

### Introduction

In economic terms, Argentina is a special case. It occupies a central place in accounts of economic history and financial newspaper headlines. The beginning of the 21st century saw Argentina's longest and largest economic crisis, which has been followed by recovery and expansion at rates of economic growth equalling those of China.

This recovery has reopened the debate on Argentina's long-term development strategy. Several authors emphasize the need to strengthen and promote Argentina's non-traditional tradable sectors, to consolidate the recent economic process and to finally overcome Argentina's recurrent internal and external imbalances (Gerchunoff and Ramos, 2005; Kacef, 2004; Porta, 2005).[1]

Between 2003 and 2008 positive international conditions and the competitive exchange rate policy followed by the government are both said to have encouraged strong macroeconomic fundamentals in Argentina (see Serino 2007). The implications of global conditions and the exchange rate policy for productive and export diversification, however, need to be discussed in more detail – especially as Argentina's structural features, commonly overlooked in aggregate macroeconomic studies, do play a role.

[Ψ] I received helpful comments on an earlier version of this paper from Professors R. Frenkel, M. Murshed, R. Vos, I. van Staveren. I also received comments from Juan Santarcangelo, an anonymous referee and various colleagues and participants at the 2nd Annual Conference on Development and Change and the 5th Conference on Labour Market and Equity in Argentina. The usual disclaimer applies.

Discussion of productive diversification in Argentina and the impact of natural resource shocks and policies hypothesized in this research, needs to take account of one of the country's most important structural features: a resource sector whose natural advantages make it more competitive internationally than other tradable sectors, and which produces wage-goods that are exported and consumed domestically. These structural characteristics matter for two reasons. First, the high productivity in Argentina's agriculture sector (and the recently developed mining sector) poses limitations on the development of other tradable sectors and therefore hampers competitive diversification (for classical and recent literature focusing on Argentina and other Latin America's countries see Chena and Perez Candreva, 2008; Chena and Feliz, 2008; Diamand, 1972; Nicolini-Llosa, 2007a, 2007b; Schlydlowsky, 1993). Although the interaction between the natural resource and industrial sectors is complex and its effects can work in different directions.

Second, because exchange rate devaluations can have particular effects in countries which, like Argentina, are exporters of wage-goods. Nominal devaluations can be contractionary, as emphasized in traditional and recent macroeconomic studies of Argentina (see e.g. Braun and Joy, 1968; Porto, 1975; Keifman, 2005). On the other hand, they can be expansionary, as noted by Frenkel and colleagues (see Frenkel and Taylor, 2006; Frenkel and Ros, 2006; Frenkel and Rapetti, 2007).

The second group of studies emphasizes many implications of nominal devaluation (i.e. the contribution to employment growth and the achievement of macroeconomic balances, Central Bank's sterilization capacity). However, it does not analyse the impact of a competitive exchange rate policy that takes account of Argentina's particular structural features. Although there has been much discussion in Argentina on the impact of devaluations in a wage-goods producing country, there are no macroeconomic studies discussing this issue with the proper analytical and sectoral detail.

This chapter develops (an unemployment version) of the Scandinavian dependent economy model, which is used to discuss how the recently mentioned structural features of Argentina constrain industrial competitiveness and determine the impact of the competitive exchange rate policy that has been pursued to encourage productive and export diversification among other things.

The model presented in this chapter has two novel features compared to the traditional Scandinavian model (see e.g. Dornbush, 1980; Murshed, 1997). First, it includes a wage equation, linking factor payments to average factor productivity, as in Rattsø and Torvik (2003). This extension shows how Argentina's natural advantages in agricultural production constrain the competitiveness of other tradable sectors and the macroeconomic implications this can have. It illustrates that a positive shock in the agriculture sector can increase unemployment and create current account imbalances, thus becoming an issue of concern for the economic authorities.

This make a new contribution to the work of classical authors such as Diamand, Kaldor and Schylidowski, within a macroeconomic framework, and also exemplifies the conditions required for a positive shock to promote internal and external imbalances: (i) a natural resource sector that is not the largest tradable sector and cannot ensure that the positive income effects of the resource shock predominate over the negative substitution effects; (ii) countries have a high propensity to import; (iii) there are large productivity differences between the natural resource and other tradable sectors, and (iv) industries that are very dependent on price competitive advantages.

The second innovative feature of the model is the inclusion of a productivity equation linking productivity growth to aggregate demand. The model in this chapter, therefore, considers the price and non-price dimensions of industrial competitiveness, and discusses how they are affected by a competitive exchange rate policy, such as that implemented in Argentina in 2003 to 2007.

Focusing on real-side issues, this chapter analyses the impact of exchange rate devaluations in countries with different structural characteristics. It shows that, for productive and export diversification to be achieved not at the expense of falling real wages, devaluations in wage-goods exporting countries like Argentina need to be implemented together with export taxes.

Another novelty of this model is that it incorporates Kaldor-Verdoon effects through a productivity equation. It shows that, by encouraging aggregate demand, exchange rate devaluations can boost productivity growth and improve non-price competitiveness in the tradable sector.

Neither the implications of nominal devaluations in wage-goods exporting countries nor their contribution to productivity growth, to my knowledge, have been considered in discussions relating to Argentina's competitive exchange rate policy in the early 2000s.

The chapter is organized as follows. After a brief conceptual discussion, the model is presented in Section 2. Section 3.1 is devoted to analysis of the adjustment to a positive resource shock and Section 3.2 discusses the general impact of exchange rate devaluation and its impact in wage-goods exporting countries. Section 3.3 extends the model to discuss the productivity aspects of the competitiveness problem and Section 4 summarizes the findings from this chapter.

## The Scandinavian Model

### *Some Conceptual Issues*

To understand the structural limitations to competitive diversification associated with resource abundance and to discuss alternative policies contributing to structural change, this chapter presents a simple analytical model along the lines of the Scandinavian model. The Scandinavian version of the dependent economy model is a Ricardian-type model in which labour is the only factor of production (see Dornbusch 1980, ch. 5; Murshed 1997, ch. 3).[2] The version developed in this chapter assumes that there is factor unemployment for this permits a discussion of Latin America's competitiveness issues that takes into account some of the propositions from Diamand, Kaldor and Schydlowsky (henceforth refereed as classical authors) within a macroeconomic framework.

According to these authors, the relatively high productivity of Latin America's agricultural or mineral sector handicaps competitive diversification because:

> these sectors can operate profitably at an [appreciated] exchange rate at which other [less productive] producers [sectors] in the economy would make losses (Schydlowsky, 1993: 28, parentheses added).

Though largely discussed, macroeconomic issues, such as the achievement of full-employment and external balances, are not considered formally by classical authors.

To work within a macroeconomic framework, the model considers the nominal exchange rate as a policy variable and assumes that factor prices reflect the productivity of the tradable sector(s).[3] Prices reflecting the (high) productivity of the (natural resource) tradable sectors do not necessarily clear the factors market, an assumption that is in line with the propositions from classical authors. Another implication of the assumption of factor unemployment, combined with the linear production function, is that the model explicitly takes account of the competitiveness of the tradable sectors.[4] Industrial competitiveness is analysed, therefore, in terms of the relation between factor productivity and prices, whether nominal wages or the exchange rate.

This competitive measure is highly simplified. As acknowledged in the literature, a sector's competitiveness depends on many other factors than the exchange rate, wages and productivity variables, like for instance the presence of specialized inputs and other relevant production costs.[5] There is a trade-off between analytical simplicity, and tractability with analytical completeness. As the purpose of this chapter is to give the competitiveness discussion within a macro context, the option for simplicity ruled. The price and productivity variables, therefore, are conceived in a broad sense, to imperfectly represent other price and non-price competitiveness determinants.[6]

## The Model

The Scandinavian model is a three goods-sectors model that distinguishes between tradables and non-tradables. To keep the model simple, labour is the only factor of production in this economy and is labelled $L$. The model does not consider factors' accumulation, neither investment. Economic sectors differ in terms of their factor productivity – it is equivalent to their total factor productivity ($TFP$) and is assumed to capture differences related to natural resource endowments and capital intensity, which, for simplicity, are assumed away.

Two of the three sectors in the economy are tradables: the natural resource sector, $R$, and the non-resource or manufacturing sector, $I$. The third sector is the non-tradable sector, $N$.

The following assumptions are defined to simplify the analysis; some of them will be removed as the discussion progresses. First, it is assumed that, due to competition, $TFP$ in the tradable sectors is higher than in the non-tradable one. A second (temporary) assumption is that all the production from sector $R$ is exported. This is a useful assumption to study the effects of structural factors for competitive diversification. For this analysis, what the sector produces is irrelevant, and $R$ can alternatively be rent. In the discussion on economic policies, however, this assumption is removed so as to consider the case of countries specialized in the production of food products.

The third assumption is that natural resource commodity prices are determined in the international market and that, at such prices the country can sell all its production abroad. The fourth assumption is that manufacturing goods produced at home and abroad are imperfect substitutes. Therefore, it is the external terms of trade for the goods produced in sector $I$, and not the law of one price that matters in this sector. The fifth and sixth assumptions are that: imports only compete with production from sector $I$ and intermediate inputs are non-tradable in nature. This implies that there are no imported intermediate inputs. Although imported intermediate inputs can have important macroeconomic implications, as recognized in the literature (see e.g. the seminal paper by Krugman and Taylor, 1978), they are not taken into account in this chapter to keep the algebra simple and to maintain the focus of the discussion on the effects of nominal devaluations on industrial competitiveness and real wages.[7]

Supply in the natural resource sector depends on labour and $TFP$, as indicated in equation (1.1) by $L_R$ and $A_R$, corresponding supply in the natural resource sector depends on labour and *TFP*, as indicated in equation (1.4) by $L_R$ and $A_R$, correspondingly

$$R = R(A_R; L_R) \atop {+ \quad +}$$

(1.1)

Output is demand-driven in the other two sectors, and the price of these domestically produced goods in terms of their unitary factor costs equals

$$P_i^h = \frac{1}{A_i} \cdot W + \bar{H}$$

(1.2)

Subscript *i* refers to sectors *I* and *N*; superscript *h* is the price of domestically produced goods; $A_i$ is the average product of labour in sector *i* and constitutes the productivity variable; *W* is the average wage or factor price, and $\bar{H}$ is other non-tradable input costs, assumed to be constant for the sake of simplicity.

Normalizing to 1 the international price of tradable goods $P_i^{int}$, this price in domestic currency units equals the nominal exchange rate *E*

$$P_i^f = E$$

(1.3)

The nominal exchange rate is defined as domestic currency units per unit of foreign currency, so that *E* increases (falls) with devaluations (revaluations). In the equation above subscript *i* concerns sectors *R* and *I*. The previous assumption regarding the natural resource sector implies that the law of one price prevails and that, at this particular time, this is the only price that counts in sector *R*.[8] For goods produced in sector *I*, $P_i^f$ denotes the price for the imperfect manufacturing substitutes produced in the rest of the world.

Nominal factor prices or wages are defined as in Rattsø and Torvik (2003) and equal

$$W = \omega \cdot Q^\tau$$

(1.4)

In eq. (1.4) $\omega$ relates wages to factor productivity, as approximated by $A_i$, and defined by

$$\omega = A_R^{\gamma R} \cdot A_I^{\gamma I} \cdot A_N^{1-\gamma R - \gamma I}$$

(1.5)

Where exponents $\gamma_i$ weight sectoral productivity according to the relative size of the sector $\left( \text{with } \sum_i \gamma_i = 1 \right)$. Variable *Q* in equation (1.4) indexes wages to the evolution of the consumer price index (*CPI*), which equals

$$Q = \left( P_I^f \right)^{\alpha_{If}} \cdot \left( P_I^h \right)^{\alpha_{Ih}} \cdot \left( P_N^h \right)^{1-\alpha_{If} \alpha_{Ih}}$$

(1.6)

with prices as defined above and exponents indicating weights in the consumption basket reproduced in the price index. Note, that, due to the assumption regarding the external destination of natural resource products their price does not enter the index. This is one of the assumptions that is removed in subsequent sections.

The degree of wage indexation depends on the value of $\tau$, which varies between 0 and 1. If $\tau$ equals 0 there is no indexation and nominal wage rigidity; if $\tau$ equals 1, there is full-indexation of price changes and real wage rigidity. Intermediate values represent imperfect indexation. The value of the indexation parameter can be negatively associated to the level of unemployment or the degree of excess capacity. Although this point is not explicitly modelled, it will be taken into account during the discussion.

Two relevant points are worth making regarding labour market dynamics. First, factor prices follow productivity, as would be expected over the long-run. Second, according to institutional arrangements there is one wage in this economy, and this is determined in relation to average factor productivity and changes in the cost of living. As a consequence, significant sectoral productivity differences (a point that is emphasized in this thesis) or indexation can make tradable sectors uncompetitive, allowing for structural unemployment, as emphasized by the classical authors.

Real income is defined as

$$Y = \frac{W \cdot L}{Q} \tag{1.7}$$

In this model both the internal and the external terms of trade matter. This is because, as industrial output is demand-driven, the external terms of trade affect demand for the tradable commodity $I$ in the domestic and international markets and, therefore, they affect output in this sector. Note that the model differs from full-employment specifications of the dependent economy models where prices are flexible and the internal terms of trade between tradable and non-tradable goods are the key relative prices since they determine the incentives to produce in one or the other sector.[9]

The external terms of trade for goods produced in sector $I$ $(p_I^*)$ are defined as the ratio of foreign to domestic prices of these imperfect substitute goods

$$p_I^* = \frac{P_I^f}{P_I^h} \tag{1.8}$$

The internal terms of trade $p_D$ are shown below and are defined as the ratio between the tradable and non-tradable goods prices.

$$p_D = \frac{P_T}{P_N^h} \tag{1.9}$$

Depending on whether the price of non-tradable goods is compared to the imperfectly substitute manufacturing goods produced abroad or at home, the internal terms of trade equals $P_D^f = P_I^f/P_N^h$ or $P_D^h = P_I^h/P_N^h$. The assumption that productivity in the tradable sectors is higher than in the non-tradable sector implies that the latter is the most labour-intensive sector,[10] and that an increase in wages will raise the price of non-tradable goods $P_N^h$ relative to the price of manufacturing goods produced domestically $P_I^h$.

On the demand side, output is defined as:

$$Y = C_I(Y; p_D^h; p_I^*) + C_N(Y; p_D^h; p_D^f) + T \tag{1.10}$$
$$\quad\; + \; - \; + \qquad\quad + \; + \; +$$

In equation (1.10), $C_I$ denotes demand for manufacturing goods produced domestically, $C_N$ stands for the demand for non-tradables, and $T$ represents the current account, which, in this model, equals the trade balance. Domestic demand in the two sectors depends positively on real income $Y$. Demand for goods produced in sector $I$ is negatively linked to internal and positively linked to external terms of trade in the corresponding sector, $p_D^h$ and $p_I^*$ respectively. Non-tradable demand rises with $p_D^h$ and $p_D^f$ due to substitution effects.

The external balance $T$ is determined by the country's import and export performances and the evolution of export and import prices.

$$T = P_R^f \cdot X_R(R; Y^f) + P_I^f \cdot X_I(Y^f; p_I^*) - P_I^f \cdot M_I(Y; p_I^*) \tag{1.11}$$
$$\qquad\quad + \; + \qquad\qquad + \; + \qquad\qquad + \; -$$

The model assumes a fixed exchange rate regime, thus the nominal exchange rate $E$ is a policy variable. This raises issues like the long-term sustainability of the current account and monetary issues not considered in the present analysis, to focus on other real-side effects of nominal devaluations.[11]

The two assumptions regarding the natural resource sector imply that $R = X_R$: supply equals export demand for natural resource products. Natural resource exports ($X_R$) in turn are positively related to domestic supply ($R$) and foreign income ($Y^f$). Exports from sector $I$ ($X_I$) also depend positively on foreign income, and are positively affected by the external terms of trade in sector ($p_I^*$). Imports are the final component of the trade balance. Imports of manufacturing goods ($M_I$) (which are assumed to equal total imports) are negatively related to the external terms of trade in sector $(p_I^*)$ and positively linked to changes in domestic income $(Y)$.

The internal balance is analysed in terms of labour market equilibrium. As defined in equation (1.12), quantity adjustments prevail in the labour market and employment $(L)$ equals labour demand from the tradables $(R, I)$ and non-tradable sectors $(N)$, and $a_i$ (equals $1/A_i$) represents sectoral factor intensities.

$$L = a_R \cdot X_R(\underset{+}{R}; \underset{+}{Y^f}) + a_N C_N(\underset{+}{Y}; \underset{+}{p_D^h}; \underset{+}{p_D^f})$$

$$+ a_I \left[ C_I(\underset{+}{Y}; \underset{-}{p_D^h}; \underset{+}{p_I^*}) + X_I(\underset{+}{Y^f}; \underset{+}{p_I^*}) \right] \tag{1.12}$$

## Structural Constraints to Productive Diversification in Resource Rich South American Countries

This section discusses the constraints on productive diversification associated with natural resource abundance. The analysis is expected to show some specificities of the economic adjustment to a positive natural resource shock and to illustrate why this could be a matter of concern for the economic authorities. The model assumes that, as usual in the Latin American countries, the tradable natural resource sector is the most competitive one. Given the previous assumptions, the productivity ordering is as follows $A_R > A_I > A_N$.

The analysis assumes an increase in the productivity of the natural resource sector $(A_R)$ to discuss the implications of a positive natural resource shock. Assuming no indexation of prices into wages $(\tau = 0)^{12}$, the increase in $A_R$ affects real and nominal wages, which in turns affects the internal and external equilibrium of the economy. From equations (1.4) and (1.5) it follows that

$$\frac{\partial W}{\partial A_R} = \gamma_R \left( \frac{A_I A_N}{A_R} \right)^{1-\gamma_R} \tag{1.13}$$

Equation (1.13) has a positive sign and states that high productivity in sector $R$, due to a resource discovery, technical change or because such a gift of nature is a structural characteristic of the country, leads to higher nominal and real wages, an increase that is positively related to the size of the natural resource sector, as denoted by $\gamma_R$. This result is in line with the arguments proposed by the classical authors, is equivalent to the Balassa-Samuelson effect; and it is also consistent with the predictions of Dutch disease type models.[13]

## Positive Natural Resource Shocks and the Internal Balance

Studying the consequences of an increase in $A_R$ for internal balance or labour market equilibrium requires totally differentiating equation (1.12). It is also necessary to differentiate real income, as expressed in (1.7), in order to disentangle the changes associated with variations in real wages and labour demand. This latter aspect is investigated in the appendix (see equations (A.0.1) to (A.0.4)). After some manipulation, the expression in equation (1.14) emerges and shows that expansion in the natural resource sector has ambiguous effects on the labour market. The sign for the partial derivatives representing the different effects of the change in $A_R$ are shown below each term.

$$\frac{\partial L}{\partial A_R} = \frac{1}{1-\phi}\left[\underbrace{\frac{\partial aR}{\partial A_R}}_{-} + \underbrace{a_R \cdot \frac{\partial X_R}{\partial R}\frac{\partial R}{\partial A_R}}_{+} + \underbrace{\frac{\partial p_D^h}{\partial A_R}}_{-}\left(\underbrace{a_N \cdot \frac{\partial C_N}{\partial p_D^h}}_{-} + \underbrace{a_I \frac{\partial C_I}{\partial p_D^h}}_{+}\right)\right]$$

$$+\frac{1}{1-\phi}\left[\underbrace{a_N \cdot \frac{\partial C_N}{\partial p_D^f}\frac{\partial p_D^f}{\partial A_R}}_{+} + \underbrace{a_I \frac{\partial p_I^*}{\partial A_R}}_{-}\left(\underbrace{\frac{\partial C_I}{\partial p_I^*}}_{+} + \underbrace{\frac{\partial X_I}{\partial p_I^*}}_{+}\right) + \underbrace{\phi\frac{\partial Y\left(\frac{W}{Q}\right)}{\partial A_R}}_{+}\right] \gtrless 0 \quad (1.14)$$

In eq. (1.14)

$$\phi = \left(a_N \frac{\partial C_N}{\partial Y} + a_I \frac{\partial C_I}{\partial Y}\right), \quad \frac{\partial Y\left(\frac{W}{Q}\right)}{\partial A_R} = \frac{\left[1 - \alpha_I^f (a_I - a_N) - aN(1-\alpha_I^f)\right]}{1-A}\frac{\partial W}{\partial A_R}$$

and $1-A = 1 - \tau \cdot \alpha_I^h (a_I - a_N) - \tau \cdot a_N(1-\alpha_I^f)$

The second expression represents changes in real income associated with variations in wages. Equation (1.13) and the assumption that sector $N$ is more labour-intensive than sector $I$ $(a_I < a_N)$ guarantees that real wages rise with a productivity shock.

Positive effects on employment result from: (i) the expansion in output and exports from sector $R$; and (ii) the increase in real wages (the second and last terms in the square brackets in equation (1.14)).

Increases in the productivity of sector $R$ also have negative consequences for employment. These are associated with: (i) the reduction in sector $R$'s labour requirements; (ii) the substitution of non-tradable goods for manufacturing goods, produced either in the less factor-intensive sector $I$ or abroad, and the substitution of goods produced in sector $I$, for (iii) competitive imports; and (iv) foreign products, in the domestic and international markets respectively.[14]

The last two substitution effects arise because the increase in wages that follows the productivity shock in sector R reduces the external terms of trade in sector $I$ $(\partial p_I^*/\partial A_R < 0)$.

Since the natural resource sector is the less *factor-intensive*, and substitution between tradable and non-tradable goods is expected to be small, employment will expand (contract) if the positive income effect of the shock is larger (smaller) than the substitution effect crowding-out sector $I$. Table 1 at the end of this section summarizes the conditions favouring one or the other outcome.

As shown in eq. (1.13) and eq. (1.14) the expansion in employment is positively associated with the size of sector $R$ $(\gamma_R)$. Therefore, in countries with a large natural resource sector, e.g. the oil-exporting countries, employment will expand following a positive resource shock. If, as is the case in the Latin American countries, sector $R$ is not the largest tradable sector a positive resource shock may lead to a 'paradoxical' disequilibrium situation in the labour market.

Large productivity differences between tradable sectors are another factor favouring the emergence of unemployment in the context of a resource shock. The larger the productivity differences the larger will be the mismatch between wages and labour productivity in sector $I$. This means that, for given intermediate input costs ($\overline{H}$), sector $I$ will have high unit labour costs (and low sectoral external terms of trade $p_I^*$), making it harder, if not impossible, for the sector to compete internationally or take off in an open domestic market.

An additional factor promoting labour market disequilibrium (not explicitly modelled) is the degree of backwardness and dependence on price competitive advantages in sector $I$. Whereas the damaging effects of a positive natural resource shock may be large in countries with nascent industries or industries with low productivity, the same shock may have only limited effects in countries producing sophisticated industrial products, as Canada or the Scandinavian counties.

## Positive Natural Resource Shocks and the External Balance

To study the adjustment in the external balance it is necessary to totally differentiate equation (1.11). As shown in equation (1.15), a positive productivity shock in sector $R$ increases primary exports, although the final effect on the trade balance is ambiguous.

$$\frac{\partial T}{\partial A_R} = p_R^f \cdot \underset{+}{\frac{\partial X_R}{\partial R}} \underset{+}{\frac{\partial R}{\partial A_R}} + \underset{+}{\frac{\partial p_I^h}{\partial A_R}} X_I + \underset{-}{\frac{\partial p_I^*}{\partial A_R}} \left( p_I^h \underset{+}{\frac{\partial X_I}{\partial p_I^*}} - p_I^f \underset{-}{\frac{\partial M_I}{\partial p_I^*}} \right)$$

$$- p_I^f \underset{-}{\frac{\partial M_I}{\partial Y}} \underset{+/-}{\frac{\partial Y}{\partial A_R}} \gtreqless 0 \qquad (1.15)$$

The first term in equation (1.15) stands for a positive impact on the overall trade balance from higher exports from sector $R$. The second term is also positive and shows the price-income effect of the chain productivity, nominal wages, manufacturing exports price ($P_I^h$). However, the shock reduces competitiveness and export levels from sector $I$, and this has negative effects on the balance of trade.[15]

The last two terms in eq. (1.15) refer to import dynamics. These increase, worsening the trade balance, because lower external terms of trade ($p_I^*$) make imported goods cheaper than their domestic substitutes. Also, imports may increase if the productivity shock is expansionary and increases real income.[16]

Although it might be expected that high(er) productivity in the natural resource sector will lead to an improved balance of trade or to a new equilibrium with higher imports, under certain circumstances this may fail to occur. The following factors make a "paradoxical" external imbalance more likely: high marginal propensities to import; large productivity differences between sector $R$ and sector $I$ promoting unfavourable terms of trade (and terms of trade changes), and dependence on price competitive advantages.

Table 1 below summarizes the findings from this section. The analysis shows that:

- resource abundance and positive resource shocks hinder competitive diversification through substitution effects;
- countries try to diversify and modify what is a priori a favourable structural condition because, under certain circumstances, resource abundance and a positive shock can lead to internal and external imbalances;
- imbalances are more likely to occur when: (i) the size of sector $R$ or the magnitude of the shock does not ensure that positive income effects predominate over negative substitution effects; (ii) countries have a high

**Table 1: Labour Market and External Adjustment to a Positive Natural Resource Shock. Conditions Leading to Internal and External Disequilibria**

| Results | Conditions |
|---|---|
| $\partial L / \partial A_R$ − | • The shock has small positive income effects, favoured by small sector $R$<br>• There are large negative substitution effects, promoted by large sectoral productivity differences |
| $\partial T / \partial A_R$ − | • There are large substitution of sector's $I$ products in the domestic and external market, promoted by large sectoral productivity differences, and/or<br><br>• The economy has a high marginal propensity to import |

propensity to import; (iii) there are large productivity differences between the natural resource and industry sectors; and (iv) industries are very dependent on price competitive advantages. Many of these conditions echo Latin America's structural features, as identified by Bielschowsky (1998)

## Macroeconomic Diversification Policies

This section analyses the effects of macroeconomic policies to improve the competitiveness of the non-natural resource tradable sector $I$. Special attention is paid to the effects of nominal devaluations; a fundamental development policy that is expected to enhance the overall competitiveness of the economy, increasing employment and improving the external balance (Frenkel and Taylor, 2006).[17]

Two additional reasons justify the emphasis in this policy. One is that a competitive exchange rate policy has been in place in Argentina since 2003. The other is that nominal devaluations can have particular effects in countries that: already have an internationally competitive sector and that, as Argentina, export the least substitutable goods of the consumption basket: food products.

The comparative static exercises consider four cases. The first case studies the general impact of nominal devaluations, while the other three cases take account of specificities that are relevant to an analysis of Argentina. These are related to: the impact of devaluations in wage-good exporting countries, the emergence of a devaluation rent and the compensated devaluation regime combining nominal devaluations and export taxes. Before turning to the comparative statics exercise it should be noted that the analysis: (i) does not address the monetary aspects of the devaluation; (ii) looks only at the impact of nominal devaluations in the labour market (for reasons of simplicity); (iii) allows for wage indexation. The most relevant findings are summarized in Table 2 at the end of this section.

## Exchange Rate Devaluations: The 'General' Case

The analysis assumes for the moment that all production from sector $R$ is exported. Totally differentiating equation (1.12) with respect to $E$ gives

$$
\frac{\partial L}{\partial E} = \frac{1}{1-\phi} \left[ \underset{-}{\frac{\partial p_D^h}{\partial E}} \left( a_N \cdot \underset{+}{\frac{\partial C_N}{\partial p_D^h}} + a_I \underset{-}{\frac{\partial C_I}{\partial p_D^h}} \right) + a_N \cdot \underset{+}{\frac{\partial C_N}{\partial p_D^f}} \underset{+}{\frac{\partial p_D^f}{\partial E}} \right]
$$

$$
+ \frac{1}{1-\phi} \left[ a_I \underset{+}{\frac{\partial p_I^*}{\partial E}} \left( \underset{+}{\frac{\partial C_I}{\partial p_I^*}} + \underset{+}{\frac{\partial X_I}{\partial p_I^*}} \right) + \phi \underset{-}{\frac{\partial Y\left(\frac{W}{Q}\right)}{\partial E}} \right] \geq 0 \qquad (1.16)
$$

As before, $\phi = (a_N (\partial C_N / \partial \Upsilon) + a_I (\partial C_I / \partial \Upsilon))$ and $(\partial \Upsilon (W/Q) / \partial E) = (\tau - 1) / 1 - A \; \alpha_I^f$. Changes in real income due to variations in real wages are negative insofar as there is imperfect wage indexation $(\tau < 1)$.[18]

The impact of devaluation on the internal balance is ambiguous: it has two positive and two negative effects on employment. Expansion in employment is the result of substitution effects, which occur because the devaluation modifies the corresponding terms of trade $(P_D^f \text{ and } P_I^*)$. Therefore, employment rises due to: (i) substitution of imported for non-tradable goods; and (ii) substitution favouring production in the tradable sector $I$ and thus tradable diversification. As shown by the third term in the square brackets, devaluation promotes the substitution of imported for domestically produced goods and encourages non-traditional exports.

The ambiguity of the final result is associated with the negative effects of devaluation. These negative effects are the result of: (i) substitution of non-tradable goods with products from sector $I$ (because the former are more labour intensive than the latter);[19] and (ii) the reduction in real wages caused by the devaluation; these two effects are captured by the first and last terms in equation (1.16). The falls in real wages and domestic demand are positively associated to the share of imported goods in the consumption basket $(\alpha_{If})$, which are the only tradable goods fully increasing in price, and negatively related to the degree of wage indexation $\tau$.

A first result from the static analysis is that the promotion of tradable diversification with devaluations requires falling real wages. Assuming low substitution between non-tradable and tradable goods, equation (1.16) suggests that export competitiveness and the export component of aggregate demand expands at the expense of domestic demand.

## Exchange Rate Devaluations in Wage-Goods Exporting Countries

This section extends the analysis removing the assumption that natural resources are only exported. This assumption is useful to clarify the link between resource abundance and the competitiveness of sector $I$. It is a valid assumption for countries exporting mineral products that cannot be used at home, such as precious stones in African countries. It is worth removing it, however, to analyse some of the particular effects of devaluation in countries which, like Argentina, specialize in the production of wage-goods that are both exported and consumed domestically.

Three more points can be put forward to further justify the examination of this structural feature of the Argentine economy. First, according to Engels law, food products are among the less, if not the least, substitutable products in the household consumption basket. Second, wage-goods tend to represent a significant part of the basket, which measures the evolution of the *CPI*,[20] in contrast to other Latin American countries, Argentina exports many of the food products consumption basket.[21] Finally, in countries with different endowments, such as resource-poor East Asian countries, food products are expected to be more easily substitutable or rather will be non-tradable and thus not directly affected by movements in the exchange rate.

The analysis in this section is straightforward. As already mentioned, food products represent a major part of the household consumption basket, and are reflected in the CPI. This implies that the price index $Q$ must include, among the prices of tradable goods, the price of natural resource goods. The index will then equal $Q^R = (P_R^f)^{\alpha_{Rf}} \cdot (P_I^f)^{\alpha_{If}} \cdot (P_I^h)^{\alpha_{Ih}} \cdot (P_N^h)^{1-\alpha_{If}\alpha_{Ih}}$, where supraindex $R$ indicates the variables and terms affected by this extension to the model.

Domestic consumption of natural resource products adds a new term to the internal balance. This term reflects domestic demand for tradable natural resource products ($C_R$), which responds positively to changes in real income and negatively to variations in the relevant terms of trade of the sector $p_D^{f^R} = (P_R^f / P_N^h)$ and $p_I^{*R} = (P_R^f / P_I^h)$. The effects of the devaluation when the products of sector $R$ are consumed domestically are now given by eq. (1.17).

$$
\frac{\partial L^R}{\partial E} = \frac{1}{1-\phi^R}
\begin{bmatrix}
\underset{-}{\frac{\partial p_D^h}{\partial E}} \left( a_N \cdot \underset{+}{\frac{\partial C_N}{\partial p_D^h}} + a_I \underset{-}{\frac{\partial C_I}{\partial p_D^h}} \right) + a_N \cdot \underset{+}{\frac{\partial C_N}{\partial p_D^f}} \underset{+}{\frac{\partial p_D^f}{\partial E}} \\[2em]
+ \underset{+}{\frac{\partial p_D^{f^R}}{\partial E}} \left( a_R \cdot \underset{-}{\frac{\partial C_R}{\partial p_D^{f^R}}} + a_N \underset{+}{\frac{\partial C_N}{\partial p_D^{f^R}}} \right)
\end{bmatrix}
$$

$$
\frac{1}{1-\phi^R}
\begin{bmatrix}
\underset{+}{\frac{\partial p_I^{*R}}{\partial E}} \left( a_R \cdot \underset{-}{\frac{\partial C_R}{\partial p_I^{*R}}} + a_I \underset{+}{\frac{\partial C_I}{\partial p_I^{*R}}} \right) \\[2em]
+ a_I \underset{+}{\frac{\partial p_I^*}{\partial E}} \left( \underset{+}{\frac{\partial C_I}{\partial p_I^*}} + \underset{+}{\frac{\partial X_I}{\partial p_I^*}} \right) + \phi^R \underset{-}{\frac{\partial r \left( \frac{W}{Q^R} \right)}{\partial E}}
\end{bmatrix}
\gtreqless 0
$$

(1.17)

where $\phi^R = a_R\,(\partial C_R/\partial Y) + a_N(\partial C_N/\partial Y) + a_I(\partial C_I/\partial Y)$ and changes in real

income following variations in real wages equal $\partial Y(W/Q^R)/\partial E = (\tau - 1)$
[22]
$(\alpha_I^f + \alpha_R^f)/1 - C.$

The internal balance equation includes two new terms (that can be recognized by the supraindex $R$) which have positive effects on labour demand. This is because devaluation changes the domestic terms of trade between the natural resource and other domestically produced goods, promoting the substitution of food products with goods produced in the other more labour-intensive sectors.

Despite these new positive terms, which can be assumed to be quite small to the extent that they refer to substitution between food and other products, the aim is to highlight the negative income effects of the devaluation.

As shown by $\partial Y(W/Q^R)/\partial E$, which reflects changes in real wages associated with the devaluation; with natural resource commodity prices determined in the international market, a higher and more devalued exchange rate increases the price of natural resource (food) products, further reducing real wages. This reduction is larger, the larger the number of exported products which are also consumed domestically, as expressed by the new term $\alpha_{Rf}$, and is negatively associated to $\tau$, the wage indexation parameter.

This particular effect has been emphasized in the traditional and more recent macroeconomic literature on Argentina. This is first because it implies that the domestic consumption of exported commodities increases the possibility of contractionary devaluations which will occur if the negative wage effect dominates the positive substitution effects (Porto, 1975). Second, because as emphasized in a recent paper by Keifman (2005), allowing for some appreciation of the "devalued" Argentine peso will increase real wages and the ensuing expansion in domestic demand will promote employment.

A second result of this comparative statics exercise is that *since the larger decrease in real wages does not bring any additional improvement in the competitiveness of sector I, using the nominal exchange rate to promote tradable diversification is more costly in Argentina than in countries that have different structural characteristics.*

Finally, it should be stressed that, unless there is some compensating expansion in employment, the devaluation will reduce real income. In this context, employment growth will depend principally on substitution effects in sector $I$, which require favourable changes in the external terms of trade in sector $(p_I^*)$. Engineering these changes and thereby securing the effectiveness of devaluation to promote an export-led regime, requires a low or null indexation parameter. As suggested (but not explicitly modelled) in section *4.2.2*, this is likely to occur in a context of high unemployment rates, as in Argentina since the 1990s, but this has not always been the case. As noted by Gerchunoff and

Llach (2003), due to its high costs in terms of real wages, devaluations in Argentina historically have engendered political-economy conflicts that have restored real wages and reduced the economy's competitiveness.

## Exchange Rate Devaluations and Devaluation Rents

This section considers one of the consequences of an exchange rate devaluation often overlooked in the literature: the creation of a devaluation rent favouring the most productive sector $R$. The rent will rise because devaluation makes international commodity prices higher than domestic production costs. Assuming equation (1.2) is a valid approximation of the unitary production costs in sector $R$, and assuming that prior to the devaluation these costs were equal to international prices as defined by equation (1.3), the rent will equal the difference between these two equations, as defined below:

$$\Gamma = E - W \cdot \frac{1}{A_R} - \bar{H} \tag{1.18}$$

With commodity prices in domestic currency units larger than production costs, nominal wages will be

$$W = a_R \left( \omega Q^{\tau} + \Gamma \right) + (1 - a_R) \omega Q^{\tau}$$

The new wage expression denotes factor payments as determined in equation (1.4) plus the devaluation rent, making wages higher than the average wage in previous sections.

Although this extension does not add any terms to the balance equation, it modifies the terms of trade and real wage expressions. Taking into account the presence of a devaluation rent implies that: ($i$) there is a lower reduction (and the possibility of an increase) in real wages (see equations (A.0.7))[23], and therefore ($ii$) there are smaller changes in the external terms of trade ($p_I^*$) and lower incentives for tradable diversification, because the competitiveness gain from the devaluation decreases with the rent it creates (see equations (A.0.10) and (A.0.11)) in the appendix).

The presence of a devaluation rent reduces the possibilities of a contractionary devaluation. This may change, however, if the rent is not distributed across the factors of production in all economic sectors, as implied by the wage setting mechanism in the model. Under different institutional arrangements in the labour market, the devaluation will worsen the distribution of income, and the final impact of this policy will depend on the characteristics of the saving and consumption patterns characteristic of households, an issue that is not explored in this chapter.

## A Compensated Devaluation Regime

The detailed discussion above exemplifies the various (and ambiguous) effects of nominal devaluations and a competitive exchange rate regime. They are clearly positive, as they promote employment through tradable diversification, reducing a common disequilibrium in Argentina since the 1990s, and are a clear feature of other (resource rich) Latin American countries. The promotion of structural change, however, comes at the cost of lower real wages, an adjustment that is larger in wage-goods exporting countries. Moreover, in countries that already have a sector with significant natural advantages the creation of a devaluation rent counteracts and puts at risk the competitiveness gains that the devaluation seeks to promote.

Partly as a consequence of these conflicting effects, structural change is promoted using alternative and complementary policies, such as import tariffs (and quotas) and production, wages and export subsidies. As these policies are now banned by international trade agreements, they are not studied in the model.[21] Nevertheless, the model is used to analyse the effects of another policy: taxes on exports of natural resources, which commonly accompany nominal devaluations in resource abundant countries. According to Schydlowsky (1993), the combination of these two policies creates a compensated devaluation regime, which is the regime that has been in place in Argentina in 2000s, and is considered to promote the non-traditional sector without major income distribution effects.

The combination of nominal devaluations and export taxes has three main effects. First, it separates the domestic and international prices of natural resource commodities from international ones. In this way, the export tax reduces or avoids the negative effects of the devaluation on real wages (see equations (A.0.8)). Export taxes not only limit the reduction in real wages, they also reduce the impact of any wage indexation in the external terms of trade for sector $I(p_I^*)$ (see equations (A.0.10) and (A.0.11) in the appendix). As a consequence, *the compensated devaluation regime can ensure that the devaluation effectively creates a price competitive advantage favouring sector I, while limiting its negative consequences on real wages.*[25]

Second, a compensated devaluation regime creates a system of dual exchange rates, where the less productive tradable sector $I$ works at a high and competitive exchange rate, whereas sector $R$ works at a lower and stronger exchange rate, which is intended to reflect its competitiveness. In this way, the export tax avoids the most productive sector $R$ from gaining an unnecessary price advantage, and limits income transfers among the different agents in the economy and the deterioration in the distribution of income (not explored in this chapter).

Finally, export taxes redirect the rent created by devaluation to the government. This income transfer –which also can prevent devaluation from

**Table 2: Labour Market Adjustment to Exchange Rate Devaluations**

| Result | Conditions |
| --- | --- |
| (1) Exchange rate devaluations: the 'general' case | |
| $\partial L/\partial E\, +$ | • Substitution of: imported with non-tradable goods (expected to be small) and sector's $I$ goods <br> • Increase in manufacturing export demand |
| $\partial L/\partial E\, -$ | • Substitution of: non-tradables with sector's $I$ goods (expected to be small) <br> • Reduction in domestic demand due to fall in real wages (positively linked to share of imported goods in the CPI) |
| (2) Exchange rate devaluations in wage-goods exporting countries | |
| $\partial L/\partial E\, +$ | • Effects in (1) <br> • Substitution of food products for other domestically produced goods (expected small) |
| $\partial L/\partial E\, -$ | • Effects in (1) <br> • Larger reduction in domestic demand from fall in real wages larger than in (1) (positively linked to share of wage-goods in the CPI) |
| (3) Exchange rate devaluations and devaluation rents | |
| $\partial L/\partial E\, +$ | • Effects in (2), with smaller substitution effects promoting diversification |
| $\partial L/\partial E\, -$ | • Effects in (2), smaller reduction in real wages due to devaluation rent |
| (4) A compensated devaluation regime | |
| $\partial L/\partial E\, +$ | • Substitution effects as in (1) |
| $\partial L/\partial E\, -$ | • Effects in (3), with smaller negative real wage adjustment and income redistribution to the government |

worsening the distribution of income– has important fiscal effects and constitutes a source of income to finance alternative diversification policies, the topic of the next section in this chapter.[26]

## Do Macroeconomic Policies Suffice?

Section 4.4 discussed the contribution of macroeconomic policies to the complex task of competitive diversification in resource abundant economies. But are macroeconomic policies sufficient? Do they tackle the central constraint on competitive diversification in countries like Argentina?

The answers to these questions are yes, and no. Yes, macro policies can make the non-resource sector competitive, and do so by tackling the price aspect of competitiveness. However, the productivity aspect of competitiveness is overlooked. If I study the problem dynamically, the answers are still yes and no. Macroeconomic policies can contribute to increasing the productivity of the industrial sector, but these policies may not be sufficient to resolve the competitiveness handicap of the sector.

The analytical framework is extended in two directions in order to discuss these points in more detail. The first extension is linked to the proposition that reductions in sectoral productivity differences and decreases in non-wage production costs are a fundamental condition for competitive and sustainable diversification in resource abundant countries. Productive and export diversification due to a stagnant agricultural sector or due to the presence of structural unemployment and low wages, cannot be considered a viable or sustainable option.

The second extension is the addition of an equation that captures the dynamics of productivity in sector $I$.[27] TFP is modelled as in Thirlwall (2002) and Rada and Taylor (2004) and presented in (1.19)

$$A_I = \Lambda + \delta \Upsilon (X_I) \tag{1.19}$$

Equation (1.19) states that productivity depends on exogenous factors, captured by the term $\Lambda$. Human capital accumulation and/or access to foreign technology are clear examples of these factors. The equation also includes a Kaldor-Verdoorn component linking productivity growth to output or demand growth.[28]

Productivity is expected to increase with aggregate demand because, as it enlarges, demand facilitates the achievement of static and dynamic economies of scale. The creation, expansion (and in certain circumstances protection) of demand promotes experience and with it learning, as well as the achievement of economies of specialization, with positive effects on industrial productivity. Because in reality the importance of complementarities and economies of scale, both static and dynamic, tend to be larger in firms and sectors operating on a global scale, the model associates the Kaldor-Verdoorn component with the evolution of exports in the non-resource tradable sector $(X_I)$.[29]

The exchange rate, tariffs and subsidy policies have no direct incidence on productivity. Yet, they may contribute indirectly to productivity growth by increasing demand. It is possible, therefore, to reassess the contribution of macroeconomic policies to productive diversification and the internal equilibrium of the economy. In line with the analyses in the previous sections, the comparative statics exercise focuses on the effects of nominal devaluations, and presents the results only for the last case of a compensated devaluation regime.

The employment response to an exchange rate devaluation when productivity is endogenous is given by

$$
\frac{\partial L^R}{\partial E} = \frac{1}{1-\phi^R}
\begin{bmatrix}
\underset{+/-}{\frac{\partial p_D^h}{\partial E}} \left( a_N \cdot \underset{+}{\frac{\partial C_N}{\partial p_D^h}} + a_I \underset{-}{\frac{\partial C_I}{\partial p_D^h}} \right) + a_N \cdot \underset{+}{\frac{\partial C_N}{\partial p_D^f}} \underset{+}{\frac{\partial p_D^f}{\partial E}} + \\[2ex]
\underset{-}{\frac{\partial p_D^{f^R}}{\partial E}} \left( a_R \cdot \underset{-}{\frac{\partial C_R}{\partial p_D^{f^R}}} + a_N \underset{+}{\frac{\partial C_N}{\partial p_D^{f^R}}} \right)
\end{bmatrix}
$$

$$
+ \frac{1}{1-\phi^R}
\begin{bmatrix}
\underset{+/-}{\frac{\partial p_I^{*R}}{\partial E}} \left( a_R \cdot \underset{-}{\frac{\partial C_R}{\partial p_I^{*R}}} + a_I \underset{+}{\frac{\partial C_I}{\partial p_I^{*R}}} \right) + a_I \underset{+}{\frac{\partial p_I^{*}}{\partial E}} \left( \underset{+}{\frac{\partial C_I}{\partial p_I^{*}}} + \underset{+}{\frac{\partial X_I}{\partial p_I^{*}}} \right) \\[2ex]
+ \phi^R \underset{+/-}{\frac{\partial \Upsilon\left(\frac{W}{Q}\right)^R}{\partial E}} + \underset{-}{\frac{\partial a_I}{\partial A_I}} \underset{+}{\frac{\partial A_I(X_I)}{\partial E}}
\end{bmatrix} \gtreqless 0
$$
(1.20)

where $\phi^R$ is as in equation (1.17) and, as before, the supraindex $R$ indicates that products from sector $R$ are consumed domestically and exported, and designates the variables and terms concerned.

Endogenizing productivity growth adds a new term to the internal balance, which is the last term in equation (1.20). It also affects real wages, which increase because the devaluation promotes industrial exports and this productivity growth, an effect that feeds back through equation (1.4).[30] The impact of the devaluation on average wages will depend positively on $\gamma_I$, which denotes the size of sector $I$, and on the Kaldor-Verdoorn coefficient, which is commonly assumed to be 0.5.[31] In turn, these effects modify real income and the different terms of trade of equation (1.20).

Considering all these effects it is possible to disentangle how employment responds to nominal devaluations when this also contributes to productivity growth. As in previous cases, the final effect of the devaluation is ambiguous. The negative effects on employment result from: (i) substitution between non-tradable and food products;[32] and (ii) reduction in the factor intensity of sector $I$, as indicated by the third and last terms within the square brackets. The positive effects on employment are associated with: (iii) substitution of imported goods for non-tradables, and (iv) increases in the competitiveness of sector $I$ and associated import substitution and export growth. As the *devaluation promotes learning and productivity growth, the increased competitiveness of sector I has a price and a non-price component and is larger than in the cases analysed before.*

Indeed, this adjustment is the reverse of the effects of exchange rate appreciations emphasized in dynamic Dutch disease models.[33] Whereas exchange rate appreciations may cause permanent losses when the knowledge accumulated in a particular sector or firm disappears; devaluations may, on the contrary, create long-term competitiveness gains. This can occur if exchange rate devaluations allow new firms to enter foreign markets, and overcome the set up costs associated with exporting. This dynamic effect of exchange rate devaluation is rarely considered.

As shown in equation (1.20) some effects can be positive or negative depending on parameter values.[34] The most important for this discussion is the response of real wages, which can be positive or negative and equals

$$\frac{\partial \Upsilon\left(\frac{W}{Q^R}\right)}{\partial E} = \frac{1}{1-F}\left\{ \begin{array}{l} a_R(1-\Omega)+\left[\tau\left(1-a_R^{\ 2}\right)\right]\alpha_I^f + \\[2ex] \delta\frac{\partial A_I(X_I)}{\partial E}\left[\gamma_I\left(\frac{A_R A_N}{A_I}\right)^{1-\gamma_I}\left(1-a_R^{\ 2}\right)(1-\Omega)-\left[\tau\left(1-a_R^{\ 2}\right)-1\right]\alpha_I^f\right] \end{array} \right\},$$

where $\Omega = \left[\alpha_R^h\left(a_R - a_N\right)+\alpha_I^h(1-a_N)+(1-\alpha_I^f)a_N\right]$ and $1-F=1-\left(1-a_R^2\right)\cdot\tau\cdot\Omega$, and are both positive.

The main consequence of considering Kaldor-Verdoorn effects is the addition of the second large term within the curly brackets. This is positive due to the increase in nominal wages and the reduction in $P_I^h$ that results from the rise in $A_I$.[35] Therefore, the Kaldor-Verdoorn effect reduces the negative consequences of devaluations on real wages and may even augment real wages. Indeed, increases in real wages are possible for plausible parameter values like a Kaldor-Verdoorn effect of 0,3, a manufacturing sector representing 20% of total output, food products constituting 30% of the consumption basket and an indexation parameter of 0,2. Yet, the rise in real wages also results from the presence of a devaluation rent and export taxes.[36]

## Some Final Comments

To contribute to the ongoing debate on Argentina's long-term development strategy, this article discusses the problem of competitive economic diversification in resource abundant countries, and in countries which, like Argentina, are producers and exporters of wage-goods. This chapter focuses on macroeconomic adjustment and discusses shocks and policies emphasizing specificities relevant to Argentina and other Latin American countries.

The analysis in Section 3.1 showed that natural resource abundance creates a "price" handicap for the emergence of a competitive manufacturing sector. Most importantly, the analysis showed that a positive natural resource shock can promote internal and external imbalances. The conditions encouraging these outcomes are: (i) the natural resource sector is not the largest tradable sector and cannot ensure that the positive income effects of a resource shock predominate over the negative substitution effects; (ii) countries have a high propensity to import; (iii) there are large productivity differences between the natural resource and other tradable sectors; and (iv) industries are very dependent on price competitive advantages.

Section 3.2 discussed the contribution to competitive (productive and export) diversification of exchange rate devaluations and the competitive exchange rate policy in place in Argentina. The analysis showed that devaluations can promote structural change, but at the cost of falling real wages. The reduction in real wages is larger in wage-goods exporting countries, hence the policy tends to be more costly in Argentina than in those with different structural characteristics. To prevent large reductions in real wages and to ensure that devaluation is effective in providing a price competitive advantage for the manufacturing sector, the model was used to show that nominal devaluations need to be implemented in combination with export taxes on natural resource exports.

The final section of this chapter addressed the productivity side of the competitiveness problem adding a productivity equation to the model. This extension represents an innovation over other versions of the dependent economy model, and serves to broaden the economic policy debate by showing that macroeconomic policies can promote productive and export diversification through price and non-price channels. Nominal devaluations, tariffs and subsidies have no direct effects on productivity, but they can improve it indirectly by increasing demand, and hence producing second round positive competitiveness effects that limit the reduction and can even lead to a rise in real wages.

However, it is important to note that, in order to contribute to competitive diversification exchange rate policy, as well as other tariff and subsidy policies, needs to be implemented as a temporary and selective measure. The reason for this is that the productivity of sector $I$ depends on other factors such as innovation and the development of competitive linkages, in which producers will have no incentives nor will they be compelled to invest if government guarantees them a permanent price competitive advantage.

## Appendix

### *Changes in Real Income and Real Wages*

To know the response of real income to changes in exogenous variables we use equation (1.7). In logarithm form the equation equals

$$\ln Y = \ln \omega + (\tau - 1) \ln Q + \ln L \tag{A.0.1}$$

Using equation (1.6), substituting into it the price expressions as defined in equations (1.2) and (1.3) and nominal wages as defined in equation (1.4), we obtain the following expression of the CPI in logarithm form:

$$\ln Q = \frac{\alpha_I^f \cdot \ln E + \left[\alpha_I^h \cdot (a_I - a_N) + a_N \cdot (1 - \alpha_I^f)\right] \cdot \ln \omega + (1 - \alpha_I^f) \cdot \ln \bar{H}}{1 - A} \tag{A.0.2}$$

where $1 - A = 1 - \tau \cdot \alpha_I^h \cdot (a_I - a_N) - \tau \cdot a_N \cdot (1 - \alpha_I^f)$, which is positive due to our assumption about factor intensities $(a_I < a_N)$.

Plugging (A.0.2) into (1.1) we thus obtain

$$\ln Y = \left[ \frac{\left[1 - \alpha_I^h \cdot (a_I - a_N) + a_N \cdot (1 - \alpha_I^f)\right] \ln \omega}{1 - A} + \frac{(\tau - 1) \cdot \left[\alpha_I^f \ln E + (1 - \alpha_I^f) \cdot \ln \bar{H}\right]}{1 - A} \right] + \ln L \tag{A.0.3}$$

The first two terms in equation (A.0.3) represent changes in real wages and the third one income changes due to variations in labour demand.

Differentiating (A.0.3) with respect to $A_R$ we know how increases in the productivity of sector R affects real wages (equation (A.0.4) below shows the result for $\tau = 0$).

$$\frac{\partial Y\left(\frac{W}{Q}\right)}{\partial A_R} = \frac{\left[1 - \alpha_I^f \cdot (a_I - a_N) - a_N \cdot (1 - \alpha_I^f)\right]}{1 - A} \cdot \frac{\partial W}{\partial A_R} > 0 \tag{A.0.4}$$

with $(\partial W / \partial A_R) = \gamma_R \left(A_I A_N / A_R\right)^{1 - \gamma_R}$, as defined in equation (1.13).

Differentiating equation (A.0.3) with respect to E we obtain the effects of nominal devaluations on real wages, when all products from sector R are exported (equation (A.0.5) shows the result for $\tau < 1$).

$$\frac{\partial \Upsilon\left(\dfrac{W}{Q}\right)}{\partial E} = \frac{(\tau-1)}{1-A}\cdot\alpha_I^f < 0 \tag{A.0.5}$$

To know the impact of nominal devaluations when products from sector $R$ are exported and consumed domestically we use $Q^R = (P_R^f)^{\alpha_{Rf}}(P_I^f)^{\alpha_{If}}\cdot(P_I^h)^{\alpha_{Ih}}\cdot(P_N^h)^{1-\alpha_{If}-\alpha_{Ih}}$ to obtain a new expression of real income. Differentiating it with respect to $E$ gives

$$\frac{\partial \Upsilon\left(\dfrac{W}{Q^R}\right)}{\partial E} = \frac{(\tau-1)\left(\alpha_I^f + \alpha_R^f\right)}{1-C} < 0 \tag{A.0.6}$$

where $1-C = 1-\tau\cdot\alpha_I^{h}\cdot(a_I - a_N) - \tau\cdot a_N(1-\alpha_I^f - \alpha_R^f)$ which is positive and larger than $1-A$, because there is a new price increasing with the devaluation.

When there is a devaluation rent and natural resource goods are exported and consumed domestically the response of real wages to a nominal devaluation equals

$$\frac{\partial \Upsilon\left(\dfrac{W}{Q^R}\right)}{\partial E} = \frac{1}{1-D}\left\{\begin{array}{l}a_R\left[1-\alpha_I^h(a_I - a_N) + a_N(1-\alpha_I^f - \alpha_R^f)\right]\\[6pt] + \left[\tau\cdot\left(1-a_R^{2}\right)-1\right](\alpha_I^f + \alpha_R^f)\end{array}\right\} \tag{A.0.7}$$

where $1-D = 1-(1-a_R^{2})\cdot\tau\cdot[\alpha_I^{h}(a_I-a_N) + a_N(1-\alpha_I^f-\alpha_R^f)]$. Equation (A.0.7) can be positive or negative; therefore wages fall less than in previous cases due to the presence of a devaluation rent, whereas increases in real wages are only possible for low values of $\alpha_I^f$ and $\alpha_R^f$.

When the government imposes a tax to natural resource exports the price of natural resource goods in the domestic market will equal their production costs. Approximating this with equation (1.2), using this new expression instead of $P_R^f$ in the consumer price index $Q^R$, doing some manipulations and differentiating with respect to $E$ we obtain

$$\frac{\partial \Upsilon\left(\dfrac{W}{Q^R}\right)}{\partial E} = \frac{1}{1-E}\left\{\begin{array}{l}a_R\cdot 1-\alpha_R^h(a_R - a_N) - \alpha_I^h(a_I - a_N)\\[6pt] -a_N(1-\alpha_I^f) + \left[\tau\left(1-a_R^{2}\right)-1\cdot\alpha_I^f\right]\end{array}\right\} \tag{A.0.8}$$

where $1-E = 1-(1-a_R^{2})\cdot\tau\cdot[\alpha_R^{h}(a_R-a_N) + \alpha_I^h(a_I-a_N) + a_N(1-\alpha_I^f)]$. Real wages decrease less or increase more than when there are no export taxes.

## Changes in the External Terms of Trade the Industrial Sector

To know the effects of exogenous changes in the external terms of trade we use equation (1.8) and its components as given by equations (1.2) and (1.3). Taking logs of this expression and differentiating with respect to $E$ we obtain the effects of the devaluation when goods from sector $R$ are exported and consumed domestically.

$$\frac{\partial p_I^*}{\partial E} = \left| 1 - \frac{a_I \cdot \tau \cdot \left( \alpha_I^f + \alpha_R^f \right)}{1 - C} \right| > 0 \qquad (A.0.9)$$

When there is a devaluation rent and natural resource commodities are consumed domestically the effects of the devaluation equal

$$\frac{\partial p_I^*}{\partial E} = \left| 1 - \frac{a_I \cdot \left[ a_R + \tau \cdot (1 - a_R^2) \cdot \left( \alpha_I^f + \alpha_R^f \right) \right]}{1 - D} \right| > 0 \qquad (A.0.10)$$

Due to the presence of the new terms $a_R$ and $(1 - a_R^2)$ the competitiveness gain is smaller than in (A.0.9).

In presence of a devaluation rent, natural resource products exported and consumed domestically and export taxes, the response of the terms of trade to changes in $E$ is given by

$$\frac{\partial p_I^*}{\partial E} = \left| 1 - \frac{a_I \cdot \left[ a_R + \tau \cdot (1 - a_R^2) \cdot \alpha_I^f \right]}{1 - E} \right| \qquad (A.0.11)$$

where $1-E$ as defined in equation (A.0.8). Because the domestic price of natural resource products is not affected by the devaluation equation (A.0.11) is larger than (A.0.10).

The final case corresponds to the compensated devaluation regime considering Kaldor-Verdoorn effects. The response of $p_I^*$ to the devaluation is now given by

$$\frac{\partial p_I^*}{\partial E} = \frac{1}{1 - F} \left[ a_R + \tau \cdot (1 - a_R^2) \cdot \left( \alpha_I^f \right) \right]$$
$$+ \delta \frac{\partial A_I(X_I)}{\partial E} \left[ 1 - \frac{(1 - a_R^2)}{1 - F} \left[ \gamma_I \left( \frac{A_R A_N}{A_I} \right)^{1 - \gamma_I} - \tau \cdot \alpha_I^h \right] \right] \qquad (A.0.12)$$

Due to the presence of a new positive term, associated to the Kaldor-Verdoorn effect, the devaluation further increases the competitiveness of sector $I$.

# Notes

1. The former is associated with the declining but still high unemployment rates and an unequal income distribution; the latter is associated with the frequently present external constraint (Porta, 2005).

2. The dependent economy model was developed by the Australian economists, W.E.G. Salter and T.W. Swan, in the late 1950s and early 1960s (see Salter, 1959; Swan, 1960). The traditional version of the dependent economy model, in contrast to the Scandinavian version, has two factors of production and a concave production function and is referred to as the Australian model. This model is commonly used to study real exchange determination and the pattern of trade specialization in small open economies (industrialized and developing), and countries' responses to exogenous shocks and commercial or exchange rate policies.

3. The analysis differs from classical authors, in that these authors consider that the exchange rate is the variable that reflects the productivity of the tradable sector. Their argument can be stated formally as follows. Let there be two tradable economic sectors, the traditional natural resource sector $R$ and the industrial sector $I$, where sector $R$'s factors productivity $(A_R)$ is larger than that in sector I $(A_I)$. For given factor prices $W$, production costs $(1/A_i \cdot \overline{W}$, with i = $R$ and $I$) in sector $R$ will be lower than those in sector $I$. The core of the argument concerns the comparison of domestic production prices $P_i^h$ (determined by domestic production costs), with international prices expressed in domestic currency $(E \cdot P_i^{int}$, where $E$ denotes the nominal exchange rate and $P_i^{int}$ stands for the prices prevailing in the international market). In a country with large sectoral productivity differences, the nominal exchange rate will only guarantee equality between $P_i^h$ and international prices, thus, the law of one price in one of the two sectors. If, as is claimed by classical authors, the exchange rate reflects the productivity of the most competitive and largest tradable sector $R$, this value of $E$ will make $P_R^h = E \cdot P_R^{int}$ and $P_I^h > E \cdot P_I^{int}$. The non-traditional sector $I$, therefore, will either not exist or its competitiveness will be seriously reduced.

4. In full-employment versions of the dependent economy model the only price that counts is the one that clears the non-tradable market and, therefore, competitiveness aspects are not taken into account.

5. This point becomes clear in Chudnovsky and Porta's (1990) review of the different approaches to the competitiveness problem.

6. It is possible to think of an adjusted productivity variable, which increases (decreases) in relation to the presence (absence) of other non-price competitiveness factors, e.g. innovation capabilities, and logistics or publicity services.

7. The main implications of imported intermediate inputs for the discussion in this chapter would be to limit the price competitiveness gain achieved through nominal devaluations. This effect is excluded here to keep the algebra simple, but will be taken into account in the CGE analysis elaborated in subsequent chapters.

8. It is important to bear in mind that the international price can be higher than the costs of production of natural resource commodities in the home economy, since it can be approximated, e.g. by its unitary production costs. This is relevant to the economic policy discussion in the following section.

9. See La Marca (2004) for a comprehensive analysis of real exchange rate adjustments in macroeconomic, trade and general equilibrium models.

10. This is a realistic and common assumption in analyses of resource abundant countries.

11. The discussion on the sustainability of the current account is omitted because the analysis is concerned with changes that are expected to release external constraints on the economy. Regarding the monetary aspects of the fixed exchange rate regime it should be noted that, in a context of capital inflows (e.g. associated with the expansion of exports in response to a devaluation), the monetary authority is able to avoid a revaluation of the exchange rate. This requires accumulation of reserves and sterilization of the money supply using the methods discussed in Frenkel (2005).

12. Allowing for wage indexation will only reinforce the adjustment. The same will apply if price adjustments prevail in the non-tradable sector or if non-tradable inputs costs are flexible.

13. This effect predicts that increases in the productivity of the tradable sector will lead to higher non-tradable prices or a real exchange rate appreciation.

14. These effects are captured by the 1st, 3rd, 4th and 5th terms in the square brackets in equation (1.14).

15. This is the first effect captured in the 3rd term in equation (1.15).

16. Real income will increase due to higher real wages. Yet, as discussed in the previous section, employment may well increase, further increasing real income and demand for imported goods, or may decrease and counteract the effect of higher real wages on import demand.

17. Williamson (2008, 2003) also makes a case in favor of a policy of exchange rate devaluation in developing countries. The articles by Prasad, Rajan and Subramanian (2007), Montiel and Serven (2008), Gala (2007) and Hausmann, Pritchett and Rodrik (2004), on the other hand, provide empirical support for this argument.

18. The derivation of changes in real wages is provided in the appendix to this chapter (see equations (A.0.3) and (A.0.5). The assumption regarding factor intensities $(\alpha_N > \alpha_I)$ ensures that the denominator is positive.

19. This effect requires some wage indexation and is captured by the 1st term in the square brackets in equation (1.16).

20. In Argentina food products are the group of commodities that has the highest weight (30%) in the basket used to measure changes in consumer prices.

21. As explained by Gerchunoff and Llach (2003), Argentina, in this respect, differs from Colombia and Brazil where increases in the price of coffee following an exchange rate devaluation will have no significant impact on real wages.

22. Where $1 - C = 1 - \tau \cdot \alpha_I^h \cdot (a_I - a_N) - \tau \cdot a_N (1 - \alpha_I^f - \alpha_R^f)$ , which is positive and larger than 1–A.

23. The extreme case of higher real wages with low indexation, however, requires that imported and natural resource products are not relevant in the consumption basket.

24. Tariffs promote tradable diversification only in the domestic market and, unless there are exceptions to specific imported commodities, they reduce real wages. On the other hand, subsidies promote tradable diversification in the domestic and international market. Since this diversification implies the expansion of exports and has no or positive effects on real wages, subsidy policies are superior to exchange rate and tariff diversification policies. However, they are costly and need to be financed.

25. This model assumes that the government saves the income collected via export taxes. Yet, as explored in the applied section, export tax revenues can finance increases in government consumption and thus fuel other sources of inflation.

26. An additional implication of the compensated devaluated regime, related to the wage-setting mechanism but not formally explored in the model, is its contribution to the equalization of factor prices. Without this effect the devaluation may not suffice to promote sector $I$, its original purpose.

27. The analysis considers only endogenous productivity changes in sector *I*. This is because this is the variable and sector of interest in this study,and also because, as often stressed in the literature, the manufacturing sector shows the highest endogenous productivity growth. See papers by Torvik (2001) and Rattsø and Torvik (2003) for an extended discussion of this issue.

28. A comprehensive list of productivity and competitiveness determinants must include: (i) human and physical capital accumulation; (ii) access to foreign technology; (iii) technological policies; (iv) the degree of backwardness or gap with the best international practice; (v) Kaldor-Verdoorn effects; (vi) innovation capacity; (vii) infrastructure, and (viii) the presence of competitive productive linkages.

29. Martin (2002) finds that it is the exporting sectors and firms that experience the highest productivity growth, providing support for this argument.

30. The derivative of equation (4.4) with respect to $E$ equals $\dfrac{\partial \omega}{\partial E} = \gamma_I \left( \dfrac{A_R A_N}{A_I} \right)^{1-\gamma_I} \delta \dfrac{\partial A_I(X_I)}{\partial E}$.

31. The devaluation also has a negative impact on nominal wages because the productivity increase reduces prices and this translates into wages through the indexation mechanism.

32. This effect takes place because there are export taxes and thus the devaluation does not affect the domestic price of food products. Without export taxes the relative price change and substitution effects would be reversed.

33. See, e.g. Matsuyama (1992) and Sachs (1999).

34. The first concerns the response of $p_D{}^h$, which will be negative similar to the employment effects resulting from the substitution between goods produced in sectors $N$ and $I$, unless the devaluation has no or very limited effects on productivity growth. The second is related to the change in relative prices and substitution between food and domestically produced industrial goods, an effect which, according to Engels law, is expected to be low.

35. These are denoted by the 1st and $2^{nd}$ terms within the second set of large curly brackets.

36. The share of imported and domestically produced manufactured goods in the *CPI* is considered to be 0.2. With similar parameter values but no devaluation rent or export taxes, devaluation reduces real wages.

# References

Bielschowsky, R. (1998) 'Evolución de las Ideas de la CEPAL', *Revista de la CEPAL* Número Extraordinario.

Braun, O. and L. Joy (1968) 'A Model of Economic Stagnation. A Case Study of the Argentine Economy', *Economic Journal* 78(312): 868–887.

Canitrot, A. (1975) 'La Experiencia Populista de Distribución de Ingresos', *Revista Desarrollo Económico* No. 59, vol. 15 (October – December).

Chena, P. and L. Pérez Candreva (2008) 'Heterogeneidad Estructural en Argentina', in *Interpretaciones Heterodoxas de las Crisis Económicas en Argentina y sus Efectos Sociales*, Fernando C. Toledo and Julio Neffa (eds.), Miño y Dávila, CEIL-PIETTE/Trabajo y Sociedad, Buenos Aires, 304 págs.

Chena, P. and M. Feliz (2008) 'Ciclos y devaluaciones en Argentina. Un enfoque heterodoxo', in *Interpretaciones Heterodoxas de las Crisis Económicas en Argentina y sus Efectos Sociales*, Fernando C. Toledo and Julio Neffa (eds.); Miño y Dávila, CEIL-PIETTE/Trabajo y Sociedad, Buenos Aires.

Chudnovsky, D. and F. Porta (1990) 'La Competitividad Internacional. Principales Cuestiones Conceptuales y Metodológicas', CENIT Documento de Trabajo No. 3.

Diamand, M. (1972) 'La Estructura Económica Desequilibrada Argentina y el Tipo de Cambio', *Revista Desarrollo Económico* 45 (12), (abril-junio).

Díaz Alejandro, C. (1963) 'A Note on the Impact of Devaluation and the Redistributive Effect', *Journal of Political Economy* vol. 71, No. 6: 577–580.

Díaz Alejandro, C. (1965) 'Exchange-rate Devaluation in a Semi-Industrialized Country', in *The Experience of Argentina* 1955–1961, MIT Press.

Dornbusch, R. (1980) *Open Economy Macroeconomics.* New York: Basic Books.

Frenkel, R. and J. Ros (2006) 'Unemployment and the Real Exchange Rate in Latin America', in *World Development* vol. 34, Issue 4: 631–646 (April).

Frenkel, R. and L. Taylor (2006) 'Real Exchange Rate, Monetary Policy, and Employment', UN DESA Working Paper No. 19. New York: DESA.

Frenkel, R. and M. Rapetti (2007) 'Política Cambiaria y Monetaria después del Colapso de la Convertibilidad', in *Ensayos económicos* N° 46; Buenos Aires, Investigaciones Económicas, Banco Central de la República de Argentina.

Gala, P. (2007) 'Real Exchange Rate Levels and Economic Development: Theoretical Analysis and Empirical Evidence', *Cambridge Journal of Economics* 32: 273–288.

Gerchunoff, P. and A. Ramos (2005) 'Los Problemas Económicos Argentinos (el Enigma del Felino)' in M. Rikles and P. Isbell, (eds) *Anuario Elcano*: América Latina 2004–2005.

Gerchunoff, P. and L. Llach (2003) 'Ved en Trono a la Noble Igualdad. Crecimiento, Equidad y Política Económica en Argentina, 1880–2003', Documento de Trabajo Fundación Pent No. 2003–003. Buenos Aires: Fundación Pent.

Hausmann R., L. Pritchett and D. Rodrik (2004) 'Growth Accelerations', NBER Working Paper No. 10566.

Kacef, O. (2004) 'Apuntes para la Definición de una Estrategia de Inserción Internacional para la Argentina', Documento de Trabajo Fundación Pent No. 2004–001. Buenos Aires: Fundación Pent.

Kaldor, N. (1967) *Strategic Factors in Economic Development.* New York, Cornell University Press.

Kaldor, N. (1981) 'The Role of Increasing Returns, Technical Progress and Cumulative Causation in the Theory of International Trade and Economic Growth', *Economie Appliquée 34*, vol. 6, 633–648.

Kaldor, N. (1989) 'Devaluation and Adjustment in Developing Countries', in Targetti and A. P. Thirlwall (eds) *Further Essays on Economic Theory and Policy*, chapter 13.

Keifman, S. (2005) 'Tipo de Cambio y Empleo; a Treinta Años de Canitrot y Porto', paper presented at XL Jornadas de la AAEP, La Plata.

Krugman, P. (1987) 'The Narrow Moving Band, The Dutch Disease and the Competitive Consequences of Mrs Thatcher: Notes on Trade in the Presence of Dynamic Scale Economies', *Journal of Development Economics* 27(1/2): 41–55.

Krugman, P. and L. Taylor (1978) 'Contractionary Effects of Devaluations', *Journal of International Economics* vol. 8(3): 445–456.

La Marca, M. (2004) 'Real Exchange Rate, Competitiveness and Policy Implications: a Formal Analysis of Alternative Macro Models', CEPA, New School for Social Research, New York.

Montiel, P. and L. Serven (2008) 'Real Exchange Rates, Saving and Growth: Is There a Link?' World Bank Policy Research, Working Paper No. 4636.

Murshed, M. S. (1997) *Macroeconomics for Open Economies.* The Dryden Press.

Nicolini Llosa J. L. (2007a) 'Tipo de Cambio Dual y Crecimiento Cíclico en Argentina' *Desarrollo Económico – Revista De Ciencias Sociales*. Ides, Buenos Aires, vol. 47, No. 186, 249–283 (julio-setiembre).

Nicolini-Llosa, J. L (2007b) 'Essays on Argentina's Growth Cycle and the World Economy', PHD Dissertation, University of Amsterdam.

Porta F., C, Bianco and F. Vismara (2008) 'Evolución Reciente de la Balanza Comercial, Recuperación y Nuevos Dilemas. La Economía Argentina 2002–2007', in *Crisis, Recuperación y Nuevos Dilemas. La Economía Argentina 2002–2007*, Bernardo Kosacoff (ed.). Buenos. Aires: CEPAL.

Porta, F. (2005) 'Especialización Productiva e Inserción Internacional', documento preparado en el marco del proyecto PNUD FO/ARG/05/012.

Porto, A. (1975) 'Un Modelo Simple sobre el Comportamiento Macroeconómico Argentino en el Corto Plazo', *Desarrollo Económico* 59 (15).

Prasad, E., R. Rajan, and A. Subramanian (2007) 'Foreign Capital and Economic Growth' *Brooking Papers on Economic Activity* 1: 153–209.

Rada, C. and L. Taylor (2004) 'Empty Sources of Growth Accounting, and Empirical Replacements à la Kaldor with Some Beef', The Schwartz Center Working Paper No. 2004–5.

Rattso, J. and R. Torvik (2003) 'Interactions Between Agriculture and Industry: Theoretical Analysis of the Consequences of Discriminating Agriculture in Sub-Saharan Africa' *Review of Development Economics* 7 (1): 138–151.

Sachs, J. D. (1999) 'Resource Endowments and the Real Exchange Rate: A Comparison of Latin America and East Asia', in T. Ito and A. Krueger (eds) *Changes in Exchange Rate in Rapidly Developing Countries*, pp. 133–153. Chicago: University of Chicago Press.

Salter, W. E. G. (1959) 'Internal and External Balance: The Role of Price and Expenditure Effects', *Economic Record* 35: 226–238.

Schydlowsky, D. (1993) 'Foreign Exchange Regimes for Dutch Disease Prone LDCs', Institute for Research on the Informal Sector (IRIS) Working Paper Nº 46, University of Maryland.

Serino, L. (2007) 'Competitive Diversification in Resource Abundant Countries: Argentina After the Collapse of the Convertibility Regime', ISS Working Paper No. 441 (May).

Swan, T. W. (1960) 'Economic Control in a Dependent Economy', *Economic Record* 36: 51–66.

Thirlwall, A. (2002) *The Nature of Economic Growth: An Alternative Framework for Understanding the Performance of Nations*. Edward Elgar.

Torvik, R. (2001) 'Learning by Doing and the Dutch Disease', *European Economic Review* No. 45: 285–306.

Williamson J. (2008) 'Exchange Rate Economics', Working Paper Series WP 08–3, Peterson Institute for International Economics (February).

Williamson, J. (2003) 'Exchange Rate Policy and Development', Paper presented to a conference of the Institute for Policy Dialogue ( June).

# Chapter 7

# FOREIGN PORTFOLIO INVESTMENT, STOCK MARKET AND ECONOMIC DEVELOPMENT: A CASE STUDY IN INDIA

## Parthapratim Pal

### Abstract

The objective of this study is to examine the impact of Foreign Portfolio Investment on India's economy and industry. As FPI essentially interacts with the real economy via the stock market, the effect of stock market on the country's economic development will also be examined. The findings of this chapter show that the perceived benefits of foreign portfolio investment have not been realized in India. From the results of this study it can be said that the mainstream argument that the entry of foreign portfolio investors will boost a country's stock market and consequently the economy, does not seem be working in India. The influx of FIIs has indeed influenced the secondary market segment of the Indian stock market. But the supposed linkage effects with the real economy have not worked in the way the mainstream model predicts. Instead there has been an increased uncertainty and skepticism about the stock market in this country.

On the other hand, the surge in foreign portfolio investment in the Indian economy has introduced some serious problems of macroeconomic management for the policymakers. Uncertainty and volatility associated with FPI have not only reduced the degrees of maneuverability available to the policymakers but have also forced them to take some measures which impose significant fiscal cost on the economy.

Though this study focuses on India and draws policy implications based on the Indian experience, the results and policy implications of this study can be used to draw lessons for other developing which are at the same or similar level of development.

## Introduction

In 1992, India opened up its economy and allowed Foreign Portfolio Investment (FPI) in its domestic stock markets. Since then, FPI has emerged as a major source of private capital inflow in this country. The objective of this chapter is to examine the impact of Foreign Portfolio Investment on India's economy and industry. As FPI essentially interacts with the real economy via the stock market, the effect of stock market on the country's economic development will also be examined. In the current global economic scenario, it is important to address these issues because of a number of reasons. During the late 1980s and early 1990s portfolio investment emerged as an important form of capital inflow to developing countries. The importance of portfolio investment to developing countries has come down after the East Asian crisis of 1997. However, unlike most other developing countries, India has generally been more dependent upon FPI than Foreign Direct Investment (FDI) as a source of foreign investment. For the period 1992 to 2005, more than 50 percent of foreign investment in India came in the form of FPI. Given such high dependence of the Indian economy on FPI, it is important to assess whether and how FPI has contributed to the economic development of the country. Secondly, the spate of financial crises since the late 1990s have repeatedly highlighted that the current global financial architecture, with its emphasis on speculative capital flows, can seriously disrupt the economic prospects of a developing country. For these countries, insulating the economy from the uncertainties of short term capital flows can impose serious fiscal costs on the economy. It can also make the management of external economy difficult by reducing the policy options available to the policymakers in developing countries. It is important to investigate these aspects of FPI in the Indian context. Also, competition among emerging markets to attract foreign portfolio investment has led to a situation in which in order to sustain inflows of portfolio investment, it has become increasingly important for developing countries to ensure attractive returns for portfolio investors. Often this means offering increasing operational flexibility and fiscal sops to portfolio investors. This increases the cost associated with portfolio investment in a developing country. It needs to be investigated whether the benefits brought by the foreign portfolio investors to the domestic economy are sufficient to justify the costs associated with the promotion of FPI in these countries.

The dependence on FPI is pushing many developing countries, including India, towards a more stock market oriented financial system. This makes it imperative to evaluate the relative merits and demerits of a stock market based financial system in a developing country. In this context, it becomes particularly important to find out how a stock market based financial system can benefit the economy and the industry of a developing country. It is also crucial to empirically investigate whether the supposedly beneficial aspects of a stock market based financial systems are actually being realized in developing countries.

Given these concerns, this chapter attempts to address the issue of foreign portfolio investment and its impact on economic development from an Indian perspective.

## How Foreign Portfolio Flow Can Help an Economy

According to standard economic theory, FPI can benefit the real sector of an economy in a number of ways. First, inflow of FPI can provide a developing country non-debt creating source of foreign investment. As developing countries are capital-scarce, such foreign capital flows can supplement domestic saving and help improving the investment rate. By providing foreign exchange to the developing countries, FPI also reduces the pressure of foreign exchange gap for such countries, thus making imports of necessary investment goods easier for them. Secondly, it is suggested by mainstream economists that increased inflow of foreign capital increases the allocative efficiency of capital in a country. According to this view, FPI, like FDI, can induce financial resources to flow from capital-abundant countries, where expected returns are low, to capital-scarce countries, where expected returns are high. The flow of resources into the capital-scarce countries reduces their cost of capital, increases investment, and raises output. However, according to another view, portfolio investment does not result in a more efficient allocation of capital, because international capital flows have little or no connection to real economic activity. Consequently portfolio investment has no effect on investment, output, or any other real variable with nontrivial welfare implications.

The third and the most important way FPI affects the economy is through its various linkage effects via the domestic capital market. One of the most important benefits from FPI is that it pushes up the stock market prices in the domestic capital market. This has an impact on the price-earning (P/E) ratios of the firms. A higher P/E ratio leads to a lower cost of finance, which in turn can lead to a higher amount of investment. This may happen because the high share prices in the secondary market may encourage a firm to issue new equities in the primary market. In such a scenario, the premium on a new equity issue will be positively related with the price of that equity in the secondary market. Assuming efficient market hypothesis holds, this implies that more efficient firms or firms with higher growth prospects will have higher secondary market prices and hence will be able to charge higher premium in the primary market. As charging higher premium on new issues is equivalent to lowering one's cost of capital, it can be said that inflow of foreign portfolio flows encourage efficient firms to invest more by lowering their cost of capital.

Figure 1: Diagrammatic Representation of how Foreign Funds encourage Domestic Secondary and Primary Market[1]

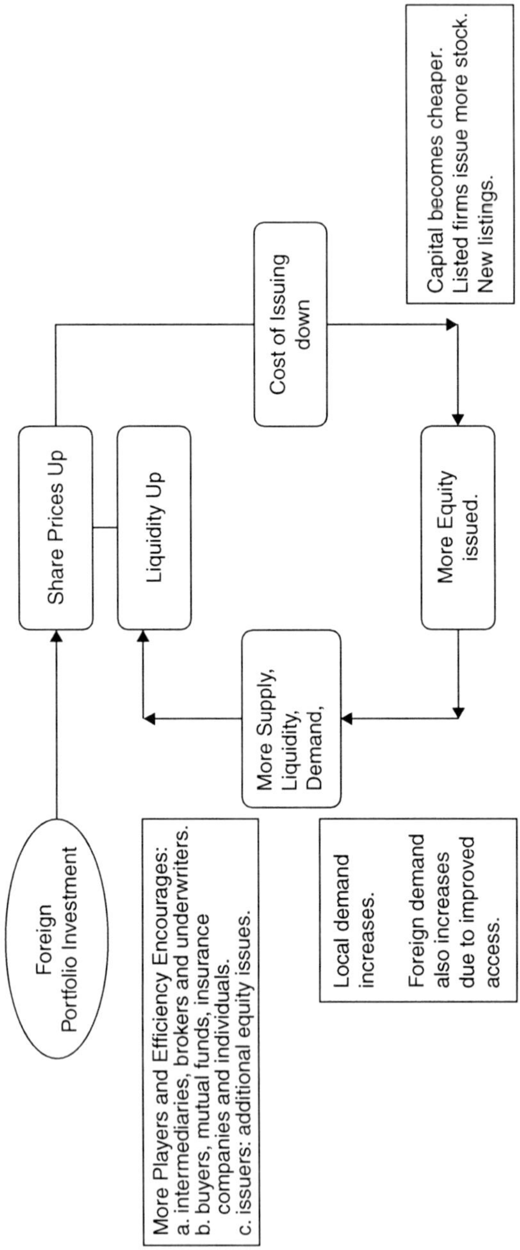

A well-developed stock market has its impact on the demand side also. It provides investors with an array of assets with varying degree of risk, return and liquidity. This increased choice of assets and the existence of a vibrant stock market provide savers with more liquidity and options, thereby inducing more savings. Increased competition from foreign financial institutions also paves the way for the derivatives' market. All this, according to the mainstream belief, encourages more savings in equity related instruments. This, in turn, raises the domestic savings rate and improves capital formation. Figure 1 schematically shows how foreign portfolio investment can affect the economy through the stock markets.

FPI also has the virtue of stimulating the development of the domestic stock market. The catalyst for this development is competition from foreign financial institutions. This competition necessitates the importation of more sophisticated financial technology, adaptation of the technology to local environment and greater investment in information processing and financial services. The results are greater efficiencies in allocating capital, risk sharing and monitoring the issue of capital. This enhancement of efficiency due to internationalization makes the market more liquid, which leads to a lower cost of capital. The cost of foreign capital also tends to be lower, because the foreign portfolio can be more diversified across the national boundaries and therefore be more efficient in reducing country-specific risks, resulting in a lower risk premium.

The above discussion highlights the broad channel through which FPI can help the domestic economy of a developing country. As India has received significant FPI since it opened up in 1991–92, it will be interesting to see the experience of India as a possible case study.

## Portfolio Capital Flow and India: The Empirical Evidence

Empirical evidence from India gives an interesting picture. Foreign Portfolio Investment has emerged as the dominant form of private capital flow to India. So far the FIIs have invested more than Rs 145,000 crore rupees in the Indian stock market and they have significant influence on India's stock markets. During the second half of 1990s, favourable external economic conditions coupled with significant increase in private foreign capital inflow have helped India to mitigate its foreign exchange shortage and build high level of foreign exchange reserves. The influx of such high volume of portfolio capital has strongly influenced the secondary market segment of the Indian stock market. But the supposed linkage effects with the real economy have not worked in India the way the mainstream model predicts.

During the decade of 1990s, the stock market registered considerable growth in India. The Bombay Stock Exchange Sensitivity Index (Sensex) went from 221 in 1982–83 to cross the 12,000 marks in 2006. Market capitalization of BSE also increased sharply over the years (Table 1). All other indicators of stock market development also show much higher level of activity since the 1990s. To illustrate the growth of the stock market, we use two indicators of stock market development. The first indicator is called stock market 'depth' which is the ratio of stock market capitalization to GDP[2]. This measure gives an indication about how stock market is growing compared to the economy. This ratio is also viewed as a rough (and inverse) indicator of the transactions cost of the capital market.

Also, to measure the relative growth in the activities of the stock markets vis-à-vis that of the banking system in India, a variant of a measure suggested by Levine (2001) is used here. This is a measure of the size of stock markets relative to that of banks and is called 'Structure-Size'. To measure the size of the domestic stock market, Levine used the market capitalization ratio, which equals the value of market capitalization of the Bombay Stock Exchange divided by GDP. To measure the size of bank, he used the bank credit ratio, which is measured by dividing bank lending to the commercial sector by GDP. Structure Size is derived by dividing market capitalization ratio by bank credit ratio[3] (Figure 2). To calculate bank credit, total bank lending to small, medium and large industries is used here. The figure shows that since 1991–92, stock market capitalization has been much higher than total bank credit to the industrial sector. For example, for the period 1982–83 to 1990–91, the average Structure-Size ratio was around 97.7 percent whereas for the period 1991–92 to 2003–04, the ratio is 352.7 percent. This is another example how the secondary market has performed in India in the last ten years.

## Table 1: Market Capitalization to GDP Ratio

| Year | Market Capitalization | GDP at Factor Cost | Market Capitalization to GDP Ratio (in %) | Year | Market Capitalization | GDP at Factor Cost | Market Capitalization to GDP Ratio (in %) |
|---|---|---|---|---|---|---|---|
| 1982–83 | 9769 | 169525 | 5.76 | 1993–94 | 368071 | 781345 | 47.11 |
| 1983–84 | 10219 | 198630 | 5.14 | 1994–95 | 435481 | 917058 | 47.49 |
| 1984–85 | 20378 | 222705 | 9.15 | 1995–96 | 526476 | 1073271 | 49.05 |
| 1985–86 | 21636 | 249547 | 8.67 | 1996–97 | 463915 | 1243547 | 37.31 |
| 1986–87 | 25937 | 278258 | 9.32 | 1997–98 | 560325 | 1390148 | 40.31 |
| 1987–88 | 45519 | 315993 | 14.41 | 1998–99 | 545361 | 1598127 | 34.13 |
| 1988–89 | 54560 | 378491 | 14.42 | 1999–00 | 912842 | 1761838 | 51.81 |
| 1989–90 | 65206 | 438020 | 14.89 | 2000–01 | 571553 | 1902998 | 30.03 |
| 1990–91 | 90836 | 510954 | 17.78 | 2001–02 | 612224 | 2090957 | 29.28 |
| 1991–92 | 323363 | 589086 | 54.89 | 2002–03 | 572198 | 2249493 | 25.44 |
| 1992–93 | 188146 | 673221 | 27.95 | 2003–04 | 1201207 | 2523872 | 47.59 |

*Source*: RBI Handbook of Statistics on Indian Economy.

Figure 2: Market Capitalization to Bank Credit to Industry Ratio (in percent)

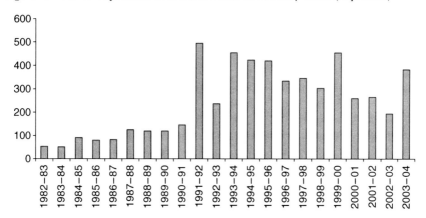

*Source*: Handbook of Statistics on Indian Economy, Reserve Bank of India.

From the above discussion, it is apparent that overall the secondary segment of the stock market has performed quite well in the post-liberalization period. Particularly after 1992, when Foreign Institutional Investors (FIIs) were allowed to put their money in the Indian stock market, its growth has been quite significant. Empirical evidence presented in Figure 2 also suggests that strong stock market growth in the 1990s has edged the Indian financial system from a predominantly bank-based financial system towards a more stock-market based one.

Given these developments in the stock market since the 1990s, and taking into account the mainstream argument that a strong secondary market promotes mobilization of resource from the stock market, there was an expectation that financial liberalization and stock market development would open up a new source of finance for Indian firms. In fact, to facilitate resource mobilization from the stock market a number of regulatory incentives were also introduced during this period. For example, before 1992, firms were required to obtain approval from the office of Controller of Capital Issues (CCI) for raising capital. New companies were allowed to issue shares only at par values. Only existing companies with substantial reserves were allowed to issue shares at a premium. This premium was decided by CCI on an estimated 'fair value'. This act was repealed in May 1992. This allowed firms to price their issues without any intervention from the authorities.

Strong growth of the secondary market, fiscal and regulatory incentives by the government and the prevalent high rate of interest in the post financial liberalization period resulted in a sharp increase of capital mobilized through equity related instruments. Money raised through new capital Issues by non-government public limited companies grew at an annual average rate of more than 43 percent during 1991–92 to 1994–95 phase. However, this upward trend continued up to 1994–95 and since 1995–96, there has been a steep decline in both the number of new issues as well as the amount of money raised through these issues. A brief recovery during 2000–01 was observed due to the global boom in Information Technology (IT) related stocks but that upturn lost its momentum quite soon (Figure 3).

To put the extent of decline into perspective one can highlight that the sum of the money raised by non government public limited companies through the primary market in the six year period between 1998–99 and 2002–03, is less than the money raised by these companies in the single year 1994–95.

It can be argued that resource mobilization from the primary market is a function of expected domestic demand and the resultant expected capital formation of the corporate sector. If the domestic demand is weak or if there are excess capacities in the private sector, then there will be low capital formation and hence low resource mobilization from the primary market. To check the validity of this statement, resource mobilization from the primary market has been benchmarked against the gross domestic capital formation and gross capital formation by the private corporate sector. These benchmarks will give an idea whether domestic demand constraints were behind the decline of the primary market in the post 1994–95 period. Also to understand how the primary market has fared vis-à-vis the secondary market, it is also benchmarked against the market capitalization of the BSE. These results are shown Figure 4.

This figure clearly shows that the decline in resource mobilization from the primary market has not happened because of lack of domestic demand. From the figure it can be seen that resource mobilization from the primary market was about 40 percent of the gross domestic capital formation by the private sector during the fiscal years 1992–93 and 1993–94. On average, between 1987–88 and 1995–96, resource mobilization from the primary was more than 26 percent of gross capital formation of the private sector. Since then, it declined very sharply and for the last six years (1997–98 to 2002–03) the ratio has been around the 5 percent mark. In 2002–03, resource mobilization from the primary market was only about 1.6 percent of gross capital formation of the private sector. As a ratio of gross domestic capital formation, resource mobilization from the primary market was only 0.33 percent in 2002–03. This gives evidence that the demand constraint has not been the binding reason behind the decline of the primary market in India.

More direct evidence of the declining importance of primary market among Indian firms comes from the rapid growth of the private placements market in

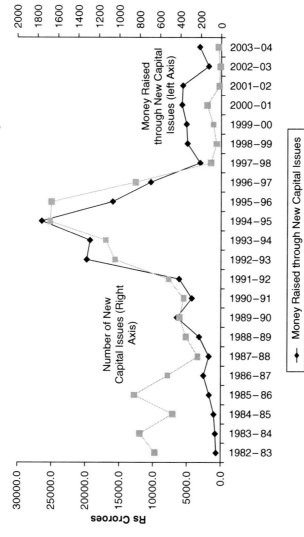

Figure 3: Resource Mobilization from the Primary Market by Non-Govt Public Limited Companies

*Source*: Handbook of Statistics on Indian Economy, Reserve Bank of India.

Figure 4: Relative Performance of the Primary Market: New Capital Issues as a percentage of some other Macroeconomics and Financial Variables

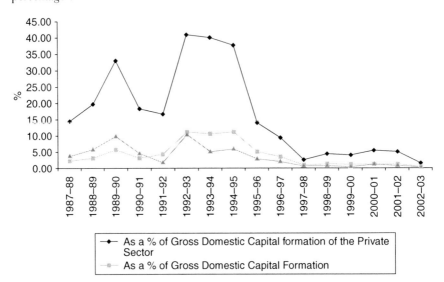

*Source*: Handbook of Statistics on Indian Economy, Reserve Bank of India.

India in the last few years. In the private placement market, resources are raised through arrangers (merchant banking intermediaries) who place securities with a small number of financial institutions, banks, mutual funds and high net-worth individuals. Since these securities are allotted to a few investors, the stringent public disclosure regulations and registration requirements are relaxed. Unlike public issues of bonds, it is not mandatory for corporate firms issuing bonds in the private placement market to obtain and disclose credit rating from an approved credit rating agency. The firms are also not required to divulge the use of funds mobilized from the private placement market. This market has largely been an unregulated market, although in September 2003 SEBI introduced a set of rules to bring it under some regulation.

Though the private placement market can involve issue of securities, debt or equity, in practice it is essentially a market for corporate debt. RBI estimates suggest that the share of equity in total private placements is insignificant.[1] The private placement market is used by both listed and unlisted private sector and the public sector companies to raise funds. Public sector financial institutions are, in fact, major players in this market.

Table 2 shows that the private placement market has been far more active than the primary segment of the stock market since 1997–98. From the table it can be seen that total private sector resource mobilization from the private

**Table 2: Comparison of Private Placement and Primary Market in India (in Rs crores)**

| | The Private Placement Market-Money Raised by | | | | | | |
| Year | Private Sector Financial Institutions | Private Sector Non-Financial Institutions | Total Private Sector (2+3) | Public Sector Financial Institutions | Total Private Sector + Public Sector Financial Inst (4+5) | New Capital Issues by non govt. pub ltd cos | (6/7) × 100 |
|---|---|---|---|---|---|---|---|
| 1 | 2 | 3 | 4 | 5 | 6 | 7 | 8 |
| 1995–96 | 2136.0 | 1934.0 | 4070.0 | 4552.0 | 8622.0 | 15997.6 | 185.5 |
| 1996–97 | 1847.0 | 646.0 | 2493.0 | 6541.0 | 9034.0 | 10409.5 | 115.2 |
| 1997–98 | 4323.7 | 4878.5 | 9202.2 | 9659.7 | 18861.9 | 3138.3 | 16.6 |
| 1998–99 | 12174.2 | 4823.5 | 16997.7 | 20382.4 | 37380.1 | 5013.1 | 13.4 |
| 1999–00 | 10875.2 | 8528.3 | 19403.5 | 17981.3 | 37384.8 | 5153.3 | 13.8 |
| 2000–01 | 13262.6 | 9843.0 | 23105.6 | 26201.2 | 49306.8 | 5818.1 | 11.8 |
| 2001–02 | 16019.0 | 12601.0 | 28620.0 | 17358.0 | 45978.0 | 5692.4 | 12.4 |
| 2002–03 | 9454.0 | 15623.0 | 25077.0 | 20407.0 | 45484.0 | 1877.7 | 4.1 |

*Source*: Handbook of Statistics on Indian Economy, Reserve Bank of India. Note that in the Indian numbering system, 1 crore is equal to 10 million.

placement market has increased six fold from Rs 4,070 crores to Rs 25,077 crores between 1995–96 and 2002–03. In comparison, money raised by non-government public limited companies from the primary market declined from Rs 15,997.6 crores to Rs 1,877 crores over the same period.

The popularity of the private placement method can be attributed to the fact that the private placement method is a cost- and time-effective method of raising funds. Secondly, it can be tailored to meet the specific needs of the entrepreneurs and most importantly, issuing securities in the private placement market, till very recently, did not come under the strict regulatory provisions applicable to public issues.

The explosive growth of the private placement market re-emphasizes the fact that the demand for funds has not declined in the economy. The corporate sector firms are simply showing their preference to source funds from a different channel and are avoiding the primary market.

Another distinctive feature of the primary market and the private placement market in India is that private and public sector financial institutions play a very big role in mobilizing resources from these markets. Table 2 shows that financial institutions account for more than 70 percent of total money raised from the private placement market in almost all the years. Similarly, if one looks at the break-up of new capital issues in the primary market, it shows that about 65 percent of total resources mobilized in this market is by banks and financial institutions (Figure 5). According to the

Figure 5: Industry-wise capital raised from the Primary Market in India (average of 1997–98 to 2002–03)

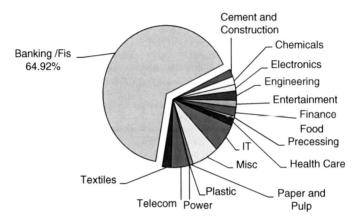

Annual Report of SEBI for 1998–99, this is a new trend in the Indian primary market where financial institutions and banks raise money from the primary market and the private placement market and then advance these funds as loans to the industry. This observation shows the preference of the Indian corporate sector towards debt-based borrowing instruments. It is not surprising that unlike new capital issues, total bank credit to industries has shown steady growth since 1993–94 (Figure 6).

The decline of the primary market coupled with the evidence that a very high percent of the money raised through this market is done by financial intermediaries indicates that actually a very small number of Indian firms are directly approaching the stock market to raise resources from this market. This finding shows that in spite of strong showing by the secondary segment of the stock market during the 1990s, the primary market has not performed well and the supposed beneficial effects of a strong secondary market have not been realized in India.

From Figures 2, 4 and 6 another interesting observation can be made. Figure 2 shows that the market capitalization to bank credit ratio has increased significantly in the 1990s, Figure 4 shows that new capital issues to market capitalization have declined sharply after 1994–95 and Figure 6 indicates that the growth of bank credit has been much higher than new capital issues after 1994–95. If we juxtapose these findings, it indicates that the primary and the secondary market have not moved in tandem in India. The growth of the secondary market during the second half of the 1990s and the first few years of this decade has not been reflected in the primary market segment of the stock market. It is notable that ratio of new capital issues to

Figure 6: New Capital Issues by Non Govt Public Limited Companies and Total Bank Credit to Small, Medium and Large Industries

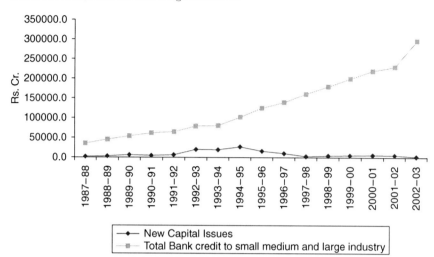

market capitalization reached the 10 percent mark both in 1989–90 and 1992–93. But the same ratio is about 0.3 percent in 2002–03 and in five of the last six years, this ratio has remained below the one percent mark. Only in 2000–01, it went above the 1 percent mark because of the global boom in Information Technology related stocks.

Evidence from firm level data, however, shows that use of equity as a source of finance has declined but the decline is much less than what is portrayed by the aggregate level data. The possible reconciliation can be made by assuming that firms are raising some equity issues from the private placements market. Firm level capital history data supports this assumption. However, it is difficult to measure how much equity is being raised from the private placement market in aggregate, because even market regulators like RBI and SEBI do not report these data.

## Possible Reasons behind the Dichotomy of Secondary and Primary Market

The dissociation between the secondary and the primary market in India is a cause for concern. Secondary market activities do not directly create any benefit for the corporate sector unless its effects spill over in the primary market to let the corporates access cheap investible resources. A weak primary market is not helping the Indian corporate sector to mobilize resources for capital formation from the stock market.

Figure 7: Composition of Household Saving in Financial Asset (in percent)

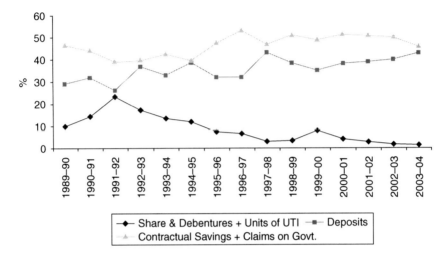

*Source*: *Handbook of Statistics on Indian Economy, Reserve Bank of India.*

A number of factors have been responsible for the decline of the primary market. One of the main reasons behind its decline is the withdrawal of domestic retail investors from the stock market. Data from RBI suggest that household saving in equity related instruments (shares and debentures + units of UTI) have gone down sharply in the recent years (Figure 7). Currently, these instruments account for only 1.37 percent of total household financial savings. In comparison, bank deposits account for about 42.8 percent of household financial savings for the same year. Two large-scale investor surveys, which dealt with retails investors and the stock market, suggest that uncertainties and irregularities associated with stock markets and lack of measures of investor protection are the main reasons behind the disenchantment of the small savers. These surveys also suggest that there is little optimism among the retail investors about the stock market and they are unlikely to invest much in equity related instruments in near future[5]. The withdrawal of retail investors from the stock market is evident from shareholding pattern of public limited companies. A report by the newspaper *The Economic Times* shows that among the companies which are actively traded in the Bombay Stock Exchange, there are more than 20 companies which have retail holdings of less than 1 percent[6].

The exodus of the retail investors from the stock market was not felt much in the secondary market because it almost coincided with the advent of the Foreign Institutional Investors (FIIs) in India. Pal (2005) shows that FIIs are currently the most dominant non-promoter shareholder in most of the Sensex companies and they also control more tradable shares of Sensex companies than any other investor groups.

However, FIIs are much less active in the primary segment of the stock market in India. According to a SEBI discussion paper[7], relatively long lock-in period due to post processing delay in listing of primary securities is the main reason behind the lack of interest of portfolio investors in the primary market. SEBI does not publish the break-up of FII investment in primary and secondary markets, therefore it is difficult to quantify the extent of FII involvement in the primary market, but it has been reported by SEBI and NSE that a very small proportion of FII flows in India enter the primary segment of the stock market. For example, the SEBI Annual Report of 2000–01 shows that in the years 1999–2000 and 2000–01, Indian residents (retail investors) were allotted 96.8 percent and 93.9 percent of amount of capital allotted to the public in the primary market. The share of FIIs was negligible in 1999–2000 and 0.1 percent in 2000–01. Marginal involvement of FIIs in the primary market coupled with the exodus of the small investors from this market are the two main reasons behind the pronounced decline in primary market activities.

Another possible reason behind the decline of primary market is the relative change in the price of debt and equity capital. One of the possible explanations of the 'Singh Paradox'[8] was that after financial liberalization, the rate of interest shot up in many emerging market and this made equity a cheaper financing option for many developing country firms. Sharp increase in stock market activities and share prices also helped the matter. It appears that the rise and fall of the primary market in India can be, to some extent, explained by change in the cost of debt financing.

During the financial liberalization of the early 1990s, the rate of interest was deregulated in India. Government of India allowed all term lending institutions to charge interest rates according to the risk perception of the concerned project, subject to a minimum rate of 15 percent. This period of high interest rate coincided with a very favourable situation in the stock market. High share prices and a buoyant secondary market induced investors to mobilize funds through the stock market. During this period there has been a shift in the financing pattern of the Indian corporate sector away from borrowing and towards equity oriented funds. The primary market opened up an alternate source of finance for Indian firms[9].

However, the favourable conditions for the primary market were not sustained. The secondary market experienced a sharp decline during the end of 1994 and early 1995. The rate of interest also declined steadily. A study by Khanna (2003) also shows that the cost of capital also did not decline steadily for Indian firms during this period. Using a sample of over 300 companies for the period 1990–2001, Khanna finds that the cost of capital to Indian firms declined initially and bottomed out in 1994, since then it increased gradually. During 1999–2001, the cost of capital for the sample firms was as high as it was in 1991. An increase in the cost of capital coupled with a decline in the rate of interest changed the relative cost of debt and equity capital in India and made borrowing a more attractive financing choice for many firms.

The third factor which contributed to the decline of the primary market is the strict disclosure norms imposed by SEBI after a series of scams and irregularities were unearthed in the primary market during 1994–95. Based on the Malegam Committee recommendations relating to disclosure requirements and issue procedures, SEBI imposed a set of entry barriers on new issues, specifying minimum issue size requirement for companies seeking listing. In addition, special requirements were imposed on finance companies seeking public funds. Many firms are trying to avoid these regulations by bypassing the primary market and tapping the private placements market which is much more informal in nature.

## Why High Portfolio Capital Inflow has not Helped the Real Economy?

These results suggest that the influx of FPI has not benefited the domestic economy the way the mainstream model predicted. The impact of foreign portfolio investment has largely been confined within the secondary market. The transmission mechanism by which secondary market activities help the real economy does not seem to be working in India.

These results are not surprising because unlike FDI, FPI does not have a one-to-one relationship with real investment. Portfolio investment is entirely concentrated in the secondary market and the beneficial effects of FPI are supposed to work only via the functioning of a stock market. Even at a theoretical level, the proposition that a vibrant stock market affects economic development is not beyond criticism. According to a vast body of literature, stock markets, under certain conditions, may actually inhibit economic development. Even in advanced countries with developed capital markets, stock markets are likely to do more harm than good to the real economy. One of the main reasons behind this deleterious role of stock markets emerges due to the dilemma posed by modern capital markets. Modern capital markets try to reconcile the social need for investment with the preference of individual investors for risk, return and liquidity. In this process, secondary markets open up prospects for speculation. Speculation leads to a situation where the players indulge in outguessing the market in foreseeing changes in short term financial ratios. This turns the secondary market in some kind of a casino where people speculate on other people's speculation (Keynes 1936). Also, Mishkin (1996) has argued that securities' markets are more prone to the problem of adverse selection, because asymmetries of information are particularly acute in these markets. Asymmetries of information make low quality firms more eager to issue securities, which exacerbates the problem of adverse selection in these markets.

The preponderance of distortionary speculative activities in stock markets and the existence of adverse selection problem ensure that the supposed positive contributions of stock markets (encouragement of savings and more efficient allocation of investible resources), hardly materialize in practice. Also, in a stock market based economy, individual investors, neither have the means nor the incentive to monitor and control corporate management. Market discipline is often exercised through hostile takeovers. Generally, it has been found that takeovers are disruptive and wasteful. More importantly, since markets try to value the enterprise largely on the basis of short-term financial performance, take-over threats create pressures and incentives for the management to think short-term. These negative features of stock markets like speculation, short termism and the turmoil of the take-over mechanism, can create a much more unfavourable impact on the third world countries with underdeveloped stock-markets, which are essentially less efficient and less transparent than their developed country counterparts[10]. Studies suggest that in developing countries, capital market development has generated more costs than benefits in recent years. These costs have included persistent misalignment of prices of financial assets, resulting in inefficiency in allocation of resources; sharply increased short-term volatility of asset prices, resulting in greater uncertainty; excessive borrowing to finance speculative asset purchases and consumption, resulting in unsustainable stocks of debt and reduced household savings.

Also as Rakshit (2002) points out, efficiency gains from short-term capital movements are crucially dependent on the absence of herd behaviour and moral hazard and on constant endeavor on the part of the investors in tracking changes in the economic fundamentals rather than in beating the gun by outguessing the psychology of the market. But according to Rakshit, it is increasingly becoming evident that short-term capital inflows do not operate under such ideal conditions. The telecommunication revolution has drastically decreased the time and cost of transferring funds from one market to the other in the recent years. The increasing ease of transferring funds between markets reduces the incentive for the investors to devote resources for assessing the health of enterprises and hence, leads to serious moral hazard problems. Here it is worth mentioning that the bailout packages adopted by the IMF to rescue the crisis ridden countries have actually exacerbated the moral hazard problem associated with foreign investment. This happens because the IMF bailout packages typically try to compensate foreign investors. This further encourages investors to undertake more risky ventures knowing that in the event of a crisis, they will be insulated from the potential losses.

Therefore, to sum up, according to the mainstream paradigm, the beneficial effects of FPI are crucially dependent upon the assumptions that well functioning stock markets promote economic development and that international portfolio investors are guided by economic fundamentals. The above discussion shows that both these assumptions are highly questionable on theoretical as well as on empirical grounds. In fact, empirical evidence from a number of cross-country studies,[11] has pointed out that among various forms of foreign investments, foreign portfolio investment is the least effective in promoting domestic investment and growth. These empirical studies reveal that contribution of portfolio investment in domestic investment is lowest among different types of capital inflow (Table 3).

However, the surge in foreign portfolio investment in the Indian economy has introduced one serious problems of macroeconomic management for the policymakers. Uncertainty and volatility associated with FPI have not only reduced the degrees of maneuverability available to the policymakers but have also forced them to take some measures which impose significant fiscal cost on the economy.

**Table 3: Summary of Some Studies on Capital Inflow**

| Author | Time Period and Country Coverage | Conclusion |
|---|---|---|
| Bosworth and Collins (1999) | 1978–95 (for 58 developing countries) | Every dollar increase in capital flows was associated with an increase in domestic investment of about 50cents (Above 80 cents for FDI, close to 10 cents for portfolio flows and about 50 cents for loans). |
| World Bank (2001): Global Development Finance, 2001, chap3. | 1972–98 (for 118 countries) This study uses the same methodology as Bosworth and Collins (1999) but uses a larger sample and longer time period. | Every dollar increase in capital flows was associated with about 80 cents increase in investment (close to 90 cents for long-term capital, 25 cents for short-term capital, above 80 cents for FDI, more than one dollar for bank lending and about 50 cents for portfolio flows). |

As foreign portfolio investors earn their returns in rupees, any devaluation of the rupee can erode the earnings of foreign portfolio investors in dollar terms (assuming the devaluation is against dollar). Therefore, devaluation or even an expectation of devaluation of the rupee can create negative sentiments among portfolio investors. As is evident from the recent spate of financial crises across the world, any sharp depreciation of a domestic currency of a developing country has the potential to trigger a sudden capital flight from that country. On the other hand, the RBI also tries to avoid nominal appreciation of the rupee, because otherwise it could seriously affect the competitiveness of the country's exports in the global market. Though officially the exchange rate of India is market determined, the dual threat of capital flight and exchange rate appreciation forces the RBI to closely monitor and intervene in the foreign exchange market, to maintain the value of rupee within a very narrow band. This compulsion not only limits the policy options available to the RBI, but it also forces the central bank to maintain high foreign exchange reserves so that it can intervene in the foreign exchange market effectively.

Secondly, faced with high capital inflows and the threat of appreciation of the domestic currency, the central bank has to absorb a very high percentage of the capital inflow to prevent the rupee from appreciating. This can affect the domestic economy in two ways. First, absorption of foreign asset increases the liquidity in the domestic economy. RBI partly neutralized the adverse impact of excess liquidity in the domestic money supply through sterilization. Sterilization is carried out through open market operations and changes in reserve requirements. However, sterilization is not costless as it imposes a quasi-fiscal cost on the economy. Secondly, to compensate the massive increase in Net Foreign Assets (NFA) and to have a check on the growth of reserve money, the RBI has to contract credit given to the domestic sector (government and commercial sector). This can increase the fiscal vulnerability of the government and can have serious repercussions for the domestic economy.

Data also show that taking advantage of the massive capital inflow and favourable external macroeconomic situation, the RBI has amassed huge amount of foreign exchange reserves since the late 1990s. Studies have suggested that the level of reserves accumulated by the RBI is much higher than level suggested by the recent literature on optimum reserves. It is possible that RBI is building up such high levels of reserves as a possible defense against the risk of sudden and large withdrawal of portfolio capital. Accumulation of reserves is costly for the economy as building reserves essentially means swapping of high yielding domestic assets with low yielding foreign assets.

Finally, as India is competing with other emerging markets to attract FPI, to sustain the inflow of portfolio investment, the policymakers in India have to ensure that India is at least as attractive as an investment destination as other emerging markets. This compels the authorities to ensure that returns on portfolio investment are high and fiscal doles given to portfolio investors are at least as attractive as the other developing countries. This induces the policymakers to a situation where they have to ensure that the returns from the domestic stock markets are high. Faced with a stagnating stock market during the second half of the 1990s, the policymakers in India had to introduce various fiscal and other sops to the stock market buoyant and the portfolio investors happy. For example, long-term capital gains tax on equities have been abolished and due to double taxation treaties between India and some other countries, capital gains on portfolio investment from these countries have been made tax free. This has not only put serious burden on the government exchequer, but it also constrains the policy options of the authorities in a country. A recent study by Chandrasekhar and Pal (2006) has estimated that tax exemption on capital gains has cost the government Rs 7,857 crores for the year 2004–05. A fallout of the sops given to the foreign investors is that portfolio investment is becoming a route for channeling illegal and allegedly terrorist money in India. The situation has become so bad that the central bank governor and the national security advisor had to warn the government about the security implications of increased portfolio flows.

Another disturbing fact about the Indian stock market is that the FIIs have emerged as the major players in the secondary segment of the stock market. Data on trading activity of FIIs and domestic stock market turnover suggest that FII's are becoming more important at the margin as an increasingly higher share of stock market turnover is accounted for by FII trading. Apprehensions have been expressed by economists that some sort of restriction is required on FII flows otherwise the domestic stock market is increasingly becoming a hostage to these players. But in spite of their dominant status in the secondary, portfolio investment has been much less active in the primary market. As a result, the supposed spillover benefits of secondary market activities are not reaching the real sector of the economy. The secondary market has become an arena for speculation where finance capital is indulging in purely speculative activities with no positive feed back on the real economy. The situation in the Indian stock markets reminds us of the famous quote from Keynes where he says: *"when the capital development of a country becomes a by-product of the activities of a casino, the job is likely to be ill-done"*- John Maynard Keynes, *The General Theory of Employment, Interest and Money*, Chapter 12. The State of Long-Term Expectation.

These observations support the arguments put forward by Grabel (1996) that reliance on foreign portfolio investment introduces mutually reinforcing problems of "compromised policy autonomy" and "increased risk potential" in a developing country. Grabel also points out that foreign portfolio investment is the riskiest form of foreign investment.

If we take into account the evidence from various cross-country empirical studies that suggests that FPI is one of the least beneficial forms of foreign investment and juxtapose it with the argument that it is also one of the most risky types of foreign investment, it is not surprising that the supposedly beneficial effects of foreign portfolio have not been realized in India.

In fact, it needs to be highlighted here that the findings of this study do not represent an isolated case where foreign portfolio investment has not been beneficial for a country. There is a growing consensus among economists that empirical results do not support the beneficial role of foreign portfolio investment. Rodrik comments:[12]

*"...persuasive evidence on the benefits of opening up to capital flows—especially of the portfolio and short-term kind—has yet to be provided"*

Even some of the IMF economists, once the staunchest supporters of financial liberalization and foreign portfolio investment, are conceding that the so-called beneficial aspects of foreign portfolio investment have not been realized in practice. Michael Mussa, Economic Counselor and Director of Research, IMF, comments:[13]

*"Many empirical studies have confirmed the common-sense appraisal of the postwar experience with trade liberalization: open policies toward international trade are an important factor contributing to stronger economic growth. Similarly persuasive evidence is not available for liberal policies toward international capital flows, particularly for portfolio flows rather than direct investment flows. Indeed, the experience in recent financial crises could cause reasonable people to question whether liberal policies toward international capital flows are wise for all countries in all circumstances."*

The lack of empirical support about the beneficial role of FPI should be viewed along with the fact that portfolio capital flows are highly volatile in nature. This is because more often than not, the expectations of the portfolio investors are based on extremely shaky informational base and can be subject to sharp changes without any underlying changes in the economic fundamentals of a country. This happens because portfolio capital flow, being entirely a market based device, is susceptible to a wide range of market failures. And as Stiglitz (1993) has pointed out, market failures in financial systems are quite common and pervasive in nature. The problem of market imperfection and asymmetric information amplifies the volatility resulting from sudden shifts in the pattern of portfolio flows. Coupled with this, herd behaviour and contagion are well documented features of financial markets where the portfolio investors operate. Together, these factors make FPI an inherently volatile form of capital flow.

Instability of portfolio flows has the potential to adversely affect growth of a developing country. Increased volatility in the domestic stock markets may reduce household saving and hinder investment. Moreover, portfolio flows can hinder export promotion by exerting upward pressures on the exchange rate and also sustain an import-cum investment boom to overheat the economy. The East Asian crisis has shown that together with the volatility of FPI, the presence of a huge amount of international speculative capital has the potential to seriously disrupt a country's economy. Given the risks associated with international speculative capital flows, the current reliance of many governments of developing countries, including India, on FPI, appears to be quite misplaced.

## Notes

1. *Source*: Adapted from "*Investment Funds in Emerging Markets*" IFC Lessons of Experience Series, July 1996. International Finance Corporation, Washington D. C., USA.
2. Stock market capitalization to GDP ratio is widely used in the literature to measure financial depth. But in strict sense this measure has a problem as we are comparing a stock variable (market capitalization) to a flow variable (GDP).
3. Levine uses the logarithm of this value, but here log is not used to avoid the negative sign.
4. NSE (2004): *Indian Securities Market, A Review (ISMR) – 2004*, National Stock Exchange, 2004, Mumbai.
5. L.C. Gupta, C.P. Gupta and Naveen Jain: Indian Household's Investment Preferences (Society for Capital Market Research and Development, Delhi 2001). Pg 21, and joint survey of household savings by SEBI and National Council of Applied Economic Research (NCAER).
6. The Economic Times, 24th January 2005.
7. '*Indian Securities Market: Agenda for development and Reform*'–SEBI Discussion Paper, undated
8. In a series of papers (Singh and Hamid 1992, Singh 1995, Singh 1998) Singh shows that there is an apparent paradox in the way firms are financed in developing countries. He shows that firms of developing countries tend to rely much more on external finance than their developed country counterparts. Also, in spite of having relatively small and immature stock markets, the contribution of the equity market as a source of finance is much higher in the firms from developing countries. These observations tend to go against theoretical predictions and a priori expectations. It is expected that an underdeveloped and imperfect capital market will discourage the firms from raising stock market finance and should induce the corporate sector to largely grow from internal sources. For example, Tirole (1991) has suggested that in an emerging market, where information gathering and dissemination activity is not adequately developed, the pricing of most firms' shares will tend to be arbitrary and volatile. And this would discourage the corporate sector from raising resources from the stock market. However, empirical evidence shows that firms from developing countries have shown a remarkably high degree of reliance on the stock market for their financing. This paradoxical situation of almost a reverse pecking order is known in the literature as the 'Singh Paradox'.

9. Sen and Vaidya (1997) say:
*"Financial Liberalization thus, had not led to a major disruption in investment activity of the private corporate sector. This ability to respond to shocks generated by interest rate deregulation was a consequence of far reaching changes in the primary issues market which opened up a new source of funds."* Pg. 136.

10. However, a wave of accounting frauds that have surfaced recently in the developed countries show that overdependence on short term financial indicators can create problems even in the markets which supposedly practice much better corporate governance and are more transparent than the developing country markets.

11. Bosworth and Collins (1999), World Bank (1999) and World Bank (2001).

12. "Exchange Rate Regimes and Institutional Arrangements in the Shadow of Capital Flows" Dani Rodrik Harvard University, September 2000, conference on Central Banking and Sustainable Development, held in KualaLumpur, Malaysia, August, 28–30, 2000.

13. "Factors Driving Global Economic Integration" by Michael Mussa, Economic Counselor and Director of Research, IMF, Presented in Jackson Hole, Wyoming, at a symposium sponsored by the Federal Reserve Bank of Kansas City on "Global Opportunities and Challenges," August 25, 2000.

# References

Bosworth, Barry, and Susan M. Collins. (1999): "Capital Flows to Developing Economies: Implications for Saving and Investment." Brookings Papers on Economic Activity 1: 143–69.

Chandrasekhar, C. P. and Ghosh, Jayati (2002): *The Market that Failed: A Decade of Neoliberal Economic Reforms in India.*

Chandrasekhar, C. P. and Pal Parthapratim (2006): "Financial Liberalization in India: An Assessment of its Nature and Outcomes" Economic and Political Weekly, Vol. XLI, No. 11, March 18–24 2006.

CMIE (2004): *Corporate Sector,* Economic Intelligence Service, May 2001. Mumbai, India.

CMIE: *PROWESS Database.*

Cobham, David and Ramesh Subramaniam (1995): "Corporate Finance in Developing Countries: New Evidence for India" CRIEFF Discussion Paper Series no 9512, University of St. Andrews, Scotland.

Corbett, J. and T. Jenkinson (1994): "The Financing of Industry, 1970–89: an International Comparison," CEPR Discussion Paper 948.

Ghosh, Jayati and C.P. Chandrasekhar (2001): *Crisis As Conquest: Learning From East Asia,* Orient Longman Publisher, New Delhi, India.

Glen, Jack and Brian Pinto (1994): "Debt or Equity? How Firms in Developing Countries Choose", IFC Discussion Paper 22.

Grabel, Ilene (1995): "Speculation-led Economic Development: a Post-Keynesian Interpretation of Financial Liberalization Programmes in Third World", International Journal of Applied Economics, vol. 9.

Grabel, Ilene (1996) "Marketing the Third World: The Contradictions of Portfolio Investment in the Global Economy", World Development 24, 11: 1761–76.

Grabel, Ilene (1997): "Savings, Investment and Functional Efficiency: A Comparative Examination of National Financial Complexes", in Pollin, Robert (ed.) *The Macroeconomics of Finance, Saving, and Investment,* Ann Arbor, Univ. of Michigan Press.

Grabel, Ilene (1999) Rejecting exceptionalism: reinterpreting the Asian financial crises, in Michie, J.and Grieve Smith, J. (eds), *Global Instability: The Political Economy of World Economic Governance*, London, Routledge 1999.

Grabel, Ilene (2000): "The Political Economy of 'Policy Credibility': The New-Classical Macroeconomics and the Remaking of Emerging Economies", Cambridge Journal of Economics, vol. 24, no. 1.

Gupta, L. C. (2001): "Household Investors' Perceptions about the Stock Market: Survey Findings and Lessons", NSE News, December 2001, Mumbai.

Gupta, L.C. C.P. Gupta and Naveen Jain (2001): *Indian Household's Investment Preferences* Society for Capital Market Research and Development, Delhi 2001.

Henry, P B (2000): "Do Stock Market Liberalizations Cause Investment Booms?" Working Paper, Stanford University, Stanford.

IFC (1991): "Financing Corporate Growth in the Developing World", IFC Discussion Paper, No. 12. Washington. D.C.

Joshi, Himanshu, (1995): "Stock Market Risk and Foreign Portfolio Investments – An Empirical Investigation", RBI Occasional Papers, Vol. 16, No. 4, December.

Keynes, J. M. (1936): *The General Theory of Employment, Interest, and Money*. New York: Harcourt Brace Jovanovich.

Khanna, Sushil (2002): "Has India Gained From Capital Account Liberalisation? Private Capital Flows and the Indian Economy in the 1990s." Paper presented at the IDEAs Conference on "International Money And Developing Countries: Theoretical And Policy Issues In The Current Context", December 2002.

Mayer, Colin (1988), "New Issues in Corporate Finance" in European Economic Review, 32, 1167–1189.

Mayer, Colin (1989), "Myths of the West: Lessons from Developed Countries for Development Finance" World Bank Working Paper no. 301.

Mayer, Colin (1990), "Financial Systems, Corporate Finance and Economic Development" in *Asymmetric Information, Corporate Finance and Investment*, R. Glen Hubbard, Editor, The University of Chicago Press, Chicago and London.

Mishkin, F. (1996), "Understanding Financial Crises: A Developing Country Perspective," NBER Working Paper Series, No. 5600, May.

Nagaraj, R. (1997): "What Has Happened since 1991? Assessment of India's Economic Reforms", Economic and Political Weekly, November 8, 1997.

NSE (2001): *Indian Securities Market: A Review*, Volume IV, 2001, National Stock Exchange, Mumbai.

Pal, Parthapratim (1998): "Foreign Portfolio Investment in Indian Equity Markets: Has the Economy Benefited?" Economic and Political Weekly, Vol. 33, No. 11, March 14.

Pal, Parthapratim (2001): "Stock Market Development and its Impact on the Financing of the Indian Corporate Sector" National Stock Exchange (NSE) Research Initiative, Working Paper No. 4. National Stock Exchange, Mumbai. 2001.

Pal, Parthapratim (2006): "Volatility in the Stock Market in India and Foreign Institutional Investors: A Study of the Post-election Crash" in the *Economic and Political Weekly*, February 19, 2005.

Rakshit, Mihir (2002): The East Asian Currency Crisis, Oxford University Press, New Delhi.

RBI: *Handbook of Statistics on Indian Economy*, Reserve Bank of India, Mumbai, Annual issues, 1999 to 2005.

Rodrik, Dani (1998). Who needs capital account convertibility? Princeton Essays in International Finance 207, 55–65.

SEBI (1998): "Indian Securities Market: Agenda for Reform" in *Banking and Financial Sector Reforms in India*. Edited by Raj Kapila and Uma Kapila, Academic Foundation, New Delhi.

SEBI: *Annual Report*, Various Issues, Securities and Exchange Board of India, Mumbai.

Sen, Kunal and Rajendra R. Vaidya (1997): *The Process of Financial Liberalization in India*, Oxford University Press. New Delhi.

Singh, A (1993): "The Stock Market and Economic Development: Should Developing Countries Encourage Stock Markets?", UNCTAD Review No. 4. pp. 1–28.

Singh, A (1995): *Corporate Financial Patterns in Industrializing Countries: A Comparative International Study*. IFC Technical Paper No. 2. Washington D.C.

Singh, A (1997): "Financial Liberalization, Stock Market and Economic Development," Economic Journal, May.

Singh, A (1998): "Liberalization, the Stock Market and the Market for Corporate Control: A Bridge too Far for the Indian Economy?" in India's Economic Reforms and Development: Essays for Manmohan Singh edited by Isher Judge Ahluwalia and I. M. D. Little, Oxford University Press, New Delhi.

Singh, A (2001): "Financial Liberalisation and Globalisation: Implications for Industrial and Industrialising Economies", in Jomo, K.S. and Nagaraj, S (eds.), *Globalisation versus Development*, Palgrave.

Singh, A and Hamid, J (1992): "Corporate Financial Structures in Developing Countries", IFC Technical Paper 1, Washington D.C.

Singh, Ajit and Weisse, Bruce A. (1998): "Emerging Stock Markets, Portfolio Capital Flows and Long-Term Economic Growth: Micro and Macroeconomic Perspectives", Cambridge Discussion Papers in Accounting and Finance, AF30, University of Cambridge, March 1998.

Stiglitz, Joseph (1993): "The Role of State in Financial Markets" Proceedings of the World Bank Annual Conference on Development Economics.

Stiglitz, Joseph (2000) "Capital Market Liberalization, Economic Growth, and Instability" World Development, June, Vol. 28, No. 6, pp. 1075–1086.

Taggart, Jr. R. A. (1985): "Secular Patterns in the Financing of US Corporations" in B. M. Friedman ed. Corporate Capital Structure in the United States, Chicago University Press, Chicago.

Tirole, J. (1991) Privatization in Eastern Europe: Incentives and the Economics of Transition, in O. Blanchard and S. Fischer, eds., NBER Macroeconomics Annual 1991.

World Bank (1999): Global Economic Prospects and the Developing Countries: Beyond Financial Crisis, Washington D.C.

World Bank (2001): Global Development Finance, 2001 Washington D.C.

# Chapter 8

# TRANSNATIONAL CORPORATIONS AND THE INTERNATIONALIZATION OF RESEARCH AND DEVELOPMENT ACTIVITIES IN DEVELOPING COUNTRIES: THE RELATIVE IMPORTANCE OF AFFILIATES IN ASIA AND LATIN AMERICA

## Célio Hiratuka

State University of Campinas (UNICAMP) and Researcher at the Center of Industrial and Technology Economics (Núcleo de Economia Industrial e da Tecnologia-NEIT) of UNICAMP

**Abstract**

The aim of this chapter is to analyze the internationalization of research and development activities carried out by transnational corporations. Based on information about U.S. transnational corporations, provided by the Bureau of Economic Analysis, this chapter seeks to assess how such corporations allocate their R&D resources abroad, comparing the role of Asia and Latin America affiliates.

**Introduction**

As of the 1990s, after a period of retraction resulting from the 1980s debt crisis, Latin American (LA) countries have started to attract significant volumes of Foreign Direct Investment (FDI) again, especially to the largest countries in the region: Brazil, Mexico, and Argentina. From an average share of about 5.7% in FDI world flows in the period 1985–1990, LA countries reached an annual average of about US$ 26.7 billions between 1991 and 1996, and of US$ 89.1

billions between 1997 and 2000, which represented about 10% of the world total in each period.

As a result, the already high degree of internationalization of the productive structure in LA countries became even higher. Considering the 500 largest corporations in the region, the foreign companies answered for an average of about 25% of sales from 1990 to 1992. In the period 1998–1999, this percentage increased to 43%. Regarding the 100 largest LA companies in the manufacturing sector in the same period, the foreign share increased from 53% to 63% (Mortimore *et al*, 2001).

It is also worth emphasizing that the boom in FDI flows and the increasing importance of foreign companies in the productive structure of LA countries occurred at the same time as a set of structural reforms, greatly inspired in the Washington Consensus. Although in different degrees, it is possible to say that most countries in the region carried out reforms involving trade liberalization, financial deregulation, stabilization programs based on exchange rate appreciation, and privatizations. Given the clear objective of reducing state participation in the economy, it was expected that transnational corporations (TNCs) would lead a new cycle of growth, in view of their intrinsic advantages in technology, knowledge, the scale of world operations, and the access to world trade flows.

Therefore, the choice of TNCs as leaders of a new pattern of growth, in a more liberal environment with less state intervention, was based on the supposition that part of the ownership advantages specific to large TNCs would spill over the rest of the productive system, bringing about an increase in the productivity and competitiveness of the industrial structure of the host countries.

In fact, the increasing presence of TNCs in developing economies over the last years has taken place within the scope of an intensive process of reorganization of their international activities. Considering the globalization of TNCs' technology activities, several authors have been stressing that, while the internationalization of R&D laboratories proceeds at a much slower pace than that seen in production and sales, these laboratories are globally more integrated. They not only adapt products and processes locally, but also leverage technology qualification, seeking intangible fixed assets abroad, which would be more advantageous with the establishment of R&D activities overseas.

According to some authors, this process would potentially deepen R&D activities in the countries where affiliates are established, increasing the possibility of positive spillover effects when compared to activities of simple adaptation. These effects would be especially important in developing countries, given the lack of technology qualification of local business systems. On the other hand, some authors stress that the internationalization process is concentrated on central countries, keeping developing countries in a position of marginal importance in the globalization of innovation activities.

Given the increasing importance of TNCs' affiliates in the productive structure of LA countries, it is fundamental to investigate how these corporations are conducting their R&D activities and contributing to the evolution of national innovation systems, particularly when we take into account that a fragile innovation structure and low R&D expenditures are two of the main factors hampering a competitive industrial development in such countries. In all LA countries, R&D activities are relatively stagnated at rather low levels, besides being financed mainly by government resources. It happens even in the largest countries in the region. In 2003, in Brazil, R&D expenditures represented 0.95% of the GDP; in Argentina, they corresponded to 0.41% of the GDP; and, in Mexico, to 0.40%. The private sector's share in these expenditures was of 41% in Brazil, 26% in Argentina, and 30% in Mexico (RYCT, 2006).

Therefore, it is crucial to understand how the TNCs are organizing their R&D activities globally, and which role is assigned to affiliates established in LA countries. This chapter attempts to collect evidence of the internationalization of large companies' R&D activities, based on information about TNCs headquartered in the United States. Its objective is to analyze the characteristics of the international R&D activities of U.S. companies' affiliates established in developing countries, comparing Latin America and Asia.

Besides this introduction, this chapter includes three other sections. In the first, we make brief remarks about the globalization of R&D activities, based on the international literature. In the second, we examine data on the R&D of U.S. TNCs' affiliates, comparing the insertion of developed and developing countries; among the latter, emphasis is placed on Asia and Latin America. In the third section are our final remarks.

## TNCs and the Globalization of R&D Activities

The literature about R&D activities in multinational corporations has been stressing both the factors that lead to the centralization of the most important R&D activities in the home country and the factors that could contribute to transfer them effectively abroad[1].

Pearce (1999) points out three factors that would make large corporations centralize R&D activities in their home countries. The first factor would be the existence of economies of scale in R&D, associated to the use of equipment, laboratories, and research teams. That is to say, the establishment of a second center of research abroad would not be economically viable while the indivisible resources destined to the central laboratory were not completely exhausted. The second factor would be that technology and innovation activities would benefit from interacting with other elements of the innovation system in the home country, such as other research centers, suppliers, the scientific community etc. The reproduction of such advantages abroad would demand intensive efforts and, primarily, an extended period of time. Finally, the third factor would be linked to the costs of coordinating and controlling the decentralization of such a strategic activity as the R&D. Besides risking the loss of focus on programs defined as priority, the TNCs would also risk the undesired diffusion of technologies developed when passing from a centralized structure to a more dispersed one.

In spite of the influence of such factors, the elements that favor a greater internationalization of R&D activities have been gaining force over the last years. Cantwell and Jane (2000) conducted a study that shows an increase in the internationalization trend, based on the analysis of patents applied for by a set of 748 TNCs in the United States. In the period 1979–1987, 11.1% of such patents resulted from research carried out outside of the TNC's home country, whereas in the period 1987–1995 this percentage went up to 16.2%.

Among the factors that explain this more intensive shifting of R&D activities is the internationalization of sales and the search for new markets on the part of TNCs. That is, technology internationalization would be linked to the greater production internationalization sought by large corporations, but would occur at a much slower pace and much less intensively. It is important to highlight that, according to this interpretation, the increase in R&D activities abroad would represent merely the intensification of a post-war trend, since technology activities abroad would basically play a supporting role in the exploitation of foreign markets, associated to the need for adapting products and processes to the specificities of the host market. The internationalization would fundamentally carry out the function of guaranteeing the exploitation of advantages generated by technological innovations developed in the home country. In this case, even though R&D activities were more frequently shifted abroad, their scope would be rather narrow, and the core activities would be kept in the home country.

However, several authors, such as Pearce (1999), Le Bas & Sierra (2002), and Narula & Zanfei (2003), have been emphasizing that the trend to internationalize TNCs' technology activities would represent not only a strengthening of the previous trend, in which R&D internationalization would be a mere reflect of an increase in production internationalization, but also a qualitative change, associated to global alterations in the strategies of resources operation and accumulation implemented by TNCs recently.

The deterioration of the conditions that supported the cycle of growth in the 1950s and 1960s and the changes in the world economic order since the economic crisis of the 1970s in the central countries encouraged a deep restructuring in large corporations. In a new environment of macroeconomic instability and volatility, with low growth rates in the main developed countries, the TNCs attempted to reinforce their proprietary advantages, stimulating fiercer competitiveness all over the world. The search for products and processes innovative capabilities and the increase in R&D expenditures was one of the most important aspects, but not the only one, since it was followed by the strategy of developing other intangible assets, such as product differentiation, trademarks, and organizational advantages.

During this process, the international organization of R&D activities changed significantly. Besides the traditional strategy of exploiting in host markets the advantages generated in the home country, Patel & Vega (1999) and Le Bas & Sierra (2002) point out two other types of R&D internationalization strategies which acquired importance recently.

The first and principal of them would be the strategy of establishing R&D laboratories abroad, with the purpose of monitoring the scientific and technological advances developed in other countries, which would potentially complement the innovation activities developed in the home country, thus reinforcing skills already developed within the corporation. In this case, the advantages of the host country, associated with the possibility of benefiting from technological externalities provided by firms and institutions in this country, would be in the same areas of technology competency found in the home country.

The second strategy, less intensively adopted than the first one, would be seeking new qualification in countries that offer advantages and technology qualifications not readily available in the home country. Therefore, unlike the first strategy, the investments to establish R&D laboratories abroad would be associated with those technology areas where there are fragilities in the national system of innovation, and the investment abroad would precisely carry out the function of balancing such fragilities.

These strategies would demonstrate that TNCs have adopted a more integrated approach in their technology activities, not only aiming at adapting products to different markets, but also developing new products and accumulating competencies associated with their R&D activities abroad. In this context, R&D laboratories outside of the home country would carry out a much more strategic function, opening up a possibility for assigning greater autonomy and, at the same time, more important tasks to these laboratories (Gerybadze & Reger, 1999).

However, it is essential to highlight that, in spite of a more internationalized approach to R&D activities, they are still rather selective in relation to the possibilities of reinforcing domestic competencies or accumulating qualifications considered strategic, but with better conditions to be developed outside of the home country. According to Cassiolato et al. (2001), the process of globalization of TNCs' technology activities would occur basically between USA, Europe, and Japan, since, when such corporations seek to interact with national systems of innovation different from those in their home countries, they do it looking for science and technology infra-structures equally developed. According to Hagedoorn (2002), of the total of agreements of technology cooperation inter-firms signed between 1990 and 1998, only 6.8% would have occurred outside of the three mentioned regions. Consequently, in developing countries, the scope and depth of these companies' R&D activities would be limited, maintaining the traditional characteristic of adapting products and processes.

If it is true that the new phase of the internationalization of R&D activities implemented by large corporations opens up the space for a higher level of technology activities carried out abroad, increasing the possible positive impacts of such internationalization on the host countries, it is also true that the selectivity in this process creates additional difficulties for developing countries.

First, it is worth emphasizing that the possibility of benefiting from this process is directly linked to the developing countries' ability to create nonnatural locational advantages associated with a science and technology infrastructure that can favor an increase in the affiliates' density of R&D activities (UNCTAD, 2005). Secondly, it is worth remembering that, even when TNCs make investments in R&D, the possibility of such investments to spill over the rest of the economic system depends largely on the absorbing capacity of the local business system. That is, it is necessary that there are some previous technology capabilities in the existing production structure to make possible the transfer of technology developed by TNCs to the host countries' economies.

These two aspects together highlight the importance of active policies for science and technology, directed not only to develop infrastructure, but also to integrate effectively this infrastructure in the technology learning activities of the business system, both in domestic and foreign companies. Especially in those countries where TNCs play a significant role in the productive system, science and technology policies should be more integrated in the industrial and foreign investment policy, aiming at contributing to the process of creating local technology skills (Lall, 2000).

In the next section, we seek to examine the TNCs' technology inter-nationalization, based on the evolution of R&D expenditures in affiliates of U.S. TNCs. Based on such data, we analyze the insertion of affiliates in Latin America and Asia.

## The Internationalization of U.S. TNCs' R&D Activities: The Insertion of Latin American and Asian Developing Countries

This section aims at analyzing the internationalization of the R&D activities of large U.S. TNC carried out abroad. Based on data collected by the Bureau of Economic Analysis in census surveys on TNCs' operations abroad, information

**Table 1: United States Transnational Corporations' Sales and R&D Expenditures. Total and Abroad. In US$ Millions and %**

|  | 1989 | 1994 | 1999 | 2003 |
|---|---|---|---|---|
| **R&D Expenditures** |  |  |  |  |
| Total | 59,925 | 91,574 | 126,291 | 140,103 |
| Affiliates abroad | 7,048 | 11,877 | 18,144 | 22,328 |
| Share of affiliates (%) | 11.8 | 12.9 | 14.3 | 15.9 |
| **Sales** |  |  |  |  |
| Total | 3,329,443 | 3,990,013 | 5,975,478 | 6,606,746 |
| Affiliates abroad | 1,019,966 | 1,435,901 | 2,218,945 | 2,905,867 |
| Share of affiliates (%) | 30.6 | 36.0 | 37.1 | 44.0 |

*Source*: NEIT/IE/UNICAMP, based on data from the Bureau of Economic Analysis.

was organized and classified, setting apart developed[2] and developing countries and, within the group of developing countries, Latin American and Asian countries. Besides the years of 1989, 1994, and 1999, for which census surveys were available, we also analyzed 2003, a year with sample coverage and less information than the others.

Table 1 shows the evolution of U.S. TNCs' internationalization, both in sales and R&D expenditures. As we can see, the increasing importance of affiliates' operations was steady all over the period for both indicators. However, the pace of this increasing importance of affiliates abroad was higher in sales than in R&D expenditures. Moreover, it is clear that R&D activities are still much more concentrated in the U.S. market than sales. In 2003, whereas foreign affiliates' sales corresponded to 44% of the total in U.S. corporations, the affiliates' R&D activities corresponded to 15.9%.

Considering the distribution of R&D expenditures among affiliates, Table 2 points to the fact that, in spite of the R&D expenditures in developing countries' affiliates having grown at a much higher average rate than those in developed countries' affiliates, the concentration is still higher in the latter. In 1989, developing countries answered for only 3.9% of the total. In 2003, their share reached 12.7%.

Among the developing countries, comparing the performance of Latin America and Asia, we see that until 1994 both groups increased their share, but Asia already had a higher growth rate. Even so, in that year, the share of Latin America affiliates was higher. Between 1994 and 2003, Latin America lost its relative importance, and its share decreased to 3.1% of the total, whereas Asia remained on its growth path, reaching 8.9% of the total in 2003 (Table 3).

**Table 2: R&D Expenditures Abroad by Majority-Owned Foreign Affiliates of U.S. Parent Companies. Developed and Developing Countries**

| Year | US$ Millions | | | % | | |
|------|------|------|------|------|------|------|
| | All Countries | Developed Countries | Developing Countries | All Countries | Developed Countries | Developing Countries |
| **1989** | 7,048 | 6,776 | 272 | 100.0 | 96.1 | 3.9 |
| **1994** | 11,877 | 10,941 | 936 | 100.0 | 92.1 | 7.9 |
| **1999** | 18,144 | 16,027 | 2,117 | 100.0 | 88.3 | 11.7 |
| **2003** | 22,328 | 19,490 | 2,838 | 100.0 | 87.3 | 12.7 |
| **Δ% p.a.** | | | | | | |
| **1989–2003** | 8.6 | 7.8 | 18.2 | | | |

*Source*: NEIT/IE/UNICAMP, based on data from the Bureau of Economic Analysis.

**Table 3: R&D Expenditures in Developing Countries by Majority-Owned Foreign Affiliates of U.S. Parent Companies: Latin America and Asia**

| Year | US$ Millions | | | % | | |
|------|------|------|------|------|------|------|
| | Developing Countries | Latin America | Asia | Developing Countries | Latin America | Asia |
| **1989** | 272 | 153 | 77 | 3.9 | 2.2 | 1.1 |
| **1994** | 936 | 477 | 408 | 7.9 | 4.0 | 3.4 |
| **1999** | 2,117 | 613 | 1,400 | 11.7 | 3.4 | 7.7 |
| **2003** | 2,838 | 689 | 1,987 | 12.7 | 3.1 | 8.9 |

*Source*: NEIT/IE/UNICAMP, based on data from the Bureau of Economic Analysis.

Therefore, we see that, at least for U.S. TNCs, the internationalization of R&D expenditures is not restricted to central countries, shifting toward developing countries, even though at a relatively slow pace. However, this was a movement concentrated in Asian developing countries, especially in the second half of the 1990s.

Data on Table 4 detail this previous information, showing the main countries in each region. As for Brazil, we observe that, in 1989 and 1994, the affiliates established in this country represented the higher share among the developing countries under analysis. In 1989, R&D expenditures in Brazilian affiliates came to represent about 1/3 of the total for developing countries, dropping to about 25% in 1994, and to 11.5% in 2003. Compared to the total for all countries, the Brazilian share went down from 2% in 1994 to 1.5% in 2003.

Therefore, the loss of relative importance of Brazilian affiliates in the international technology activities of large U.S. corporations is evident.

**Table 4: Majority-Owned Foreign Affiliates of U.S. Parent Companies –
Share of Selected Developing Countries in R&D Expenditures Abroad**

| Region/Countries | Share in R&D Expenditures Abroad | | | |
|---|---|---|---|---|
| | 1989 | 1994 | 1999 | 2003 |
| **Latin America** | **2.2** | **4.0** | **3.4** | **3.1** |
| Argentina | 0.1 | 0.2 | 0.1 | 0.1 |
| Brazil | 1.3 | 2.0 | 1.6 | 1.5 |
| Chile | 0.01 | 0.02 | 0.02 | 0.0 |
| Venezuela | 0.1 | 0.1 | 0.2 | 0.1 |
| Mexico | 0.5 | 1.5 | 1.3 | 1.3* |
| **Asia** | **1.1** | **3.4** | **7.7** | **8.9** |
| China | 0.0 | 0.1 | 1.8 | 2.5 |
| Hong Kong | 0.1 | 0.4 | 1.2 | 1.0 |
| India | 0.03 | 0.04 | 0.1 | 0.4 |
| Korea, Republic of | 0.1 | 0.1 | 0.6 | 0.9 |
| Malaysia | 0.04 | 0.2 | 0.9 | 1.1 |
| Philippines | 0.1 | 0.1 | 0.2 | 0.2 |
| Singapore | 0.4 | 1.4 | 2.3 | 2.3 |
| Taiwan | 0.3 | 0.9 | 0.7 | 0.3 |
| Thailand | 0.01 | 0.03 | 0.04 | 0.1 |

* Data for 2002.
*Source*: NEIT/IE/UNICAMP, based on data from the Bureau of Economic Analysis.

Nevertheless, Brazil continues to show the higher relative importance in Latin America, ranking above Mexico, even considering the increasing importance of Mexican affiliates in sales, which is almost twice higher than the Brazilian share. The other Latin American economies have an even lower importance, ranking well below Brazil and Mexico.

When compared to Asian developing countries, the contrast is obvious, since in Asia the trend to an increasing share occurs in almost all countries, except for Taiwan and Hong Kong. The evolution of affiliates established in China and Singapore deserve to be mentioned, for these two countries became the centers with the higher importance among all developing countries analyzed. It is also worth of noticing the rapid growth of Korea, Malaysia, and India in the period under study.

In Table 5, it is also interesting to compare, for each country, the affiliates' share in the total of R&D expenditures to their share in sales. Whereas Latin American countries are invariably more important as markets than as centers for R&D, the Asian countries' share in sales is not so different from their share in R&D. Some of them even stand out for having higher relative importance in R&D activities than in sales. This is the case for India, South Korea and China.

**Table 5:  Majority-Owned Foreign Affiliates of U.S. Parent Companies –
Share of Selected Developing Countries in R&D Expenditures and Sales
Abroad, 2003**

|  | Share in Total Sales | Share in R&D Expenditures | Share in R&D Expenditures/ Share in Sales |
|---|---|---|---|
| **All countries** | **100.0** | **100.0** | **1.0** |
| **Developed countries** | **72.2** | **87.3** | **1.2** |
| **Developing Countries** | **27.0** | **12.7** | **0.5** |
| **Latin America** | **11.5** | **3.1** | **0.3** |
| Argentina | 0.7 | 0.1 | 0.2 |
| Brazil | 2.2 | 1.5 | 0.7 |
| Chile | 0.3 | 0.0 | 0.1 |
| Venezuela | 0.4 | 0.1 | 0.1 |
| Mexico* | 3.9 | 1.3 | 0.3 |
| **Asia and Pacific** | **11.8** | **8.9** | **0.8** |
| China | 1.7 | 2.5 | 1.5 |
| Hong Kong | 1.9 | 1.0 | 0.5 |
| India | 0.3 | 0.4 | 1.1 |
| Korea, Republic of | 0.7 | 0.9 | 1.3 |
| Malaysia | 1.1 | 1.1 | 1.0 |
| Philippines | 0.4 | 0.2 | 0.6 |
| Singapore | 3.4 | 2.3 | 0.7 |
| Taiwan | 0.9 | 0.3 | 0.3 |
| Thailand | 0.7 | 0.1 | 0.2 |

\* Data for 2002.
*Source*: NEIT/IE/UNICAMP, based on data from the Bureau of Economic Analysis.

China, especially, draws our attention, since in 2003 Chinese affiliates
represented 1.7% of all affiliates' sales, but 2.5% of R&D expenditures, that is,
the share in R&D expenditures was one and a half times higher than the share
in sales. In Brazil, the share in R&D expenditures represented 70% of the
share in sales. Therefore, in 2003, Brazil was still a more important center of
production and sales for U.S. corporations than China, but less important in
technological activities.

Concerning the other Latin American countries, Brazil ranks above them
and also surpasses some Asian countries, such as Thailand, Taiwan and
Philippines. It is also worthy of note the case of Mexican affiliates, which have
the highest relative share in sales among developing countries (3.9%), but
represent only 1.3% of the total spent in R&D.

Another indicator that reveals the higher relative importance of innovation
activities in Asian developing countries than in Latin American ones is the ratio
between R&D expenditures and sales. According to Table 6, considering the

**Table 6: U.S. TNCs – R&D Expenditures/Sales Ratio, Total and Affiliates Abroad – in %**

|  | 1989 | 1994 | 1999 | 2003 |
|---|---|---|---|---|
| **TNCs' total** | **1.8** | **2.3** | **2.1** | **2.1** |
| **Affiliates' total** | **0.7** | **0.8** | **0.8** | **0.8** |
| **Developed countries** | **0.8** | **1.0** | **1.0** | **0.9** |
| **Developing countries** | **0.2** | **0.3** | **0.4** | **0.4** |
| **Latin America** | **0.2** | **0.4** | **0.2** | **0.2** |
| Argentina | 0.2 | 0.2 | 0.1 | 0.1 |
| Brazil | 0.3 | 0.7 | 0.5 | 0.5 |
| Chile | 0.05 | 0.04 | 0.04 | 0.1 |
| Venezuela | 0.3 | 0.3 | 0.4 | 0.1 |
| Mexico | 0.2 | 0.5 | 0.3 | 0.3* |
| **Asia** | **0.1** | **0.3** | **0.6** | **0.6** |
| China | 0.0 | 0.2 | 1.6 | 1.2 |
| Hong Kong | 0.1 | 0.2 | 0.5 | 0.4 |
| India | 0.6 | 0.5 | 0.4 | 0.8 |
| Korea, Republic of | 0.2 | 0.3 | 0.9 | 1.0 |
| Malaysia | 0.1 | 0.2 | 0.7 | 0.8 |
| Philippines | 0.2 | 0.3 | 0.4 | 0.5 |
| Singapore | 0.2 | 0.4 | 0.5 | 0.5 |
| Taiwan | 0.3 | 0.8 | 0.7 | 0.2 |
| Thailand | 0.02 | 0.04 | 0.05 | 0.1 |

*Source*: NEIT/IE/UNICAMP, based on data from the Bureau of Economic Analysis.

total of TNCs' world operations, including their headquarters, the ratio between R&D expenditures and sales increased from 1.8% in 1989 to 2.3% in 1994, decreasing a little both in 1999 and 2003 to 2.1%. Taking into account the same indicator for all affiliates' operations, the ratio reached 0.7% in 1989, increased to 0.8% in 1994, and remained at this level in 1999 and 2003.

As it was expected, in affiliates established in developed countries, the intensity of innovation efforts is higher than the average for the total of affiliates, increasing from 0.8% to 1% in 1994 and 1999, and decreasing to 0.9% in 2003. In the developing countries as a whole, the same indicator shows a trend to increase, going up from 0.2% in 1989 to 0.3% in 1994 and 0.4% in 1999 and 2003. Therefore, the difference in relation to the level observed in developed countries decreased.

Analyzing each region separately, we noticed that, in Latin America, the percentage rose significantly between 1989 and 1994, increasing from 0.2% to 0.4%, but decreased again to 0.2% in 1999 and 2003. Whereas at the end of the 1980s this indicator was at the same level as the average for affiliates established in developing countries, at the end of the 1990s the percentage for Latin America was rather lower.

In the Brazilian economy, the increase in the ratio between R&D expenditures and affiliates' sales was even more pronounced, going up from 0.3% to 0.7% between 1989 and 1994. In 1994, among the countries mentioned in the table, Brazil shows the second highest ratio, ranking below Taiwan only. However, between 1994 and 1999, it decreased again to 0.5%, and remained at this level in 2003.

In the other Latin American countries, the ratio was always below that of the Brazilian economy. In 2003, affiliates in Argentina, Chile and Venezuela reached 0.1%, whereas Mexican affiliates spent 0.3% of sales in R&D (data for 2002).

On the other hand, in Asia, the ratio between R&D expenditures and sales showed a tendency to increase, mainly between 1994 and 1999, proving that some Asian countries did manage to attract important investments to technology development. As a whole, Asian developing countries underwent an increase in R&D intensity, from 0.1% in 1989 to 0.3% in 1994, and 0.6% in 1999, where it remained in 2003.

Again, we must emphasize the Chinese case, which increased from 0.2% in 1994 to 1.6% in 1999 and 1.2% in 2003, a level that is even higher than the one observed in developed countries as a whole. India also deserves emphasis, since, from the beginning of the period analyzed, its affiliates' ratio between R&D expenditures and sales was substantially higher than that of other countries in the region. In spite of a decrease from 0.6% to 0.4% between 1989 and 1999, in 2003 this indicator reached 0.8%.

Two other important Asian countries, considering R&D intensity, are South Korea and Malaysia. In Korea, the ratio was 0.2% in 1989, went up to 0.9% in 1999, and reached 1% in 2003. In Malaysia, it increased from 0.1% in 1989 to 0.8% in 2003. The negative example is Taiwan, which, as in data related to shares, also shows a decrease in the ratio between R&D and sales. In 1994, Taiwan's ratio was the highest among Asian developing countries. However, since then, this indicator has decreased, going down to only 0.2% in 2003. This is probably associated with the shifting of R&D centers to other countries in the region.

In sum, we observe that large U.S. TNCs increased their R&D expenditures abroad, internationalizing their technology activities, but at a slower pace than that seen in the internationalization of sales. However, the most relevant fact is that, in this process of internationalization, developing countries acquired importance in relation to developed countries. Even though the latter are still answering for the greatest amount of R&D expenditures outside the United States, the increasing importance of the former is obvious.

In a certain way, this fact could counter the conclusion in Cassiolato *et al.* (2001), that the internationalization process remains limited to the Triad. In spite of that, the data analyzed show how selective TNCs are when choosing the location of their R&D activities, and their uneven distribution among developing countries. It is clear the difference established between Asian and Latin American countries during the 1990s, especially in its second half. The increase in Asia's relative importance and the decrease in Latin America's share show up in all indicators analyzed.

Certainly, the increase in Asia's importance as a preferential region for production, mainly of products associated to electronics/information technology, played an important role in this process.[3] However, it is reasonable to observe that, even within Asia, the increasing importance of R&D activities was not uniform, and remained limited to some countries. A rather selective movement is in action, concentrated on Asian developing countries and, within this region, on some few countries, which not only increased their share in the R&D expenditures of U.S. TNCs, but also show a high ratio between R&D expenditures and sales, similar to that observed in the central countries.

A common trait among the countries which showed this quality, especially China, Korea, Malaysia, Singapore and India, is the adoption of active technology policies directed to the development of important locational advantages for highly technology-intensive activities (labor qualification, technical and higher education, support to basic research, funding and incentives to R&D activities), combined with selective investment policies. These policies were structured with the objective of raising the technology content of foreign affiliates' activities and the degree of complementarity and integration with local companies and institutions (UNCTAD 2005; Lall, 2000 and 2003).

From this perspective, considering the situation in Latin America, Katz's study (2001) points out that the structural reforms implemented in this region in the 1990s, based on trade liberalization, capital flows liberalization, privatizations, and reduction of the public sector role, although have had positive impacts on the modernization and the (static) efficiency of the production system, resulted in a reduction of domestic technology efforts, both in national and transnational corporations. First of all, the possibility of counting on imported inputs and capital goods meant the replacement of the technology efforts made by corporations previously operating in the local market for technology embedded in the imported goods. From the TNCs' point of view, this new pattern of technology use, more consistent with international patterns, meant a reduction of efforts to adapt products and processes to the local market. Second, the privatization of utilities, especially energy and telecommunications, was followed by the closing of the R&D and engineering divisions set up during the previous stage. Finally, expenditures in science and technology infrastructure, which in Latin American countries have always been a state responsibility, suffered the impact of successive cuts in resources, due to the need for fiscal adjustments.

To these factors, we can add the policy directed to foreign investment, which, unlikely that seen in Asian developing countries, was not concerned with the implementation of measures to develop technology activities either in the established affiliates or the new ones that entered the region during the recent boom of FDI. Contrary to a selective sectoral policy or to a policy focused on more technology-intensive areas, in general Latin American countries adopted a horizontal policy, in which the main concern was to abolish restrictions to FDI and to the operation of foreign companies and to remove profit remittance regulations.

The data analyzed reveal a loss of status in the international distribution of R&D expenditures by U.S. TNCs regarding Latin American affiliates, especially Brazilian affiliates. Although Brazil remains as the Latin American country where foreign affiliates spend more in R&D, its share is much lower than that observed at the end of the 1980s. The recent boom in foreign investment, in the 1990s, did not change the role of Latin American affiliates, which remained restricted as regards to more dense R&D activities.

## Final Remarks

Recently, Latin America has been receiving high volumes of FDI, translated in an increasing presence of TNCs in the production and foreign trade structure of the countries in this region. This process reflects largely a fiercer competition among large transnational corporations, which has encouraged their process of production internationalization toward developing countries. It also reflects the fact that, from the beginning of the 1990s, Latin American countries have adopted a much more favorable approach to the inflow of direct investment, materialized in policies of deregulation and elimination of barriers to foreign capital to provide a much "freer" environment to affiliates' operations. Moreover, the privatization processes in the region also fostered, explicitly or not, the entering of foreign corporations, speeding up the denationalization of the productive basis.

In the transition from the import substitution model to a new, more liberal one, there was an expectation on the part of economic policy makers and most economists that TNCs would be fundamental to make Latin American countries resume a sustainable growth path. According to this line of thought, besides the benefits associated to the inflow of foreign capital through FDI, TNCs would be able to contribute to update the production structure of host countries, making viable a greater insertion in the international trade. It was believed that, on account of these companies' characteristic ownership advantages, such as technology knowledge and organizational, marketing and managerial skills, part of them would be transferred to host countries. One of the most important vectors of this process would be an increase in R&D expenditures, which, in Latin American countries, could contribute to raise the ratio between R&D expenditures/GDP and the share of private expenditures in the total R&D expenditures, besides heightening the potential spillover effects on domestic firms.

So far the data analyzed in this article show that these optimistic expectations about TNCs' contribution to improve the national innovation systems in Latin American countries were not met. Based on the U.S. TNCs' operations, we see that, although an increasing part of R&D activities is being shifted to affiliates, this process is still highly concentrated in affiliates located in other developed countries. In 2003, about 16% of the total R&D expenditures were made by affiliates abroad. Of this total, although developing countries have been acquiring importance, only 12.7% was made by affiliates in developing countries in the same year. However, even among developing countries, we can see a rather marked concentration on some countries, in general located in Asia.

Latin American countries have lost their share in the total, due to both the stagnation of R&D investments in the region and the higher relative growth observed in Asian countries. That is, in spite of the inflow of foreign investments and the increasing foreign presence in Latin American countries, this process was not followed by an increase in the technology activities of foreign companies in the region. In Asia, otherwise, several countries succeeded in attracting massive investments in R&D at the same time as FDI flows increased.

While policies favoring the inflow of foreign capital have been adopted in these two groups of countries, in the Asian one, even considering the characteristics of each country, in general policies to stimulate investment were more selective, directed to sectors and activities of higher technology content. Besides, policies to attract FDI were coupled with active science and technology policies to encourage an increase in the innovative activities performed by foreign affiliates and a higher degree of complementarity and integration with domestic companies and institutions.

In Latin American countries, regarding the FDI policy, the creation of a favorable environment to large TNC' operations has prevailed, by means of trade liberalization, deregulation, and remove of restrictions to foreign capital, without a defined policy to focus on more technology-intensive sectors and activities. In general, the affiliates adjusted to this new environment prioritizing the rationalization of activities, increasing the import of more technology-intensive capital goods and inputs, and often reducing R&D activities previously directed to adapt products and processes to local markets, made unnecessary in view of the convergence of production and consumption patterns provided by liberalization and globalization. At the same time, policies to strengthen the science and technology infrastructure in Latin American countries became vulnerable, and resources were frequently limited by the need of fiscal adjustments.

Thus, the massive presence of large transnational corporations' affiliates in Latin America, which are world leaders in their sectors and carry out an intense innovation activity globally, for the time being remain as a potential of technology transfer yet to be realized. Certainly, the affiliates operating in these countries could play a much more relevant role in technology development and in the generation of spillovers to further economic development as a whole. However, this is not a trivial task, since, as stressed above, the increasing globalization of R&D activities has been much more selective, demanding locational advantages related to science and technology infrastructure and labor qualification, and also a public sector able to coordinate actions to attract investments or to encourage the already established TNCs to become more integrated with the national innovation system and more able to generate externalities. This is a task that was not satisfactorily performed by Latin American countries in the last cycle of foreign investments, and that remains as a challenge in the beginning of this century.

## Notes

1. In Hirschey and Caves' terminology (1981), these would be the centripetal and centrifugal forces, respectively.
2. The United States, Canada, European Union (15), Japan, Australia, New Zealand, Israel, and Switzerland were considered developed countries. The others were considered developing countries.
3. See *Boletim NEIT* n. 6, for a detailed analysis of the geographic distribution of U.S. affiliates' activities.

## References

ARAÚJO, R. D. (2004). Desempenho inovador e comportamento tecnológico das firmas domésticas e transnacionais no final da década de 90. Dissertação de Mestrado. IE/UNICAMP.

BOLETIM NEIT, n. 6. http://www.eco.unicamp.br/Neit/boletim.htm

BUREAU OF ECONOMIC ANALYSIS. *US investment abroad: financial and operation data*, several years.

CANTWELL, J. e JANNE, O. (2000). The role of Multinational Corporations and National States in the globalization of innovatory capacity: the European perspective. *Technology Analysis & Strategic Management*, vol. 12, n. 2.

CASSIOLATO, J.E.; LASTRES, H.; SZAPIRO, M. e VARGAS, M.A (2001).Local Systems of Innovation in Brazil, development and Transnational Corporation: a preliminary assesment based on empirical results of a research project. *DRUID conference paper*.

COUTINHO, L., LAPLANE, M. e HIRATUKA, C. (org.). (2003) *Internacionalização e desenvolvimento da indústria no Brasil*. São Paulo: Ed. Unesp.

DUNNING, J. (1993). *Multinational Enterprise and the global economy*. Londres: Addison Wesley.

GERYBADZE, A. e REGER, G. (1999). Globalization of R&D: recent changes in the managament of innovation in transnational corporations. *Research Policy*. Vol. 28.

HAGEDOORN, J. (2002). Inter-firm R&D partnership: an overview of major trends and patterns since 1960. In *Research Policy*, vol 31.

HIRSCHEY, R.C. e CAVES, R.E. (1981). Internationalisation of research and transfer of technology by multinational enterprise. In *Oxford Bulletin of Economic and Statistics*, n. 42.

KATZ, J. (2001). Structural Reforms and technological behavior. The sources and nature of technological change in Latin America in the 1990s. In *Research Policy*, vol. 30.

LALL, S. (2000). Export performance technological upgrading and foreign direct investment strategies in the Asian newly industrializing economies with special reference to Singapur. *Desarollo Productivo*, n. 88. Cepal.

LALL, S. (2003). Reinventing industrial strategy: The role of government policy in building industrial competitiveness. *Mimeo*, paper presented to G-24.

MORTIMORE, M. MORTIMORE, M., VERGARA, S. e KATZ, J. (2001). La competitividade internacional y el desarrollo nacional: implicancias para la política de Inversión Extranjera Directa (IED) en América Latina. CEPAL, *Série Desarrollo Productivo*, n. 107.

LAPLANE, M. F., SARTI, F., HIRATUKA, C., SABBATINI, R. (2001). El caso brasileño. In CHUDNOVSKY. D. (Editor) *El boom de las inversiones extranjeras directas en el MERCOSUR*. Buenos Aires: Siglo XXI.

Le BAS, C. & SIERRA, C. (2002). Location versus home country advantages in R&D activities: some further results on multinationals locational strategies. In *Research Policy*, vol. 31.

NARULA, R. e ZANFEI, A. (2003). Globalisation of innovation: the role of Multinational Enterprise. *DRUID working papers*, n. 03–15.

PATEL, P. e VEGA, M. (1999). Patterns of internationalisation of corporate technology: location versus home country advantages. In *Research Policy*, vol. 28.

PEARCE, R. (1999). Descentrelised R&D and strategic competitiviness: globalised approaches to generation and use of technology in multinational enterprises. In *Research Policy*, vol. 28.

RYCT (2006) El Estado de La Ciencia. Red Iberoamericana de Ciencia Tecnologia.

UNCTAD (2002). *World Investment Report: TNCs and export competitiviness*. United Nations, New York.

UNCTAD (2005). *World Investment Report: TNCs and the internationalization of R&D*, United Nations, New York.

# Chapter 9

# EXTERNAL DEBT NATIONALIZATION AS A MAJOR TENDENCY ON BRAZILIAN EXTERNAL DEBT IN THE TWENTIETH CENTURY: THE SHIFTING CHARACTER OF THE STATE DURING DEBT CRISIS

## Luiz M. Niemeyer
Catholic University of Sao Paulo-PUC-SP

**Abstract**

This chapter discusses the shifting character of the Brazilian State in several major debt crises throughout this century including its more recent one that started in 1999 and is considered to end in 2005 when Brazil paid in advance its debt with IMF. The intention here is to review the role of the Brazilian State during these debt crises. It is shown that pressures from the international capital market and the country's private sector forced the Brazilian State to assume the debt risk and obligations of the private sector. This process is called "the nationalization of the debt" of the Brazilian external debt. Our major purpose is to see whether the recent debt process (1994–1998) and its repercussion until 2005 shows the same trend as the 1976–1982 period – that is, to see whether the State ended up bailing out the risks of the huge amount of portfolio investment that the country received.

The tendency for external debt "nationalization" is present in the recent external debt of Brazil (1992–1998). But, contrary to the debt cycle of 1967–1982, the external debt "nationalization" of the 1990s follows the pattern similar to the external debt cycle of 1947–1962.

## Objective

The objective of this chapter is to analyze the role of the State in the process of the external debt of Brazil. Specifically, our thesis is to find out if historically the State assumed all the risk by "nationalizing foreign obligations" – in which economic losses are socialized while economic gains are privatized – as was the case in the 1982 debt crisis (Cruz 1984).

Using the historical method, this chapter will help us understand the shifting character of the Brazilian State during the recent process of external borrowing by the country (1994–1999) and its repercussion until 2005 when the country paid in advance its loan with IMF.

We will see whether the recent debt process (1993–1998) shows the same trend as the 1976–1982 period – that is, whether the State will end up bailing out the risks of the huge amount of portfolio investment that the country received. We are considering the analysis of the 1982 debt crisis as a benchmark because with this crisis the Brazilian economy interrupted the outstanding growth path that the country had from the 1930s to the early 1982.

The idea of "socialization of losses" in Brazilian economy dates back at least to the beginning of this century when the coffee valorization scheme reached its apex. Furtado (1963) described how the coffee producers succeeded in transferring to the whole society the burdens of the ups and downs of the coffee trade cycle by keeping the exchange rate below the par.

Since Brazil in this century can be considered one of the leading borrowing countries, its experience gives ground to the understanding of the role of State on external debt crisis in major developing economies.

In order to search for historic trends about the behavior of the Brazilian State in external debt crisis, we will analyze and compare different and critical periods in recent Brazilian economic history in which the external debt played a significant role in the economic life of the country. It is relevant to mention a methodological aspect that will be taken into consideration.

The periods chosen ended up in debt crisis. Therefore, in the topic that we are approaching (that is, the role of the state), it's very difficult to identify if they are related to the causes or the consequence of the debt crisis.

In order to analyze this relevant point in each historical period, we will start with a subperiod of relative stability and then we will move to a subperiod that ended in debt crisis. That is, each historical period under analysis will consist of two periods, one "stable"[1] and another one that resulted in a debt crisis. The periods to be compared, which will represent a section of the chapter each, are 1906–1930; 1947–1962; 1967–1982; 1992–1998. In the last section we present our conclusions.

**Nationalization of External Debt in Historical Subperiods**

| Period | 1906–1932 | | 1947–1962 | | 1967–1982 | | 1993... |
|---|---|---|---|---|---|---|---|
| Subperiod | Stable | Unstable | Stable | Unstable | Stable | Unstable | N/A |
| Years | 1906–1914 | 1920–1931 | 1947–1955 | 1956–1962 | 1968–1974 | 1975–1982 | 1994... |
| Bailed out | NO | Yes | YES | Yes | No | Yes | Yes |

## The Old Republic 1906–1930

In this period, the Brazilian State was the principal external debtor. As observed by Topik (1987), international capitalists have frequently encouraged state presence in the economy to ensure a safe investment climate. The Brazilian state borrowed heavily to finance its budget deficit, infrastructural investments, railroads and the coffee valorization scheme. The state's role in the foreign debt was powerfully affected by the Taubate Convention of 1906 and its policy of coffee valorization, since the basic funding of the Convention was external debt.

Suzigan and Villela (1973:332) report that, during the period from 1890 to 1931, Brazil received new loans amounting to £ 343,4 million, paid £ 365,4 million and increased its external debt by £ 245,9 millions[2]. This discrepancy stopped between 1932 and 1945. Until 1934, 75 per cent of the trade surplus was used in the payment of the external debt while this percentage dropped to 40 per cent between 1934 and 1945.

The 1906–1914 period was a rare time of economic stability in Brazilian history. Inflation was not a relevant issue and did not affect the outflow of capital. In strong contrast, the Brazilian economy in the 1920s faced high instability coupled with inflation.

In order to check if the state ended bailing out the debts of the private sector, we will focus on the international financing of the coffee valorization. At the beginning, the operation was managed by the Sao Paulo State together with the major international coffee importers, who provided two thirds of the resource needed.

Exports accounted for between one third and one fifth of GDP during the Old Republic. Coffee and rubber[3], often responsible for over 80 per cent of the country's exports, propelled the economy. Sao Paulo was by far the major coffee producer responsible for around 80 percent of the coffee crop.

The decentralized Old Republic suited the interests of powerful export oriented groups, and the ancient patron-client system found its political expression in the *politica dos governadores* by 1900. Sao Paulo State more than the rest, chose the route of foreign borrowing (Love 1980).

In the period under study Sao Paulo State was the major player on the valorization of the coffee, hence we will concentrate on the behavior of this state:

**External financing of coffee valorization and the extensive penetration of Sao Paulo by foreign capital led to a degree of foreign political control, at least to the extent of restricting Sao Paulo's political options. Love (1973: 251)**

## Brazil 1906–1914: Federal Government's Indirect Participation

Marischal (1987:171) reports that by 1914 Latin American government debt reached more than US$ 2 billion. Fifty percent of this amount was contracted during the previous century. The other half was contracted in the loan boom of 1904–14. During the World War I period, Latin America, which has been a net capital importer since the middle of the XIX century, for some years became a net capital exporter, using part of its trade surplus to repatriate some of the debt.

The quasi-gold standard, established in Brazil in 1906 through the creation of the Conversion Office (TCO) which financed and supported the coffee industry, eased the way for capital flows into the country. Hence the maintenance of a relevant level of gold reserves worked as a window dressing to attract large flows of capital. When the Bank of England raised its interest rate, its immediate effect was on short-term capital movements and then on international gold. Brazil became short of commercial finance since this type of capital flowed to UK, and Brazil had to use its gold reserves in order to honor its international obligations. Additionally, Lewis (1938: 149) adds that, "accumulation of short-term capital in a country was paralleled by a large inflow of gold, and presumably their exit from the country will be marked by an outflow of the metal". Together with these inflows we have the presence of the abnormal short-term capital and the consequent capital flight associated with it. Hence, gold convertibility made possible a huge capital outflow (Furtado 1963:229).

In the first subperiod, we do not see the state bailing out the debt of the private sector or the debt of Sao Paulo state, which acted throughout this period in the interest of the private sector. Hence, the socialization of the losses can be found in the work of the TCO through its exchange rate policy rather than through the nationalization of the foreign debt.

The complicated valorization scheme to defend the coffee economy worked relatively well until the 1930s (Furtado: 1963: 224). Furtado points out that the coffee producers succeeded in transferring to the whole society the burdens of the ups and downs of the coffee trade cycle. He characterized this transferring as "the socialization of losses". By keeping the exchange rate below par, the rest of the society subsidized exporters. For instance, when the coffee prices declined in the international markets, the exporter's milreis earnings fell less because of currency's devaluation; on the other hand, coffee producer's costs rose more slowly.

As observed by Delfim Netto (1979: 67) the first coffee valorization, inaugurated in 1906 and inspired by the Taubate Convention of the same year, was a *market corner* promoted by private capital operating in the behalf of the government. For Love (1980), valorization was essentially simple: a foreign loan would be obtained to purchase coffee from planters and stockpile it; in year of bad harvests this supply would be released on the international market; and meanwhile all exported coffee would be taxed at a high enough rate to repay the foreign loan. In theory, coffee debts were self-liquidating through the gold surtax.

Due to Federal Government resistance, Sao Paulo State took the lead and together with the major coffee importer Hermann Sielken promoted the first valorization. The "Sielken syndicate" worked as follows: the major coffee importers from the USA and Europe provided 80 per cent of the required funding to buy the coffee and the remaining 20 per cent was to be provided by Sao Paulo State, who in turn borrowed it from international banks.

As Delfim Netto (1979:50) reports, in August 1908 Sao Paulo State borrowed £ 1 million from the Bank fur Deutschland; in December of the same year a £ 2 million loan was negotiated with the Schroroder & Co. of London and a £1 million loan from National City Bank of New York; both loans carried a four year term with a grace period up to 1908. By June 1907 the Sao Paulo State had bought and stockpiled 8 million sacks of coffee.

By the end of 1908, Delfim Netto reported the following liability position related to the stockpiling of 7 million sacks of coffee: a) a £ 2 230 thousand debt to Schoroeder City Bank; b) and a £ 10 457 thousand debt related to advances provided by the importers. In order to consolidate this debt, a £ 15 million "funding" loan was floated in December by the Sao Paulo State to roll over the valorization debt.

According to Fausto (1985: 222), the Sao Paulo State loan was floated with a group of banks such as Schroroder & Co, Banque de Paris et Pays Bas and Societe General de Paris. Bearing in mind that the first Brazilian funding loan of 1898 amounted to £ 10 million, this huge 10 year loan was floated thanks to the guarantee of the Brazilian Federal Government under Afonso Pena. It is also relevant to mention that, under the loan agreement, the Sao Paulo State also provided as a guarantee 7 million sacks of coffee that were stockpiled.

Another cost of the valorization was the lost of control of coffee marketing to foreign lenders after 1908. In a sense, valorization was a strong response to foreign control. However, financing arrangements instead gave exporters and foreign financiers even greater control. (Love 1980: 49). The sale of the coffee given in guarantee was controlled by a committee of seven members. Four members were designated by Schoroder & Co, which became the manager of the valorization. Two members were nominated by Societe General de Paris. The remaining member was appointed by the Sao Paulo State.

In June 1913, the £ 15 million loan was paid in advance and the coffee valorization defenders throughout the Old Republic would use this payment as "a real proof" of the viability of the coffee valorization scheme. In my opinion, the advance payment was a bigger evidence of an attempt to get rid of the foreign control over coffee exports than of any strong economic viability of the program. My reasoning is based on the fact, previously reported, that in 1922 the federal government floated a £ 9 million 10 year loan carrying a proviso that Brazil should avoid a new coffee valorization plan. This loan was paid in advance in 1923 to fight this proviso.

With the beginning of the World War I in July of 1914, the flow of capital stopped. Brazil was facing a 30 per cent increase in imports and an 80 per cent increase in amortization (Brazil started to repay the 1890 funding loan in 1911). Technically, Brazil did not default on its external obligations, but in August, due to a massive run, the TCO closed and the foreign exchange market collapsed. The country had to sign the second "funding loan" (a "debt renegotiation" loan; the first one was signed in 1898) of £ 14502 thousand in 1914, which was disbursed in 1915.

## Federal Government Direct Participation and Sao Paulo's Response (1920–1931)

Eichengreen, (1990:239) reports that the gold standard of the inter-war period was a hybrid, neither a pure gold standard, which prevailed in various countries prior to World War I nor a fiat money system like that which succeeded the breakdown of Bretton Woods. With the gold standard of 1925–1931, London was subject to new and powerful competition from New York and, on a minor scale Amsterdam.

For Jorgensen and Sachs (1989:52), however, the overall level of international capital flows never recovered to that of its heyday in the period 1870 to 1914; flows of real private investment between 1914 and 1930 were only two-thirds as great as those between 1900 and 1913.[4] Furthermore, during the inter-war period, developmental finance for the periphery was eclipsed by lending, for reconstruction and servicing the war debt, between the industrialized countries. Latin American countries date the start of the Depression from the second half of 1928 due to the abrupt halt in foreign lending in June 1928, when the New York stock market started its meteoric rise and interest rates tightened on the call money market (Klinderberger: 1984: 317). When comparing the debt crisis of the 1930s with the ones from the previous century, Eichengreen (1991: 151) stressed as the major difference the universal character of the former. The majority of sovereign debtors suspended interest payments and initiated protracted negotiations. The 1929 depression marks the beginning of a period of about 15 years, during which hardly any foreign capital flowed into Latin America.

## 1920–1923

In the beginning of 1921, encouraged by the success of the two previous valorizations,[5] the Federal government, under the presidency of Epitacio Pessoa, promoted the third coffee valorization scheme, the first one under his control. As reported by Delfim Netto (1979: 78), the prompt participation of the Federal government was due to financial difficulties of the Brazilian state and the profitability associated with the operation, and the need to solve the alleged national problem of the coffee industry.

In 1921, the central government created the "provisional" Rediscount Department at the Bank of Brazil (BB). The storage of the 4.5 million coffee sacks[6] was financed with money issuance. Part of this issuance was backed by a £ 5.5 million short-term loan.

In the beginning of 1922, the Brazilian government was unable to repay this short-term debt. Using as a guarantee the 4.5 million coffee sacks previously acquired, the Federal government in May floated a 10 year, £ 10 million loan. Delfim Netto (1979: 78) reports that, as in the first valorization, a committee of bankers was created. The members of this committee were designated by Rothschild, Schroeder, the federal government and the Brazilian Warrant, an international trading company that dominated coffee markets, fiscal and future. The loan carried the proviso that Brazil should avoid a new valorization plan. It also ruled that the Federal Government could defend the coffee through the Brazilian Warrant only.

## 1924–1929 Sao Paulo Takes Control

In early 1924, the Federal government paid in advance the £ 9 million loan to combat the strict covenants. Additionally, Delfim Netto (1979: 88) reports that the coffee planters, unhappy with the previous strict control in the industry, pressed the Federal government, which then transferred the control of the valorization to Sao Paulo State.

In January of 1926, as previously reported, the Instituto Paulista de Defesa Permanente do Café (IPDC) made a £ 10 million short-term loan from

Lazard Brothers. In the second semester of this year, the recently organized Sao Paulo State Bank was granted a £ 5 million per year credit line. At the Federal level, in 1926 the Stabilization Office (SO) was established to provide stable, cheap milreis to the coffee exporters. In 1927 the amortization of the 1914 funding loan began, and Washington Luiz had to balance the requirements of the Paulistas and the Treasury.

At the outset of the Depression, the coffee sector enjoyed an "automatic" benefit when capital flight and the end of gold convertibility for the milreis produced a devaluation of the currency; part of the coffee sector's losses could thereby be transferred to the population at large through rises in the prices of imports, while planters received more and more milreis (Furtado 1963).

## 1930–1931

In early 1930, there was an increasing tension between the powerful coffee planters. President Washington Luis' first response to the crisis was to protect the milreis rather than planters. Fausto (1985:248) reports that the tension reached its peak during the coffee planter's conference in the end of December 1929 and early January 1930. Several requests were presented to the president, among them a request for the £ 10 million held by the Banco do Brasil, to be used to finance the coffee producers.

As reported by Love (1980:59), due to the prompt refusal of this request by the Federal government, Sao Paulo State, before the fall of Washington Luiz (Brazilian President from 1927 to 1930), floated a 10 year, £ 20 million British Valorization Loan with its collateral stock supervised by foreign banks who established the amount of coffee to be remitted.

By 1930, Topik (1987: 27) reports that the Brazilian currency, the milreis, lost about 80 per cent of its value. The revolution lead by Getulio Vargas in October of 1930 – interpreted as a reaction against an economic system defended by Paulista politicians – marks the end of the Old Republic. In December 1931 Sao Paulo's IPDC turned over its responsibilities to a newly created federal government organization and the coffee industry returned to the federal government supervision. The Vargas provisional government abandoned the exchange rate system and a new exchange control was introduced in March 1932. By December 1932, most state and federal loans had gone into default.

The Sao Paulo £ 20 million British Valorization Loan was turned over to the central government. "Consequently, the Paulistas got off at less than the full cost of the capital they borrowed for valorization" (Love 1973: 248). If one accepts the view that throughout this period Sao Paulo State was a representative of the private sector (since the coffee valorization program served mainly the interest of the private sector), we can say that, contrary to the period of 1906–1914, in the 1920–1931 period there was a "nationalization of foreign obligations" when a debt crisis occurred, as was the case in the 1932 debt crisis.

**A federal decree of March 2, 1932 divided Brazil's loans into seven grades. The more famous "Aranha Plan" of February 5, 1934, added one more category, but basically kept to the same scheme of establishing priorities for payment of interest and the repayment of principal. In both plans, the first grade was reserved for Brazil's three federal Funding Loans (1898, 1914 and 1931), and the second exclusively for the Sao Paulo coffee Realization loan. The first grade called for loan repayments and full interest as scheduled; in the case of SP loan, only interest was to be paid on schedule, but the repayment of the principal was to be stretched out. In the 1932 plan, no state loans other than those of Sao Paulo were assigned a priority higher than grade four...In the 1934 scheme, Sao Paulo was the only state to have loans in the first five grades (of which only the first two repaid any principal...**(Love 1980:251).

## The Years of Rapid Economic Growth (1947–1962)

Because of the sharp increase in external capital inflows during the 1950s, Brazil's total capacity to import grew at a substantial rate. This enabled the country to sustain high rates of economic growth – following an Import Substitution (ISI) path – until the early 1960s. Throughout the 1950s the terms on which Brazil obtained sufficient external financing for its foreign exchange (FE) gaps progressively deteriorated, and the country had to face an upward trend of effective interest rates combined with a downward trend in the maturities-structure of outstanding debt. Beginning in 1960, the economy was plagued by a severe cash-squeeze liquidity crisis and the country was forced to negotiate with the IMF (Donnelly 1970: 137).

Andrew Gunder Frank (Bandeira 1978: 91) reports that during the period from 1947 and 1960, Brazil received new loans and FDI amounting to US$ 1814 million and paid US$ 2459 million as a service for the debt and FDI. Gunder Frank also reports that to this negative net balance of US$ 645 million between inflows and outflows of capital we should add US$ 1022 million related to clandestine capital flights.

**The accumulation of commercial arrears and their subsequent renegotiations proved unsatisfactory to both creditor and**

**debtor countries. … This situation hastened the transition to organized financing systems for medium-term suppliers' credits (credits of between one and five years), since central banks became increasingly unwilling to continue financing the accumulation of commercial arrears. … In this way, a number of governments sought to transfer gradually an increasing share of the responsibility for the provision of export financing to the supplier, or rather, in view of the latter's nominal reliance on bank credit, to the private banks.** (United Nations 1967: xi).

In the period under study our analysis will be centered on the debt rescheduling of payments of commercial arrears and suppliers' credits. According to IBRD (1967: 21), the rescheduling operations during this period often had been confined to this type of credits alone and were conducted by informal debt rescheduling clubs, constituted by the principal creditor countries involved, e.g., the "Paris Club" and the Hague Club. The idea behind these clubs was to share equally among its members the burden of refinancing and also to adopt a uniform position in relation to the debtor country. Brazil had to face this kind of negotiation in 1953, 1961 and 1964.

## The Second Vargas Government and the Commercial Arrears (1947–1955)

It was the time of "the world dollar shortage", and private capital exports from developed countries from 1947 to 1954 achieved only 50 per cent of the 1920's volume. Developing countries were very dependent on official loans and grants. Due to developing countries' developmental effort and the related import burst, it's a time of lower priority on reserve accumulation.

We are considering the period under study stable in the sense that the economy kept its path of growth despite the inflation peak of 25.6 per cent in 1954. Politically, however, the final two years were extremely unstable, chiefly in mid-1954 when Vargas was overthrown and committed suicide in August.

Getulio Vargas (1951–54) was elected in October 1950. He had made clear during his election and in the beginning of his term that his government would not be liberal to the international capital as was his predecessor Eurico Dutra (Malan 1985: 72). In January of 1952, the Vargas government decided to impose restrictions on profit remittances. This severely affected the relations of the US[7] and Brazil.

In the end of 1952, as previously reported, Brazil amassed US$ 541 million commercial arrears, with the U.S. exporters and European exporters being its principal creditor. On the external front, Vargas had to face an interruption of external financing. Skidmore (1967: 117) remembers that in 1953, the Joint United States-Brazilian Economic Commission was terminated as the Truman government[8] was replaced by the Eisenhower administration. The new administration was "openly suspicious of the need for any special measures to aid in the economic development of the poorer nations."

Additionally, Vianna (1987: 17) reports about the intention of the World Bank to influence more deeply the economic policy of the borrowing countries. The foreign exchange crisis of the end of 1952 furnished the ammunition for the argument of the World Bank.

During the negotiations of the US$ 300 million loan from the Eximbank to pay the US exporters arrears, Vianna raised an important point. The author (Vianna 1987: 87) stressed the conflict between the Eximbank and World Bank. While the first one was susceptible to the lobby of American exporters, the second one to the claims of the New York banking community. While the U.S. government was pro-World Bank, the Congress was pro-Eximbank.

During the exchange crisis at the end of 1952, the World Bank wanted to intervene in the Brazilian economy and was against the US$ 300 million loan from the Eximbank. The Eximbank was acting in the interests of the U.S. exporters and was not in favor of the intervention proposed by the World Bank. In the end, the American exporters succeeded in lobbying the US Congress and in April of 1953 the loan was approved despite the resistance of the US Government. Due to World Bank pressure, the loan carried hard conditions for Brazil.

The US$ 541 million commercial arrears of 1952 was related in a major part to the acquisition of capital goods and the equipment needed to maintain the industrialization drive[9]. In the case of USA, commercial arrears were covered through US$ 300 million loan from Eximbank. In the case of England, a loan was made with the Bank of London in 1953 for the amount of US$ 158 million. The negotiations involving the refinancing of these arrears are very important for the subject matter of our dissertation.

As reported by Sprott (1965: 83), many of these commercial arrears were related to orders from the private sector, which anticipated that adequate exchange would be available in the exchange auctions. As reported previously, in the exchange rate system of 1948–1953 import licenses meant big profits. Licenses were granted on the basis of estimated quantities of exchanges likely to be available in US dollars.

Since the exchange was not available, this short-term private debt, due to the negotiations that followed, magically turned on the largely increased public medium and long-term debt that jumped from US$ 638 million in

1952 to US\$ 1159 million[10] in 1953. That is, the Brazilian State ended bailing out the risk of the private sector.

**The commerce and industry association of New York protested to the Brazilian Ambassador that American business confidence was being jeopardized by the slowness to bail out exporters-*exporters, it should be remembered whose bad judgement of a financial situation alone accounted for their difficulties, a mistake in judgement for which presumably the Brazilian government was not to blame* (Hansen 1953: 28).**

## Planned Import Substitution (1956–1962)

The dollar shortage debate associated with the Triffin dilemma dominated discussion in the 1950s and early 1960s. After 1955, together with balance of payments loans, suppliers' credit became a major source of financing for developing countries. According to Guth, a decisive factor for the large share of supplier's credit was that exporters were able, in the majority of industrial countries, "either to use credit facilities of government-subsidized institutions or at least to offset their own risk by relying to a considerable extent on government guarantees"(Guth 1963: 35). The large share of this type of financing in developing countries gave rise to concern since the usual term of these loans is 5 years. Guth also observed that long-term private loan finances to developing countries had almost disappeared during this period.

The high rate of growth and the high instability that characterized the years of 1956–1962 was reflected in the increasing rate of inflation. The Kubitschek government (1956–1960) relied strongly on supplier's credit to finance the imports of the Target Plan. Donnelly (1970: 141) reports that in 1960, the suppliers' credit[11] represented 38 per cent of the total external debt (Group I and II) or 58 per cent of private resources accounted as project credits.

On March 15 1961, the president Quadros' new government promoted the devaluation by 100 per cent (Skidmore: 389). In April 1961, this government started to negotiate a rescheduling agreement[12] with other institutions such as the "Hague Club" and the Eximbank.

To explain how the Brazilian government bailed out the private sector, the major borrower of suppliers' credit, we go back once more to the excellent research work provided by Donnely (1970). When he presents the breakdown of the external debt of Brazil (Donnely 1970: 96) we see that balance of payments credits (compensatory finance) jumped from US\$ 600 million per year, from 1954 till 1960, to US\$ 1115 million in 1961. This sudden increase is the result of the debt rescheduling program promoted by the Quadros

Government. To better understand the bail out process promoted by the Brazilian state we quote Donnelly, bearing in mind that "compensatory credits" (balance of Payments loans) are obtained only by countries' governments:

> **The rescheduling agreement that resulted provided from relief over a five-year period, 1961–1965. As obligations on supplier's credit came due to exporters in the various countries, Brazil received fresh loans (i.e., refinancing credits) from these governments in order to meet its obligations on schedule. Since these refinancing were really balance of payments loans, the liquidation of suppliers' credits- was thus accompanied by an increase in compensatory credit accounts as medium-term loans for *balance of payments support*** (Donnely 1970: 145).

## President Goulart and the Generals (1962–64)

In the words of Celso Furtado, a member of the Goulart government (1962–1964), the financial minister of this government, pressed by the IMF, BIRD, the Hague Club and Washington, had to renegotiate the foreign debt every three months and they seriously considered the alternative of rupture with IMF, as did Kubitschek (Bandeira 1978: 93). By early 1963, the president was inclined to a moratorium since the debt service became unbearable (Bandeira 1978: 109). The crisis that ended in the military overthrow of the elected president in the end of March 1964 is common knowledge and is outside the scope of our research. However, the negotiations and the rescheduling agreement of July 1964 reinforce our point about the shifting character of the Brazilian state.

As Donnely (1970: 150) stresses, this agreement covered basically medium term project credits of roughly US$ 385 million falling due over a two-year period. Official project credits represented 24 per cent, and the remaining 76 per cent were suppliers' credit, whose breakdown against the total is as follows: Extended Hague Club (Japan) – 46 per cent; the U.S. – 30 per cent.

In general, the mechanics of the refinancing with the majority of the creditor countries worked as follows: resources from individual governments, through official credits were available for 70 per cent of the debt service payment due in 1964 and 1965. The remaining 30 per cent the country was supposed to remit. Provided that Brazil would make debt service payments to original creditors in full, "the official agencies of these countries would, once proof of payment was presented, extend credits to the Banco do Brasil in amounts equal to the 70 per cent of the effected remittances" (Donnely

1970: 145). Since the Banco do Brasil was the country's monetary authority it is easy to see the mechanics of the state assuming the private sector debt.

When we compare the 1961 and 1964 rescheduling agreements, it's relevant to mention that in 1961 the refinancing was available without evidence of payments to the exporters. However, the total debt relief for 1964 and 1965 was roughly three times that of 1961.

Finally, to stress our point of the State bailing out private credits related to suppliers' credit, we quote Diaz-Alejandro, a major researcher of Latin America economy during this time:

**One may question the desirability of mechanism used in industrialized countries, first to promote their exports of capital and other goods by liberal use of official insurance and credit schemes, and then to pressure recipient countries to consolidate private bad debts that are thus transformed into public debt on both the exporting and importing side, this system reduces entrepreneurial risk incentives to refine cost-benefit calculations and objectively to evaluate commercial risks.** Diaz-Alejandro (1971: 449).

### The Return of Private Bank Loans and the Debt Crisis (1968–1982)

The increasing nationalization of the Brazilian external debt in the 1970s is of common knowledge likewise the burden of the Brazilian external debt in the 1980s. This burden was translated mainly by the exponential increase of the country's public internal debt and the consequent fiscal crisis engendered by it. Therefore, the following two sections just show a brief summary of the classical analysis presented by Cruz (1983) and Nogueira Batista (1983) on the subject of the shifting character of the Brazilian state in the 1968–1982 period.

### The Brazilian Economic "Miracle" (1968–1974)

Since 1966 there was no need for compensatory loans due to the positive inflow of autonomous capital and foreign direct investment (FDI). It is also relevant to mention that private bank loans replaced the supplier's credit of the late 1950s and early 1960s.

Pereira (1974:7) reports that the government intervention during this phase, coined as the "debt administration phase", was to adapt the country legislation to changes that were taking place on the international capital markets. As previously reported, private sector was responsible for 67 per cent of the total external debt. The information bellow illustrates this fact:

From 1966 to 1971 the breakdown of the external credits was as follows: 48 per cent import financing and 52 per cent international private banks credits. At least 65 per cent of the import finance was related to public sector and state controlled companies' investment in infrastructure and civil construction (Pereira 1974: 194). Regarding the bank loans, we have an opposite situation with at least 73 per cent of the private bank credits driven to the private sector.

## The Nationalization of the External Debt (1975–1982)

Swedberg (1987: 327) reports that debts of non-oil developing countries in 1974 were about US$135 billion. In 1982, at the time of the debt crisis that started with the default of Mexico in August, these debts skyrocketed to US$ 500 billion in nominal terms and over 30 countries were in default. At the end of 1982, short-term debt amounted to about US$ 130 billions. Brazil, for instance, was rolling over about US$ 10 billion on a day-to-day basis. The Brazilian economy was captured (together with other developing economies) by international capital movements in search of new markets.

The Brazilian economy embarked on an ambitious import substitution program when the world economy was managing the result of the oil price shock. The growth-cum debt strategy resulted in an increasing external debt.

An impressive fact of the Brazilian external debt during the 1970s was the increasing "nationalization" of foreign obligations that started to take shape in 1977. This debt starts predominantly as a private debt[13] and during the decade is transformed into public external debt. In 1975, the private sector share on external debt dropped to 50 per cent, while by the end of 1980, the public sector was responsible for almost 77.5 per cent of the external funding obtained in 1980 (Cruz 1983: 72). From 1977–1978, the public companies started to fund themselves with foreign loans. They were used as a vehicle to roll over the foreign debt. The Central Bank required the banks to lend the public sector (including state-owned companies) at least 30 per cent of their assets. It's not the projects anymore that attracted the financing but the need to roll over the external debt that "create" the projects.

Another major element in the process of "nationalization" of the external debt was the introduction, in September 1977, of RES. 432. Basically, RES. 432 established a device of "socializing" the losses related to more accentuated exchange rate devaluation. For instance, in the case of companies indebted with foreign loans, this device proved to be very helpful by the time the "maxidevaluation" occurred in the end of 1979 (Cruz 1983: 89).

The original intention of RES. 432 was to reduce the increase of the monetary base due to capital inflows. RES. 432 allowed the banks involved in the lending of external resources to transfer their hard currencies debt to the Central Bank which in turn become responsible for almost all the costs involved. In this way, the Central Bank assumed the position of the lender of last resort. The purpose of this device was to match the management of the external debt profile (minimum term for amortization of 8 years), with the short-term credit demand (minimum tenor of 3 months). If the banks could not get clients to borrow from their hard currency lending (minimum tenor of amortization of 8 years), they always had the possibility of depositing these idle resources at the Central Bank. Thanks to this device, the banks that operated with RES. 63 type of loan (bank intermediate loans) were almost free from the exchange risk; in the absence of a client there was always the possibility of transferring the risk to the Central Bank (Nogueira Batista 1983:140).

In 1982 when the external debt crisis erupted, the public sector was responsible for more than 70 per cent of the external debt, and the idea of socializing the losses and privatizing the profits, inaugurated with the Taubate Convention in 1906, was present once more. That is, the Brazilian public sector, that was forced to be involved in debt rollover in 1977–1978, had to manage alone the burden of heavy debt in a very unfavorable international situation. To make a long story short, these large amounts of external debt "were converted" into internal debt that in turn became the principal problem faced by the Brazilian economy in the 1980s.

## The Return of Compensatory Finance 1994–1998

A significant development in global finance in the 1990s is the growth of international portfolio investment (PI) in emerging markets. The growth of portfolio investment in Latin America, replacing the bank lending which precipitated the debt crisis of 1982, has reduced the credit constraint under which these economies have suffered since the early 1980s. It also opens the door for new attempts of stabilization. In the 1990s, capital inflows combined with high economic activity and exchange rate appreciation favored stability.

Latin America region remained practically isolated from international capital markets from the time of 1982 Mexican moratorium and the signing of the first Brady Plan to the restructuring of the external debt of Mexico in 1990. One can say that the resolution of the debt crisis of 1982 was obtained via "securitization" (Brady Plan) and conversions. The Brady Plan was implemented by official agencies such as IMF, World Bank and U.S. Treasury. The debt with international banks, related to the 1982 debt crisis was "securitized" by its value on the secondary market, roughly 50 per cent of its book value. This debt were negotiated and transformed into bonds. That is, the countries issued bonds (15 to 20 years maturity) backed by this debt. These bonds carried as a collateral US T bonds.

By 1993, the fall of international interest rates had eased the external debt burden and led to an agreement with creditor banks. This agreement was concluded in April 1994. Brazil was a latecomer to the Brady agreement; the exchange of instruments in debt stocks and arrears amounted to US$12.1 billion debt with the Paris Club and to roughly US$ 47.7 billion in commercial bank debt restructuring.

In December 1997, Brazilian government granted a US$ 1 billion credit line, for companies operating in the stock market, to buy their "undervalued" share due to the Hong Kong stock exchange turmoil of the second week of November. This follows a pattern of coffee valorization schemes of the beginning of the century, since the government was bailing out private losses. That is, in the risk of stock exchange crash the State was pressed to assume all the losses. For the time being the data available is small. However, this move tends to be bigger since an important share of the short-term capital flow was driven to the easy gains on the Brazilian stock exchange market.

At least until 1997, roughly fifty per cent of the registered public debt is related to the external debt carried over from the 1980s. This debt was negotiated and transformed into bonds (Brady Plan), that is, US$ 47 billion debt restructuring with commercial banks and US$ 12 billion with the Paris Club. If we discount from the registered debt of the public sector (as a rough estimate) US$ 55 billion per year from 1994 to 1997 and US$ 45 billion from

**Table 1: Gross External Debt (US$ Billion)**

| Year | 1992 | 1993 | 1994 | 1995 | 1996 | 1997 | 1998 | 1999 |
|------|------|------|------|------|------|------|------|------|
| **Registered** | 110,8 | 114,2 | 119,7 | 129,3 | 144 | 163,3– | 203 | 203 |
| **Nonregistered** | 25,1 | 31,4 | 28,2 | 29,9 | 35,8 | 36,7 | 21,2 | 22,2 |
| **Gross** | **135,9** | **145,8** | **147,9** | **159,2** | **179,9** | **200** | **224,2** | **225** |

*Source*: For 1992 to 1995 Boletim do Banco Central (BBC), November 1996; for 1996 to 1997 BBC (June 1999); for 1998 to 1999, Boletim do Banco Central (BBC) Maio 2002.

**Table 2: Private and Public Sector Share in the Gross External Debt in Percentage**

| Year | 1992 | 1993 | 1994 | 1995 | 1996 | 1997 | 1998 | 1999 |
|------|------|------|------|------|------|------|------|------|
| **Public** | 69 | 62 | 59 | 57 | 47 | 38 | 42 | 48 |
| **Private** | 31 | 38 | 41 | 43 | 53 | 62 | 48 | 52 |

**Table 4: Private and Public Share on the Registered Debt in US$ Billions**

| Year | 1992 | 1993 | 1994 | 1995 | 1996 | 1997 | 1998 | 1999 |
|---|---|---|---|---|---|---|---|---|
| **Public** | 86,6 | 83 | 87 | 90 | 84 | 76 | 92 | 97 |
| **Private** | 23,4 | 30 | 33 | 39 | 60 | 92 | 110 | 106 |

*Source*: For 1992 to 1995, Boletim do Banco Central (BBC), November 1996; for 1996 to 1997, BBC, June 1999; For 1998 to 1999, Banco Central annual Report, 1999.

**Table 5: Private and Public Share on the Registered Debt in Percentage**

| Year | 1992 | 1993 | 1994 | 1995 | 1996 | 1997 | 1998 | 1999 |
|---|---|---|---|---|---|---|---|---|
| **Public** | 78 | 73 | 73 | 60 | 58 | 45 | 46 | 48 |
| **Private** | 22 | 27 | 27 | 40 | 42 | 55 | 54 | 52 |

1998 to 1999, the total debt of the public sector incurred in the 1990s would be as follows:

**Table 6: Adjusted Gross Public Debt in US$ Billions**

| Year | 1992 | 1993 | 1994 | 1995 | 1996 | 1997 | 1998 | 1999 |
|---|---|---|---|---|---|---|---|---|
| **Public Debt** | 86,6 | 83 | 31,6 | 35 | 29 | 21 | 47 | 52 |

*Source*: Tables 5 and 6.

It is important to mention that almost all the nonregistered debt until 1999 are from the private sector (related mainly to trade finance credit lines). Therefore, we can conclude that the *flow* of the Brazilian external debt in the period was driven to the private sector. The chart bellow illustrates this point:

**Table 7: Gross Private Debt in US$ billions**

| Year | 1992 | 1993 | 1994 | 1995 | 1996 | 1997 | 1998 | 1999 |
|---|---|---|---|---|---|---|---|---|
| **Private Debt** | 42,1 | 55,4 | 60 | 68 | 95 | 124 | 107 | 117 |

*Source*: Tables 2 and 3.

In the second half of 1998, the foreign exchange situation of Brazil became critical. The uncertainty increased and the private creditors of the country resisted to rolling over the debt that was becoming due. This fact, among others, explains the heavy loss of reserve experienced during this period. On the other hand, the negotiations underway with IMF, US Treasury, World Bank, etc, were signaling in the direction of a big financial rescue package. Therefore the conditions for a new wave of "debt nationalization" with the government bailing out the private sector were underway.

## 1999–2005

From 1999 to 2002 Brazil faced several speculative attacks, with the more important ones being the following: a) the forced devaluation of the Real with the adoption of the floating exchange rate regime in February 1999; b) September 11 terrorist attack in the U.S in 2001 with its repercussions to the emerging markets; c) the Argentinean meltdown in the first semester of 2002; d) the uncertainty associated with the presidential elections in October. The country has signed several agreements with the IMF involving resources in the amount of US$ 86 billion (US$ 41,5 billion in 1998–1999, U$ 15 billion in August 2001 and US$ 30 billion in September 2002). From this amount, US$ 55 billion were disbursed in 2005, when Brazil paid in advance its debt with IMF.

The Table 8 below illustrates the "nationalization of the Brazilian external debt". This aspect becomes clear if we consider that the share of the public sector in the Gross External Debt started to increase from 1998 onward. However, more relevant is the presence (for the first time in the 1990s) of compensatory finance from 1998 onward. As a result of the several "rescue packages", the country disbursed US$ 55 billion from the IMF. That is, the "nationalization" of the Brazilian external debt in the 1990s, contrary to similar process in early 1980s, follows the same pattern of the resembling process in the early 1960s.

## Table 8:  Brazilian External Debt from 1998 to 2005

|                              | 1998  | 1999  | 2000  | 2001 | 2002  | 2003 | 2004  | 2005  |
|------------------------------|-------|-------|-------|------|-------|------|-------|-------|
| Gross External Debt          |       |       |       |      |       |      |       |       |
|   (GED) in USS billi (1)     | 224   | 225   | 217   | 210  | 211   | 215  | 201   | 169,4 |
| Public in US$ bill. (2).     | 92    | 101   | 100,5 | 103  | 110,5 | 111  | 125,2 | 96    |
| Public %                     | 42    | 45    | 46    | 54   | 52    | 52   | 62    | 57    |
| Private in US$ billi (3)     | 128,8 | 124,8 | 116   | 106  | 90,1  | 79   | 76,1  | 73    |
| Private in %                 | 58    | 55    | 54    | 46   | 48    | 48   | 38    | 43    |
| IMF(4) in US$ billi.         | 9,4   | 12,3  | 1,8   | 8,3  | 21    | 28   | 25    | 0     |
| GED % GDP (5)                | 28,4  | 42    | 36    | 41,2 | 45,9  | 42,4 | 33,3  | 21,4  |

(1) *Source*: for 1998 and 1999, Boletim do Banco Central (BCB), May 2002; for 2000 and 2001, BCB May 2004; for 2002 to 2005, May 2006. (2) *Source*: the same as (1) but from 2000 onwards adding "setor publico financeiro" (public financial sector) obtained from Banco Central do Brasil Annual Report (BCBAR) for the respective year. (3) *Source*: the same as (1) but from 2000 onwards subtracting "setor publico financeiro" (public financial sector) obtained from Banco Central do Brasil Annual Report (BCBAR) for the respective year. (4) *Source*: BCBAR 2001 and 2005, for 1998 and 1999 includes BIS loans of respectively US$ 4,7 bill. and US$ 3,1 billion; (5) *Source*: BCBR 2005 for 2001 to 2005, Remaining years, "Indicadores Economicos" of the Brazilian Central Bank as of March 2003.

## Conclusions

Historically, the Brazilian state bailed out the debt of the private sector during instable sub-periods. This was the case of 1920–1931, 1956–1962 and 1975–1982. The nationalization of the external debt is a consequence of an increasing economic instability coped with an increasing external debt of the country. The increasing share of the public external debt can be seen as a sign of a forthcoming debt crisis.

As for the current period (1994–2005), if we regard the impact of the IMF package loans, we can see that the country would not close its external account from 1998 onwards without "burning" additional strategic foreign exchange reserves. As we saw in Section 3, the use of compensatory financing is a sign of the return of historical process of the Brazilian State bailing out the external debt of the private sector. This aspect become clear if we consider that the share of the public sector in the gross external debt started to increase one more time in 1998. That is, the "nationalization" of the Brazilian external debt in the 1990s, contrary to similar process in early 1980s, follows the same pattern of the resembling process in the early 1960s.

## Notes

1. In Latin America economies it is very difficult to find five-year periods of stability. That is why we are using the term "relative stability."
2. For Oliveira (1977:16), the coffee production, responsible for an important share of the external debt, was a kind of production that consumed itself in its own financing.
3. The rubber production faced a crisis in 1910 due to the competition that never recovered.
4. James (1992: 596), reports that in 1911–13, the average annual capital export of Britain, German, France and the U.S. to the rest of the world was $1400 million. In the period 1924–28, when capital flows were at their greatest, the annual figure was $860 million (or $550 million in prewar prices).
5. The second valorization program, funded with federal government credit, was adopted during World War I and lasted from 1917 to 1920.
6. One sack of coffee equals 60 kilograms or 132 pounds.
7. As a background, Vianna (1987: 67) informs us that between 1949 and 1954, the net investment in manufacturing by the USA in Brazil represented 53% of the USA's manufacturing investment in Latin America and 17 per cent of its world wide investments in this sector (34 per cent if Canada is not included). Therefore in response to several pressures that were created, the "free foreign exchange" market was included in the Res.70 of Sumoc of February 1953. The Vargas Administration established a "free"cruzerio market, which could be used for the unlimited remissions of profits by foreign investors.
8. Through its Point Four Program the Truman Government was sympathetic to the financial problems of developing countries. The technical studies by the Joint Commission were developed from July 1951 to July 1953.

9. According to Bresser Pereira (1984: 23), the Brazilian exchange system between 1947 and 1953 was transformed into a powerful stimulus to industrialization.

10. In most instances, importers who had received import licenses were able to pay the cruzeiro counterpart to the Banco do Brasil. But owing to the insufficiency of foreign exchange, the Banco do Brasil was unable to pay foreign exporters when presented with import documents for collection. The subsequent accumulation of commercial arrears, which, in effect, constitute loan "forced" from foreign exporters took the form of official short-term debt (Group IV) since they represented the official responsibility of the BB (Donnelly 1970:99).

11. 9 per cent of all suppliers' credits outstanding was related to six countries, with U.S. credits responsible for 30 per cent.

12. The terms of the agreement and the amount involved can be found in Cabral (1962: 300).

13. The large local companies and shiftily the multinational companies were the major ones responsible for the first cycle of external borrowing in the 1970s (1969–1973).

## Bibliography

ABREU, M. de PAIVA (1973).. *The Niemeyer Mission: an episode of British financial imperialism in Brazil* (University of Cambridge, Centre of Latin American Studies, Working Paper no. 10, Cambridge).

BANCO CENTRAL do BRASIL (1999). Boletim do Banco Central do Brasil.

BANDEIRA, L. A. Moniz (1978). O Governo João Goulart. Rio de Janeiro: Civilização Brasileira, 4th edition.

BATISTA Jr, Paulo Nogueira (1983). *Mito e Realidade na Divida Externa Brasileira*. São Paulo: Editora Paz e Terra.

CABRAL, Castilho (1962). *Tempos de Jânio (e outros tempos)*. Rio de Janeiro: Civilização Brasileira.

CRUZ, Paulo Davidoff (1984). *Divida Externa e Política Econômica*. São Paulo: Brasiliense.

DELFIM NETTO, A. (1979). *O Problema do Café no Brasil*. Rio de Janeiro: Ed. Fundação Getulio Vargas.

DIAZ ALEJANDRO, C. F. 1971. "Some Aspects of the Brazilian Experience with Foreign Aid." In Bhagwati, J. N. et all (eds.). *Trade balance of payments and growth*. Amsterdam: North Holland.

DONNELY, J. T. (1970). *External Debt and Economic Development in Postwar Brazil, 1947–1966*. Unpublished doctoral dissertation submitted to the Vanderbilt University.

EATWEEL, J. and Taylor, L. (1998). *International Capital markets and the Future of Economic Policy*. CEPA Working Papers Series III, No 9. New York; New School for Social Research.

EICHENGREEN, B., *Elusive Stability: Essays in the History of International Finance, 1919–1939*, New York: Cambridge University Press, 1990.

FAUSTO, B. (1985). "Expansão do Café e Política Cafeeira". In Fausto, B., org., *Historia Geral da Civilização Brasileira*. Tomo III Vol I.

FURTADO, C. (1963). *The Economic Growth of Brazil*. Berkley, University of California Press.

GUTH, W., *Capital Exports to Less Developed Countries*. Dordrecht-Holland: D. Reidel Publishing CH, Company, 1963.

HANSEN, B. (1961). *Foreign Trade Credits and Exchange Reserves. A contribution to the theory of international capital movements*. Amsterdam: North- Holland Publishing Company.

JORGENSEN, E. and SACHS, J., "Default and Recognition of Latin American Foreign Bonds." In Eichengreen, B. and Lindert, P.H.(eds), *The International Debt Crisis in Historical Perspective*, Cambridge, Ma: MIT Press, 1989.

Kindleberger, C. P., "The 1929 World depression in Latin America." In Thorp, R. (ed.), *Latin America in the 1930s: the role of the periphery in world crisis*, New York: St. Martins Press, 1984.

KRUGMAN, Paul (1998). "What Happened to Asia? Cambridge MA, Department of Economics, Massachusetts Institute of technology.

LEWIS, C., *America's Stake in International Investments*, Washington, D.C.: The Brookings Institutions, 1938.

LOVE (1980). *Sao Paulo in the Brazilian Federation 1889–1937*. Stanford: Stanford University Press.

MALAN, Pedro S. *Foreign Exchange Constrained Growth in a Semi-Industrialized Economy: Aspects of the Brazilian Experience, 1946–1976*. University of Berkley: Unpublished Ph. D. dissertation.

MARISCHAL, C., *A Century of Debt Cruses in Latin America: from independence to the Great Depression, 1820–1930,*. Princeton: Princeton University Press, 1989.

OLIVEIRA, F.C., *A Economia da Dependência Imperfeita*, Rio de Janeiro: Edições Graal, 1977.

PEREIRA, J.E. de C. (1974). *Financiamento Externo e Crescimento Economico no Brasil: 1966/1973*, Rio de Janeiro, IPEA/INPES 1974.

PEREIRA, L.C. Bresser (1984). *Development and Crisis in Brazil, 1930–1983*. Bolder, Color: Westview Press, 1984.

SKIDMORE, T.E. (1967). *Politics in Brazil, 1930–1964*. New York: 1967.

SPROTT, J. T. (1965). *The External Accounts and Debt Servicing of Brazil: 1950–1959* (unpublished Ph.D. dissertation, University of Colorado).

SUZIGAN, W. e VILLELA, A. V., *Política do governo e crescimento da economia brasileira*, Rio de Janeiro: IPEA/INPES, 1973.

Swedberg, Richard, " The impact of an exogenous event: The oil shocks, the private banks and the origins of the debt crisis", *International Social Science Journal*, August 1987, pp. 323–333.

TAYLOR , L. (1998). *Lax Public Sector, Destabilizing Private Sector: Origins of Capital Markets Crises*. CEPA Working Papers Series III, No 6. New York; New School for Social Research.

THORP, R. ed.(1984?). *Latin America in the 1930s: the role of the periphery in world crisis*. New York: St. Martins Press.

TOPIK, S. (1987). *The Political Economy of the Brazilian State, 1889–1930*. Austin: University of Texas Press.

UNITED NATIONS (1954). *The International Flow of Private Capital 1946–1952*. Department of Economic Affairs. New York: United Nations

UNITED NATIONS (1965). *External Financing in Latin America*. Department of Economic and Social Affairs- ECLA. New York: United Nations.

VIANNA, S.B. (1987). *A Política Econômica do Segundo Governo Vargas (1951–1954)*. Rio de Janeiro: BNDES.

# Chapter 10

# PRUDENTIAL REGULATION AND SAFETY NET: RECENT TRANSFORMATIONS IN BRAZIL

## Ana Rosa Ribeiro de Mendonça

CERI (Center of International Economics Studies) and NEIT (Center of Industrial and Technology Studies)

**Abstract**

This chapter examines the contributions that the original Basel Accord took and that Basel II might make toward changing the banking regulation framework in Brazil. It will be argued that risk weighted capital requirements imposed by the Original Accord, which took effect in 1994, meant not just an important change, but almost the creation of a bank regulation framework in Brazil. It will be argued that the adoption of Basel II may increase not only the concentration level, which is already very high, but also the participation of the foreign capital in Brazilian banking system.

**Introduction**

Financial markets are submitted to more well-developed regulatory and supervisory mechanisms than those found in other sectors of the economy, a fact that is explainable due to the features that are inherent to the nature of the transactions conducted within these markets. Among such features, one may point out those which would explain the sensitivity of financial institutions, and specially banks, to crises, and the possibility that contagious movements will irradiate from such institutions, causing a systemic risk. Bank institutions, jointly with the Monetary Authority, are members of the monetary system, they receive and create cash deposits, fully liquid instruments. They operate by leverage, i.e., their assets and liabilities are higher than their capital and, generally speaking, they act as term changers: the terms of the liability transactions are shorter than the terms of the asset transactions. Financial agreements are transactions which involve obligations and rights to be exercised at a future date: the value of the agreements will depend on the reliance that they will be performed. Certain considerations may be elaborated on taking such features as a starting point. These institutions play a central role in the credit and payments system, and credibility is an essential element for their operations, given the high degree of leverage and the absence of correlation between the terms of the respective transactions. Loss of credibility of the agents in a given institution may bring about adverse movements by the depositing public – withdrawing deposits not only from the specific institution, but also from other institutions, given the rationale of the *first come first served* principle – as well as by other institutions, a circumstance which may jeopardize the asset/liability relationship, even if the accounts are in fact balanced. Thus, contagion movements might be generated, even from balanced institutions, and may cause systemic problems. And problems of liquidity/solvency within the banking system may overflow to the system as a whole, given its importance for the working of the payment and receipt system and for the credit transactions generally, whether related to new credits or to re-financing of existing credits.

These considerations justify the more thoroughly developed regulation and supervision apparatus these institutions are subject to, the stated purpose of which is to ensure the health and solidity of the system, as well as the protection of small depositors. This apparatus may be considered from two different viewpoints. First, instruments and mechanisms that can be brought into action at times when problems have already come in to being, so as to mitigate their effects and avert contagion, typifying a protection network. Among these specially relevance must be ascribed to the monetary authority, as a last instance lender, and to the presence of deposit insurance coverage. Secondly, rules and regulations that represent the prudential and supervisory regulation apparatus, and which bolster the capacity of the system to avoid or to absorb the problems discussed hereinabove.

Prudential regulation implies establishing specific rules for the behavior of the agents and for the disclosure of information, which must be supplemented by monitoring and supervision rules.[1] Generally speaking, these are preventive rules, i.e., their foremost purpose is to abort potential problems.

For a number of decades, prudential regulation as adopted in a number of different countries attempted to minimize the possibility of problems occurring, by applying mechanism restricting the sphere of action of the institutions,[2] and which were essentially supported by the regulation and control of the balances. The sphere of action of the institutions was restricted and controlled by means of limits imposed on their portfolios of assets and liabilities. Among the issues addressed by this form of regulatory framework, specially relevance is ascribed to the (il)liquidity of the asset positions of the institutions as compared to their liability positions. In this form, the guarantee of the liquidity of deposits by imposing limits on the nature of the allotments banks are allowed to make and by stimulating the maintenance of reserves to cover drafts have at all times been part of the essential elements of such structures. Among the several instruments or mechanisms found within such frameworks, the following should be pointed out: limits to indebtness and to leverage; liquidity indexes;[3] limits on the exposure of banks to individual borrowers; limits as to the composition of assets and to the class of activities that each kind of institution could carry out.[4]

Over these last decades, however, the financial markets have undergone major changes, which have rendered inoperative a significant part of this ret of control and restriction rules for ensuring the balances. And these changes arose from an important movement in terms of innovations, deregulation and financial liberalization. A series of institutional innovations introduced by agents operating in the financial markets, an intense process of financial liberalization and deregulation of the markets have ended up by minimizing or even putting out of effective action rules and regulations limiting or restricting the scope of action of the financial institutions in their constant search for profitability and, in some cases, for liquidity. Among financial innovations, special mention should be made of the expansion and dissemination of derivative instruments, the intensification of the securitization process, which has contributed towards banking de-intermediation and towards a more flexible set up of the asset portfolios of the institutions, as well as strategies for diversifying the funding sources, i.e., the development of liability management processes based on which the importance of deposits as liability instruments decreases, thus reducing the efficiency of regulation based on indicators related to deposits.

Deregulation, in turn, by softening or even eliminating barriers between banking and non-banking institutions, has expanded the field of action of financial institutions, intensifying the movement triggered by the innovations.[5] The liberalization of capital flows across boundaries provided for a greater integration of the several domestic markets and the organization of international markets.

As the limits of the existing apparatus became evident, a reorganization of the framework for the behavior and supervision rules was initiated, so as to ensure the stability and solidity of the system, and to protect depositors through restrictions and limitations on the make up of the portfolios of the institutions, together with the understanding that in the search for profits, the agents of this market are encouraged to take excessive risks.[6] Although some of the instruments and mechanisms then in force were retained, the central issue of prudential regulation moved over to focus on the risks represented by the asset positions of the institutions. The rationale for this was that the threat to financial institutions and, ultimately, to the payment system as a whole stemmed from the risks undertaken in the investments made by the banks. The strategy of regulation ought therefore to set aside the profile of the liabilities of the banks and move over to the strategies for asset investments.

The requirement under which banks must maintain a minimum capital ration is a fundamental point in the new format of prudential regulation, and is presented by some authors as being part of a financial re-regulation. Under this requirement, the regulatory authority imposed on banks the obligation to maintain a minimum ration between capital stock and the assets in its portfolios. This ratio is called the *capital index*.

The major argument for justifying the widespread use of the capital index is the stimulus generated by the necessity banks will have to earmark part of their capital stock, which would weigh up against the perverse incentive for accepting excessive risks. Prudential regulation would therefore stimulate the maintenance of safer portfolios, by imposing minimum capital requirements, since in adverse situations not only savers but also the shareholders would bear the losses.

This rationale is central to the 1988 Basel Agreement, i.e., the necessity of maintaining minimum capital indexes, in which assets are weighted according to credit risks and, after, market risks. The adhesion to this Agreement ended up by acquiring a greater magnitude than that originally envisaged,[7] and meant that institutions had now to retain a capital pro rata not only to the actual volume of the asset positions, but also to their risks.

The New Capitals Agreement, published in mid-2004 retains the central concept, i.e., the need to maintain minimum capital indexes weight according to risk. But the new structure is much more complex than the preceding one, since it goes further in the direction of measuring risks, bringing into the framework more accurate methods for the measurement of risks – as implemented by the institutions themselves – besides the treatment afforded to operational risks, in addition to the already consolidated credit and market risks. Regulation and supervision are growling focused on the quality of the risk management and on the appropriateness of its measurement. The result is a system more sensitive to risk and to private understanding of risks, since it introduces market practices into the regulations.

## Brazil

The regulatory and supervision framework that governs the Brazilian financial system underwent a major process of changes in the course of the 1990s, and these changes must be analyzed as part of a more wide-ranging process of transformations which this system underwent, both in terms of the logics of its domestic functioning as well as in terms of its integration to the international system. Among these transformations in the environment in which financial institutions operate, the following should be highlighted: (i) the financial liberalization process, which allowed foreign capital to enter the system; (ii) the reduction in the rate of inflation, resulting from the implementation of the Real Plan, with its powerful impacts on the system as a whole, given the relevance of inflationary profits for financial institutions; (iii) a wide-ranging movement of mergers and takeovers, interventions and liquidations of private banks, extinction or privatization of a major part of the State banks, implying a major reduction in the public financial sector, an increased concentration in the sector, and the participation of foreign interests; and (iv) the restructuring of Federal financial institutions.

In the second half of the 1990s, the bank system became subject to a great vulnerability, as a consequence of the combination of a number of factors: end of the inflationary profits, expansion in credit and in default, and restrictive monetary and credit policies. In the face of this vulnerability, the Central Bank of Brazil (BCB) adopted a set of emergency measures to ensure the recovery of the system. But the changes in the regulatory framework were not limited to such emergency measures. The BCB also implemented a number of measures so as to improve its regulatory and supervision structure, in face of the new needs for controlling and monitoring the financial and capitals markets, i.e., it set up a framework focused on the need to provide risk measuring, evaluation and management, a circumstance which demonstrates its connection with the more general movement experienced by regulation and supervision, as seen hereinabove.

Thus, the second half of the 1990s witnessed important changes in prudential, safety and supervision regulation, and a discussion thereof is the topic of this section, to be preceded by a presentation of the regulatory framework in force before the changes came into being. Before going on, however, it is relevant to comment on the configuration of the regulatory and supervision authority. In Brazil, the BCB is responsible for regulating the supervision of a wide range of financial institutions, banks or otherwise, including investment funds (with the exception of share funds, which are regulated by the Securities Committee – CVM), brokers and distributors, financing institutions, etc., and carries out this function based on the guidelines defined by the National Monetary Board (CMN). Thus, almost all authorized financial institutions come under the umbrella of the BCB.

Up to the mid-1990s, prudential regulation was strongly focused on the liabilities of banking institutions, involving a mix of minimum capital and net equity requirements, a limit in the diversification of risks, a limit of immobilization (90% of the net equity) and a limit of indebtness (15% of the net equity) (Lundberg, 1999b). Although some of these instruments have been maintained, e.g. the immobilization limited and the minimum net equity requirement, a great change in focus was implemented, moving from liability transactions over to risk-weighted asset transactions.

The meaning of the prudential regulation in force at the time was quite different from that we observe in the present time, given the high rates of inflation prevailing up to 1994. If, on one hand, inflation rendered regulation based on balances somewhat complex, since it reduced the significance of the information contained in the balance sheets of the banks, on the other hand it provided profitability even for inefficient banks.

Banks benefited from the high rate of gains provided by floating and index arbitration transactions. The revenues generated under a high rate of inflation were in fact so important for banking institutions that they ended up by leaving at a second plane the financial results of their activities. Under these conditions, the need for regulations and supervision was diminished, since even fragile banks were profitable. In many cases, and specially in the first half of the 1990s, the gains obtained from floating transactions made up for administrative inefficiencies and for losses incurred with doubtful accounts, under a period in which the credit activities had also been reduced.

According to Moura (1998), the supervision apparatus in place at the time was inadequate to deal with banking problems, and this inadequacy was cloaked by a slack monetary policy, typical for inflationary periods. Thus, according to Moura, only stabilization would render the weaknesses visible. Among the typical problems of the time, the following should be underlined: (i) inadequate provisions for losses on loans; (ii) credit concentrated in certain sectors and regions; (iii) shareholding investments by banks in non-financial institutions; (iv) premature liberalization of the entry rules into the banking system; and, last but not least, (v) frauds and grievous difficulties in monitoring the non-financial institutions of the banks (Moura, 1998).

The framework of prudential regulation was fragile but consistent with the dynamics of the operation of the system, and there was no traditional system for insuring deposits, which does not mean there were not safety mechanisms, at least until the late 1980. In fact, before the 1988 Constitution was promulgated, the funds accrued in the Monetary Reserve were used for the purpose of providing guarantees for holders of deposit accounts with liquidated financial institutions and for conducting remedial operations in the financial system. This Reserve was set up with funds arising from the Tax on Financial Transactions (*Imposto sobre Operações Financeiras* – IOF), collected and used according to criteria defined by the CMN, which, in the mid 1970s, authorized the use of these funds for the purposes referred to in the preceding.[8] Thus, resources originated from taxation were used to provide depositors with guarantees, and for dealing with liquidated financial institutions, and were widely used for this purpose[9] In 1988, when the resources collected through the IOF were transferred to the National Treasury, the reserve fund was not longer refurbished. Thereafter, the existing safety network in fact lost its sinews, since it no longer count on its main source of revenue. During the first years of this new phase, this was not a major problem, given that even inefficient banks managed to be profitable as a result of the inflationary winnings.

The CMN and the BCB made a major effort to create and improve the regulation and the supervision rules, as well as to create instruments with which to structure a safety network. A number of changes introduced as from August 1994 demonstrate the range and the depth of the transformation completed and in course, within the framework of bank supervision and regulation. These changes can be divided into two major groups: remedial and emergency measures, some with a limited effective term, and structural measures, which aimed at organizing a set of rules which would ensure consistency between the institutions and the risks they undertook, a greater transparency in the transactions, more complex internal control mechanisms within the institutions, as well as a greater liability of the managers and owners of the institutions.

## Remedying the System: Emergency Measures

The fragility experienced by the banking system during the period immediately following the stabilization of prices brought to the forefront the difficulties arising from an inadequate prudential regulation and supervision structure, as well as the non-existence of a protection network. Initially, it was felt that the instruments existing at the time, based on intervention, extrajudicial liquidation and temporary special administration, together with actions to be taken by Federal financial institutions – particularly by the Banco do Brasil and the Caixa Econômica Federal – in the interbank market, by providing liquidity for institutions facing problems, would be sufficient to abort the possibility of systemic risk. But the need to intervene in major private banks rendered the greater gravity of the situation explicit.[10] To face this situation, the Federal government adopted a set of measures the purpose of which was both to create instruments that would minimize the systemic effects of an already existing adverse situation as well as to enable the Central Bank to take preventive action in situations of vulnerability. These measures included the creation of a program which stimulated the restructuring and strengthening of the Brazilian Financial System (PROER/Resolustion 2,208/95), of the credit guarantee fund (FGC/Resolution 2,197/95), and the enactment of Provisional Measure no. 1,182/95, subsequently converted into Law 9,447/97, which provided for an institutional split model, whereby the "good" and the "bad" bank could be separated.

The central ideal of the PROER was to provide for the piecemeal or total takeover of less efficient or insolvent institutions by other more efficient and adequately capitalized institutions. For this purpose, the purchasing banks were provided with a Central Bank credit line with which to carry out the administrative reorganization of the banks they took over, and benefited from a special tax treatment, providing for the deferment of losses and costs incurred in the transaction, including with the demobilization of assets. Access to this credit was subject to authorization by the Central Bank, and was granted on a case-by-case approach and upon the acceptance of a clear rule: the transfer of the controlling interest in the institution to be taken over, including to foreign capital institutions. It should be pointed out that under its efforts to restructure and strengthen the system, the BCB resorted to a legal loophole, whereby an increase in foreign participation in the system was permitted.

Concurrently, and so as to render possible the implementation of the PROER, the Federal Administration enacted Provisional Measure 1,182/95, which made it possible for an institution to be transferred in part or in full, and permitted its corporate reorganization. In the case of institutions subjected to special regimes (liquidation, intervention or RAET, the power to take this decision was conferred upon the intervener or liquidator, subject to prior authorization by the BCB. But the scope of the Provisional Measure had a wider reach. Whenever the BCB detected insufficient equity or financial means, which could eventually lead to a situation requiring intervention,[11] it could now take preventive action and order the capitalization of the institution, the transfer of its controlling interest or its corporate reorganization, including takeover, merger or split. The main innovation was the expanded scope of action of the BCB, formerly limited to decreeing special regimes, and which now gained the power to act before the situation worsened.[12]

This set of measures attempted to put in motion, in an orderly fashion and subject to rules defined by the BCB, a movement resulting in the takeover, split or merger of institution, in part or in full, and thus allow for market solutions to deal with the problems faced by certain institutions and which could generate systemic risks. The underlying logic was that the costs and risks for the system as a whole arising from the extinction of certain bank institutions, specially major banks, would be much greater than the costs of the operations. According to the BCB, the resources granted under the PROER amounted to R$ 20.36 billion, corresponding to 2.7% of the GDP of the period during which the program remained effective (1995/97) (Maia, 2003) (Table 1). In mid-2006, the credits held by BCB with the institutions under liquidation as a result of the PROER transactions amounted to R$ 41 billion (BCB, 2006).[13]

**Table 1: Proer: Values of the Transactions and Origin of the Capital of the Incorporating Banks**

| | Value of the Transactions (in billion current R$) | Mergers and Takeovers – Surviving Bank | |
| --- | --- | --- | --- |
| | | Domestic | Foreign |
| Major Banks | 14.06 | 3 | 1 |
| Minor Banks | 1.25 | 4 | 0 |
| Cash* | 5.05 | – | – |
| Total | 20.36 | 7 | 1 |

*Source*: BCB, apud Maia (2003).
* Financing for purchase of real estate portfolio.

The guarantee fund was created given the absence of an instrument providing insurance coverage for deposits or other similar mechanisms, as was the case of the Monetary Reserve funds up to 1988. The guarantee fund is a non-profit private entity, the purpose of which is to provided coverage for deposits and financial investments issued by the member institutions up to the value of R$ 20,000.00, in the event of an intervention, extrajudicial liquidation, bankruptcy, or when the BCB acknowledges that the issuer is insolvent.[14] The resources of the FGC stem from contributions paid by the member institutions, amounting to 0.025% of the monthly balances of the insured instruments. They were widely resorted to during the period immediately following the creation of the fund, given the vulnerability that affected certain banking institutions.[15]

Lundberg (1999b) presents an evaluation of the corrective process, and lists a number of positive aspects: (i) low cost as compared to other international experiences; (ii) the splitting model, as a counterpoint to the purchase model which had previously prevailed, implied a better definition of the liability of the former controllers and managers for the default; (iii) in the model adopted, the costs actually borne by the Government would be lower, given the possibility of at least a partial reimbursement from the assets of the former controllers and shareholders; and, finally, (iv) with the establishment of the FGC, not only was a vacuum in the regulatory scheme filled, but the losses incurred by the public administration were reduced, since the FGC is a private mechanism.

Despite the issues pointed out hereinabove based on the reading made by Lundberg (1999) concerning the results of the process under discussion, the remedial measures adopted not only averted a situation of overhanging crisis but were also successful in bolstering the health of the system, which emerged from the process with a higher degree of concentration and with a larger participation of foreign capital.

Still in what concerns the organization of the protection network, but taking into account the function of the monetary authority as the last instance lender, it should be noted that the enactment of the Law of Fiscal Liability (Supplementary Law 1001/00) has limited the capacity and the flexibility of the BCB in situations of vulnerability as those discussed in the preceding, making it difficult or unfeasible to set up programs similar to the PROER. In fact, in the chapter dealing with the allotment of public funds to the private sector, the law determines that any assistance to institutions belonging to the Brazilian financial system can only take place based on specific legislation and that the prevention of insolvency and of the risks inherent to the system must be dealt with employing private funds and instruments within the system itself, as is made clear in the following articles:

> Art. 28. Save as otherwise provided in specific legislation, no public funds, including credit transactions, may be used for assisting institutions pertaining to the Brazilian Financial System, even in the form of loans for recovery or funding of changes in shareholding control.
>
> § 1. The prevention of insolvency and other risks shall be undertaken by funds and other mechanisms to be set up by the institutions pertaining to the Brazilian Financial System, as provided in law.
>
> § 2. The provisions of the heading of this Art. 28 shall not hinder the Central Bank of Brazil from granting to financial institutions rediscount transactions and loans maturing in less than three hundred and sixty days.

## Improvements in Prudential Regulation

During this same period, a great effort was made to improve the framework of the prudential regulation and supervision in force within the Brazilian financial system. In order to discuss this effort and in and attempt to understand the format into which the regulation/supervision framework evolved, one may conceive of the changes along certain major axes: risk adequacy, information transparency and rules for access and internal control of the institutions. As for risks, several measures were implemented with the aim at setting up a set of more precise rules for risk measuring and evaluation. Among such measures, special mention should be made of the institution of capital requirements based on the asset positions of the institutions weighed by the risks undertaken, initially in terms of credit, then in market terms, and finally in operational terms, consistently with the stages defined under the Basel Agreements; the creation of a credit risk center an the new rules for provisioning against expected losses. As for the transparency of information, one must point out the measures that apply to the publication of quarterly information by the institution, as well as the disclosure of data in conformity with international rules, allowing for the consolidation of information by the *Bank for International Settlements* (BIS). Changes were also introduced in the rules governing access to the financial system, as well as stricter regulations concerning the qualifications and the obligations of officers and shareholders and the compulsory introduction of internal control systems.[16] Given the scope of this chapter and the relevance of risk adequacy to the current state-of-the-art of the regulatory framework, the discussion below will focus on the measures taken to address this issue.

As for the establishment of the regulatory norms, Resolution 2,099/94, which meant the adoption of the Basel Agreement, became a benchmark not only because of the changes it entailed in the format of the regulatory framework but also because it triggered a process under which a series of norms were set up, with the purpose of erecting a more precise framework for risk measuring and evaluation.[17] The adaptation of the regulatory structure to the Agreement implied certain major changes. Firstly, the change in the focus of the regulation, which put aside liabilities and net equity, and moved over to focus the asset positions of the banks. The traditional indebtness limit was replaced by a limit to asset positions, weighed according to risk, consistent with the changes in the focus of the regulatory structure as discusses in the preceding. Thus, banks had now to maintain an adjusted net equity of at least 8%, a rate which was subsequently increased to 11%[18] of their active positions weighed according to risk, as shown in Table 2.

Resolution 2,099/94 introduced relevant elements in the regulatory process also in terms of authorization for operation, of the transfer of shareholding control and reorganization of financial institutions, and in terms of the operation of facilities in the country.

As a result of these changes in the form of supervising the limits of operational leverage, moving from the liabilities to the assets weighed at risk, the amount of capital to be retained by the institutions was increased (Lundberg, 1999b).

In addition to such capital requirements related to the asset positions, banks must also retain a minimum capital to operate within the system, varying according to the type of institution. According to Moura (1998), such requirements would act as barriers to the entry of new institutions.

As claimed above, Resolution 2,099/94 was a benchmark, and initiated a process leading to a number of changes in the current regulatory framework, so as to render it consistent with the new domestic environment in which financial institutions operate and taking into account the changes proposed by the Basel Committee, always in the sense of providing rules that will ensure a more accurate risk evaluation and management. Further rules have subsequently been issued, especially in terms of risk evaluation, but also in the sense of ensuring a greater and better access to information, a regulation of the entry and

**Table 2: Risk Weights and Asset Transactions**

---

**No risk (0%)**
- cash
- deposits with the BCB
- Federal Treasury Bonds
- Term deposits with related institutions

**Reduced risk (20%)**
- bank deposits
- gold
- current foreign currency assets
- securities issued on the domestic market by financial entities of international bodies[1]

**Reduced risk (50%)**
- investments in foreign currencies, abroad
- State and Municipal Treasury Bonds
- securities of other financial institutions
- residential credits under normal circumstances

**Normal risk (100%)**
- loans
- debentures
- merchant leasing transactions
- currency transactions
- shares and investments
- pledges and guarantees

**Normal risk (300%)**
- Tax credits[2]

---

*Source*: CMN, Resolution 2,099/94.
1. Risk weighing instituted in 2002 by Circular Letter 3,140/02.
2. Initially, the weighing factor for tax credits was 100%. Given, however, the relevance of these credits in the balance sheets of certain institutions, the BCB decided to alter it to 300%.

maintenance of institutions in the system, the responsibility of officers and shareholders, and so on. Some of these changes will be discussed below, first and foremost in what concerns the measuring of risks and consistency with the amendment to the Base Agreement, under which market risks, in addition to the already considered credit risks, ought to be taken into account for the purpose of calculating capital requirements.

## a) Credit Risk Center (Resolutions 2,390/97 and 2,724/00)

Once this Center was set up, banks were compelled to identify and inform to the BCB the clients, whether natural persons or legal entities, owing them more than R$ 5,000.00, as well as the risk level of the transactions/clients, guarantees and credits already written off as losses.[19] The underlying notion is that such information will contribute towards strengthening supervision and ensure a better risk management by financial institutions, since they can be accessed whenever loan decisions are to be taken, "... *in the search for a reduction in the level of default and for a resulting increase in the volume of credit offered (credit bureau function)*" (BCB, 2002, p. 95).

## b) Risk Classification of Loans and Provisioning (Resolution 2,682/1999)

The purpose of this initiative was to render provisioning against losses more adequate to the risk profile of the credit transactions, since it now took into account a wider base and more prospective aspects, and not only late payments. Financial institutions had now to classify transactions in their credit portfolios and to set up provisions against expected losses in this portfolio based on the established criteria. For this purpose, not only did the credit transaction have to be evaluated and ranked according to features including value, purpose, type of transaction and guarantee, but also and specially the borrower and the guarantor of the transaction, taking into account aspects such as the debtor's ability to generate cash flow, the economic sector in which the debtor operates, macro-conditions and segment-bound conditions, etc.[20] The classification of the transactions must be reviewed from time to time in view of payments in arrears, and published in the balance sheets of the banks, so as to ensure a greater transparency in the information describing the risks of the credit portfolio of the relevant institution.[21] Furthermore, the BCB may order an additional provisioning in view of the liability of the borrower with the System as a whole, based on the information available at the Center.

## c) Diversification of Risk per Client (Resolution 2,844/01)

This mechanism imposes restrictions on the composition of the bank portfolios, by limiting exposure to individual borrowers to 25% of the equity of the institution. It attempts to ensure a minimum level of diversification, and avoid interrelated loans, since it prohibits credit transactions with owners and officers and their respective relatives.

## d) Treatment of the Market Risks

Among the risks that are addressed by the BCB rules are the exchange, liquidity and interest rate risks, as well as the credit risks of swap transactions. As for currency and gold transactions, the total divorce between the active and passive exposures was limited, and the institutions were compelled to maintain capital of their own related to such exposures, in conformity with the market risk amendment to the Basel Agreement. The calculation of the minimum requirements is now carried out apply an F risk factor to the exposure level and a maximum limit to the ratio between exposure and the reference equity was defined (Resolution no. 2,891).[22] The exposures to the risk represented by the variation in interest rates also became subject to capital requirements, calculated according to a method developed based on a VaR model (Resolution 2.92/00).

Defined by the BCB (Resolution 2,804, Art. 2) as "... *the occurrence of imbalances between negotiable assets and payable liabilities – a divorce between payables and receivables – which may affect the institution's payment capability* ...", the liquidity risk of the positions held by the institutions became the target of procedures aiming at the maintenance of control systems which will ensure a permanent supervision of the positions held on the financial and capital market.

The credit risk of swap transactions also came to be covered by capital requirements, in the form of aggregating to the net equity required the cost of replacing the agreements, calculated according to market marking and to potential future exposure (Resolution 2,399/97).

In December 2004, a few months after the Basel Committee issued the New Capitals Agreement, the BCB published Communiqué no. 12,746. In this document, the BCB sketched out the format of Basel II to be adopted in Brazil, as well as the schedule for its implementation. According to the BCB, "... *the Communiqué purports to adapt such* (Basel II) *guidelines to the conditions, specificities and development features of the Brazilian market*" (2005, p. 99). The guidelines laid down by this document are highlighted below, together with some brief comments.

As for the calculation of capital as related to credit risk, it was decided that the implementation of a simplified standard approach would be mandatory for all financial institutions. Thus, the BCB made it clear that the standard approach, as put together by the Committee, and supported by the evaluation conduction by external risk calculation agencies, would not be adopted in Brazil, which makes sense given that only a few of the agents active in Brazil are included in the ranking. The rationale for the simplified standard approach can be found in one of the Exhibits to the Basel II Agreement, and is, in fact, what one might term the turbinated Basel II. If, on one hand, the simplified approach is mandatory for all institutions, the larger institutions may choose to adopt the advanced approach based on internal risk evaluation models. The possibility of adopting different schemes for calculating the credit risk and the capital requirements may contribute to creating competitive unbalances between institutions of different dimensions. This is because the more accurate perception of risks to be attained by agents adopting internal models can or may lead to the need to maintain lower amounts of capital; given the costs involved in the development and implementation of internal models, this will more likely be implemented by the larger institutions, particularly foreign institutions, when safer borrowers are the target of the operations. In this manner, the adoption of differing rules may give rise to different competitive conditions for institutions using internal models. Another possible effect is that more fragile agents, whether in terms of size, segment or region in which they operate, may come to face a worsening in their conditions for accessing credit, in terms of volume or price.

**Table 3: Schedule for the Implementation of Basel II in Brazil**

| 2005 | | |
| --- | --- | --- |
| **Credit Risk** | **Market Risk** | **Operational Risk** |
| Review of the capital requirements for adopting the simple standardized approach. | Introduction of portions of the capital requirements established under the 1$^{st}$ Basel Agreement and still not provided for under the current regulations. | Development of market impact studies for the more simple approaches provided for under the New Agreement. |

| 2007 | | |
| --- | --- | --- |
| **Credit Risk** | **Market Risk** | **Operational Risk** |
| Definition of the eligibility criteria for adopting the approach based on internal classifications. | Definition of the eligibility criteria for adopting the approach based on internal classifications and plans for the validation of these models. | Definition of portions of the capital requirement under the Basic Method or under the Alternative Standardized Method. |

| 2008–2009 | | |
| --- | --- | --- |
| **Credit Risk** | **Market Risk** | **Operational Risk** |
| Definition of schedule for validating the approach based on internal classifications (Basic or Advanced IRB). | Introduction of portions of the capital requirements established under the 1$^{st}$ Basel Agreement and still not provided for under the current regulations. | Disclosure of the criteria for adopting the internal models. |

| 2009–2010 | | |
| --- | --- | --- |
| **Credit Risk** | **Market Risk** | **Operational Risk** |
| Validation of the approach based on internal classifications. | | Definition of schedule for validating the advanced approach. |

| 2011 | | |
| --- | --- | --- |
| **Credit Risk** | **Market Risk** | **Operational Risk** |
| | | Validation of the advanced approach. |

*Source*: BCB, Communiqué 12,746.

**Table 4: Basel II and the Simplified Standard Approach: Weighing the Credit Risk**

**Risk Weight 0%**
- availabilities in local or foreign currency
- investments in gold
- transactions with the BCB and with the National Treasury
- transactions with multilateral development entities
- advance payments of the FGC

**Risk Weight 20%**
- bank deposits, cash
- FCVS debts
- transaction rights of credit cooperatives

**Risk Weight 35%**
- real estate loans for residential properties, with chattel mortgage
- certificates of real estate receivables

**Risk Weight 50%**
- transactions with other financial institutions
- transactions with foreign governments and central banks
- other real estate financing transactions

**Risk Weight 75%**
- retail transactions

**Risk Weight 100%**
- credit transactions
- quotas in investment funds
- other active transactions

**Risk Weight 300%**
- tax credits

*Source*: Notice of Public Hearing no. 26 (July/2006).

As for market risks, the Communiqué includes the premises which were already provided for in the 1996 Amendment but which had hitherto not been inserted in the actual framework.

In conformity with Communiqué no. 12.746, highlighted in the preceding schedule, and after a delay of a few months, the BCB published a notice of a public hearing together with draft Resolutions to be submitted to the CMN, dealing with the revision of the capital requirements to be maintained by the institutions in view of their exposures to credit risks and to market risks.[23]

As for capital requirements related to the credit risk, the innovation was the creation of two additional risk weighing levels: (i) 35% for exposures to real estate financing (loan transactions for the purchase of residential property and real estate receivables certificates); (ii) 75% for exposures to retain loans, these being classified as credit transactions with minor agents, to a total value below 0.2% of the total retain portfolio, and not exceeding R$ 100,000.00. In fact, these innovations came as no surprise, since they are consistent with the provisions of Communiqué no. 12,746, which indicated the adoption of the simplified standard approach, i.e., a more complex version of the 1988 Agreement, which in Brazil was regulated by Resolution 2099/94, establishing further risk weighing levels. Furthermore, Basel II provides for different risk levels for real estate loans and retail transactions, in view of the benefits arising from the diversification of risks in such widespread portfolios.

In conformity with Basel II, the rules proposed in the notice take into account the effects of risk mitigation factors, e.g. guarantees, pledges, other instruments of personal guarantee, co-obligations in credit assignments, assignment in trust of securities, credit derivatives, as well as deposits in cash, gold and federal bonds, *inter alia*. When such instruments are used, the risk weighing factor is determined by these instruments. Thus, e.g., when a loan is guaranteed by the National Treasury, by the Central Bank, by Constitutional Funds or by multilateral Institutions, the risk weight factor of the credit will drop from 100% to 0%.[24]

Finally, as for the supervision of the system, some important changes have been implemented. The supervision of the financial system can be understood based on two aspects which motivate the actions of the supervising authorities, which, in the case of Brazil, is the Central Bank. Firstly, compliance with laws and regulations is verified; secondly, the BCB controls the financial health of the institutions. It is obvious that the two aspects are intimately related, given the logic underlining the regulatory framework, viz. to guarantee the health of the financial system. In Brazil, the supervision is conducted based on the regular flow of information provided by the institutions to the BCB,[25] called indirect supervision, and on direct action or field supervision, under which supervisors conduct an on site evaluation. Supervision has been conducted in a global, consolidated and continuous form, and is know as the consolidated global inspection (IGC). This implies an expanded inspection, involving a larger number of inspectors and which attempts, on a given base date, to determine the risk conditions at a global and consolidated level for a given group.

## Final Remarks

The regulation and supervision framework which governs the Brazilian financial system has undergone a major change process in the course of the 1990s, and such change must be understood as part of a wider process of transformations undergone by such system. The creation of protection mechanisms and instruments in the mid 1990s was successful inasmuch as it aborted a crisis that was becoming explicit. The BCB also implemented a major effort in creating a series of measures which represented the adaptation of its regulation and supervision structure to the new control and monitoring needs for the financial and capitals market, i.e., the setting up of a framework focused on the need to measure, evaluate and manage risks. The framework resulting from such changes is quite different from that which prevailed during the preceding period, and is much closer to the internationally prevailing standard. Since the changes were intensified, the system has gone through a context of great stability, with the exception of a few cases of intervention under the change in the foreign exchange system in early 1999, and more recently with the intervention in Banco Santos (2004). One may argue that such stability arises from the new format adopted by the regulatory framework, but, also, that this framework has not been put to test. The current challenge is to render Basel II operational: this is a process that is being scheduled and unfolded by the BCB and by the CMN in a step-by-step form, in view of the complexity of its implementation and the possible results on the system as a whole.

## Notes

1. The existence of a set of rules presupposes the existence of instruments whereby one may check whether these rules are being complied with, i.e., the monitoring and supervision rules. According to Llwellyn (1999), monitoring rules concern verifying compliance with the rules, whilst supervision rules are of a more general nature and concern the behavior of the institutions.

2. Some of these systems, e.g. in the USA, imposed geographical limitations and restrictions on the lines of products, limited the association of banks with other types of corporations, whether financial or otherwise. The logic behind the segmentation in the US regulatory structure was to avoid contagious movements among different markets.

3. Imposition of quantitative indicators for the purpose of determining permissible transactions, e.g. liquidity indexes based on the availability of primary and secondary reserves.

4. The latter applies specially when the financial system takes on a segmented format, i.e., with specialized institutions.

5. Banking institutions went over to operate in other markets and using other instruments, and this resulted in significant changes in the make up of their asset and liability portfolios.

6. Persaud presents a less naive discussion of this regulatory movement concerning risks, specially the most recent movement which aims at the measurement, evaluation and appropriateness of risks based on the understanding of the institutions themselves (Persaud, 2002).

7. The initial space for implementing the Basel Agreement was that represented by the internationally active banks of the G10. Finally, however, the Base rules were generally adopted by over 100 countries.

8. Law 5,143/66, which instituted the IOF, provided that the Fund to be set up with the resources deriving from such tax could only be used for intervening in the exchange and securities market, in assisting financial institutions, specially the BNDES, and under other circumstances to be defined by the CMN. The possibility of using these resources to provide guarantees for depositors and in remedial transactions was introduced by Decree-Law 1,342/74 (Lundberg, 1999b).

9. In the 1970s, these resources were used when Banco Halles went bankrupt and, more extensively, absorbed the losses of Banco União Comercial, which was taken over by Banco Itaú under a market transaction, and in several other situations. In the 1980s, they were employed in the course of the extrajudicial liquidation of three large private banks – Sul Brasileiro, Comind and Auxiliar (1985) – and under interventions in State banks (1987). For a more thorough overview of the volumes involved and the situations in which these resources were used, see Lundberg (199b).

10. The intervention in the Banco Econômico, in 1995, without any mechanisms for the protection of depositors, and the imminent intervention in Banco Nacional, which occurred in November of the same year, shortly after the enactment of the measures discussed hereinto. Up to then, a series of minor banks had undergone intervention and judicial liquidation, and a process of mergers and takeovers was in course. State banks had been submitted to temporary special administration (RAET).

11. The issues listed in the legislation included losses arising from reckless management, repeated infringements of bank law, and events that adversely affect the economic or financial situation of the institutions, which could eventually lead to its bankruptcy.

12. Another innovation introduced by Provisional Measure 1,182 was the expansion in the joint liability of the controllers, the extension of non-disposability to the controlling shareholders, and an acceleration of the possibility to expropriate the shares of banks facing difficulties.

13. This amount appears in the explanatory notes to the financial statements of the BCB as the fair market value related to the extrajudicial liquidations of the following banks: Nacional, Econômico, Mercantil, Banorte and Bamerindus. For the purpose of calculating the fair market value, the BCB takes into account the market value of the guarantees and the order of preference in payment defined by current legislation.

14. Instruments issued by institutions guaranteed by the FGC: cash, term and savings deposits; letters of exchange, mortgage, real estate and real estate credit instruments. At a later date (2004), the balances of investment accounts were included in the coverage afforded by the FGC, while judicial deposits were excluded.

15. The FGC faced a major financial problem in early 1997, when there was the need to guarantee the deposits with the Bamerindus. At that time, the FGC had available approx. 10% of the resources required. The solution was to grant a PROER loan to the intervener, guaranteed by the FGC (Lundberg, 1999b).

16. A major change found in Resolutions 2,723/00 and 2,743/00 refer to the financial statements of the institutions, which now are presented in a consolidated fashion, at the level of the financial group as a whole, which means with the inclusion of subsidiaries abroad.

17. The Basel Agreement was adopted in 1994, but the new rules became operative early 1995.

18. In 1997, the BCB increased the percentage first to 10% and then to 11%.

19. Initially, institutions were compelled to inform the Center of all credit operations equal to or in excess of R$ 50,000.00. This limit was gradually lowered until it reached

the current minimum value of R$ 5,000.00. According to Circular Letter 2,977/00, the following information must be provided: (i) client ID; (ii) total amount of debts outstanding, overdue and paid off (H risk); (iii) value of the co-obligations or guarantees undertaken; and (iv) risk level of the transaction (from AA to H).

20. When granting a loan, banks perform a credit analysis based on such criteria (applied to the borrower and to the transaction as such), whereupon the transaction is ranked at one of the 9 levels defined in the regulation: from AA (very low risk) to H (very high risk or default). The provisioning is defined according to the risk category in which the credit transaction is classified. Credits in arrears must be re-classified.

21. For instance, a transaction originally classified as A (requiring a provisioning of 0.5% of the value of the transaction) that is affected by a delay in payment between 15 and 30 days must be reclassified as B (requiring a provisioning of 1.0% of the value of the transaction. Thus, the bank must increase the provision to be retained for such transaction.

22. When this rule was first set up, the F factor was set at 100% and the maximum exposure limit was set at 30%. These parameters are, however, subject to changes and updating so as to become adjusted to the situation of exchange volatility prevailing in any given period (BCB, 2002).

23. Note that the content of such a notice is not necessarily final. The final wording will only be effectively known upon the publication of the respective CMN resolution. Nevertheless, this document most certainly indicates with sufficient clarity the general trend of the new rules for capital requirement.

24. Further details on the weighing factors to be considered upon the use of risk mitigation instruments can be found in the notice.

25. In Brazil, financial institutions must regularly provide information to the BCB, according to the rules defined by the Accounting Plan of the Institutions of the National Financial System (Cosif). The Cosif was created late 1987, with the purpose of unifying the several accounting plans existing at the time, and of standardizing the procedures for the registration and preparation of financial statements (BCB).

## References

BANCO CENTRAL DO BRASIL (BCB). Edital de Audiência Pública n. 26. Brasília, mai. 2006.
_____. Comunicado n. 12.746, de 9 de dezembro de 2004. Comunica os procedimentos para a implementação da nova estrutura de capital – Basiléia II.
_____. *Relatório de Estabilidade Financeira*. Brasília: BCB, mai. 2005.
_____. *Relatório de Estabilidade Financeira*. Brasília: BCB, nov. 2003.
_____. *Relatório de Estabilidade Financeira*. Brasília: BCB, mai. 2003.
_____. *Demonstrações Financeiras Sintéticas Intermediárias*. Brasília: BCB, jun.2006.
BASEL COMMITTEE ON BANKING SUPERVISION (BCBS). *International Convergence of Capital Measurement and Capital Standarts*. Basiléia, BIS, 1988.
_____. *International Convergence of Capital Measurement and Capital Standards*: a revised framework. Basle: BIS, 2004.
CARVALHO, F.C. Inovação Financeira e Regulação Prudencial: da regulação de liquidez aos Acordos de Basiléia. In: Sobreira, Rogério (org.), *Regulação Financeira e Bancária*. São Paulo: Atlas, 2005.
MOURA, Alkimar R. *A Study of the Banking Supervision in Brazil*. São Paulo, EASP/FGV/NPP. Relatório de Pesquisa n. 19, 1998.

MAIA, Geraldo V. S. *Reestruturação Bancária no Brasil*: o caso do Proer. Brasília: BCB, jun. 2003 (Nota Técnica do Banco Central do Brasil n. 38).

LUNDBERG, Eduardo. Rede de Proteção e Saneamento do Sistema Bancário. In: Saddi, Jairo (org.), *Intervenção e Liquidação Extrajudicial no Sistema Financeiro Nacional*: 25 anos da lei 6.024//74. São Paulo: Textonovo, 1999a.

————. Saneamento do Sistema Financeiro: a experiência brasileira dos últimos 25 anos. In: Saddi, Jairo (org.), *Intervenção e Liquidação Extrajudicial no Sistema Financeiro Nacional*: 25 anos da lei 6.024//74. São Paulo: Textonovo, 1999b.

LIMA, Gilberto. Evolução Recente da Regulação Bancária no Brasil. In: Sobreira, Rogério (org.), *Regulação Financeira e Bancária*. São Paulo: Atlas, 2005.

LLWELLYN, D. *The Economic Rationale for Financial Regulation*. London: FSA, apr. 1999 (occasional paper 1).

PERSAUD, Avanish. *Where Have all the Financial Risks Gone?* London: Gresham College, nov. 2002.

Chapter 11

# RE-CRAFTING BILATERAL INVESTMENT TREATIES IN A DEVELOPMENT FRAMEWORK: A COMPARATIVE REGIONAL PERSPECTIVE[Ψ]

## Biplove Choudhary
Asia Pacific Trade and Investment Initiative, UNDP Regional Centre for Asia and Pacific, Colombo, Sri Lanka

## Parashar Kulkarni
Formerly Research Officer, Centre for Trade and Development (Centad)

## Overview

### *Definition*

UNCTAD (2000) defines Bilateral Investment Treaties (BITs) as agreements between two countries for the reciprocal encouragement, promotion and protection of investments in each others territories by companies based in either country. BITs constitute to date the most important instrument for the international protection of foreign investment.[1]

While the specific elements of the treaties and the manner of their application differs across countries, typically the coverage of BITs extends to scope and definition of investment, its admission and establishment, national treatment, most favoured nation treatment, fair and equitable treatment, compensation in the event of expropriation, war and civil unrest or other damage to the investment, guarantees of free transfers of funds and

---

[Ψ] The paper has benefited by helpful comments received from Prabhash Ranjan and K.M. Gopakumar. The usual disclaimer applies.

recuperation of capital gains, and dispute settlement mechanisms both state-state and investor-state.

## Objectives

The proponents of BITs have sought to justify them in terms of the overall benefits in attracting Foreign Direct Investment (FDI). Cross border investments are seen as an important source of bridging the savings-investment gap and boosting economic growth in developing countries. They are thought to be important mechanisms for effecting technology transfer, employment generation and relaxing constraints on Balance of Payments. Profit remittances on account of foreign equity are related to the performance of investment projects unlike the inflexible repayment obligations of foreign debt. These supposed benefits from FDI have generated an intense competition amongst developing countries.

## BITS and FDI

It has often been claimed that BITs are an important mechanism to increase FDI flows. However, the evidence of the presumed linkage between BITs and inflow of FDI is of a contested nature. Thus based on an analysis of twenty years of data of bilateral FDI flows from the OECD to the developing countries, Driemeier (2003) argued that there is little evidence of BITS stimulating additional investment in host countries. Rather, BITs act 'more of a complement than a substitute for domestic institutions' leading to the conclusion that those that are benefiting from them are least in need of a BIT for demonstrating the quality of their property rights.[2] There is little discussion of the 'adverse' incentives to potential foreign investors or provision of insurance much beyond what the domestic investors enjoy with enormous impact on the policy choices available to host governments.[3]

Despite this, in recent years, countries are responding to increased global competition for FDI by becoming more proactive in their investment promotion efforts. For instance, the number of countries implementing investment-related policies, and the range of measures they used, have both grown rapidly over time.[4] Amongst the leading instruments of investment promotion, are investment agreements. While they do not contribute directly to increasing incentives to invest the way tax allowances, asset subsidies, etc. do they provide protection to foreign investment from risks such as expropriation and remittance control, which are perceived to exist in developing countries. International investment agreements come in various forms, primarily BITs and Double tax avoidance treaties (DTTs). In addition, investment chapters in FTAs and comprehensive investment cooperation agreements form other types of international investment agreements. Table 1 (Annexure I) details investment agreements based on the type and region of signatories, and type of agreements.

Overall, International investment agreements (IIAs) have proliferated at the bilateral, regional and interregional levels over the past decade. In 2005 alone, 162 international investment agreements (IIAs) were concluded, bringing the total number of IIAs to almost 5,500. BITs accounted for almost half of these agreements as seen in Figure 1 (Annexure I).[5]

Developing countries have also been active players in signing investment treaties and as outlined in Chart 1 (Annexure I), 30 percent of BITs signed until July 2004 were South-South BITs. In total, 113 developing countries have entered into BITs with another developing country. China, Egypt and Malaysia have each signed more than 40 such agreements, and have also signed more agreements with other developing countries than with developed countries.

Double Tax Avoidance Treaties also saw a rise as seen in Figure 2 (Annexure 1). The number of DTTs signed by 2005 has reached a total of 2700. The growth rate of South-South DTTs is particularly high. From 1990 to 2005, the number of South-South DTTs has increased from 96 to 312. India, China and Malaysia accounted for the largest number of such treaties.[6]

The remaining agreements were typically in the form of international trade and investment agreements. Since the last five years, such comprehensive treaties have seen a spurt. While the total number of PTIAs is still small compared to the number of BITs (less than 10 percent), they almost doubled during the past five years (Figure 3, Annexure 1). In addition, as of 1 July 2006, at least 67 agreements were under negotiation involving 106 countries.[7]

This is also the case in terms of advanced agreements such as comprehensive trade and investment treaties. For instance until July 2004, as outlined in Figure 3 (Annexure 1) only 7 percent of global trade and investment treaties did not involve developing countries. By 2004, the total number of PTIAs among developing countries had risen to 49, and 31% of all current PTIAs have been concluded between or among developing countries. This is a natural trajectory as developing countries increase their share in global inward FDI, and recently in outward FDI too. For instance in 2005, 57 transnational corporations listed in the Fortune 500 were from developing and transition economies, compared with 19 in 1990.

India has also signed a number of investment promotion agreements. As on December 2005, India had signed 56 bilateral investment treaties. Eight amongst India's top ten investors have signed an investment agreement with India (Table 2, Annexure 1). India has signed BITs with both developing and developed countries. These include 2 LDCs, 33 developing countries and 21 developed countries.

While the number of investment treaties is increasing, the number of investor state disputes on account of violation of these agreements has also increased. These trends have been examined later in the paper. In 2005, at least 50 new investor-State dispute settlement (ISDS) cases were filed, bringing the total number of treaty-based arbitration to a new peak of at least 226 by the end of 2005 (Figure 4). These cases involve 62 countries. This is the highest annual increase ever recorded. 136 out of the total of 226 cases were filed with International Centre for Settlement of Investment Disputes (ICSID). (Figure 5, Annexure 1) At least 61 Governments – 37 of them in the developing world, 14 in developed countries and 10 in South-East Europe and the Commonwealth of Independent States – have faced investment treaty arbitration.[8] Though difficult to quantify precisely, it is estimated that the financial implications of such cases are exceedingly high.

This paper would attempt to understand the development concerns in standard BIT provisions with special reference to the explosion in investment arbitration and dispute settlement systems in recent years. Subsequently, the manner in which BITs provisions have been sought to be applied by foreign investors in developing country settings would be analyzed in a comparative regional perspective with the help of two case studies: the case of Dabhol Power Corporation in India and the case of the Cochabamba water privatization in Bolivia. Both these cases attracted a lot of attention and raised a number of development concerns both in their respective countries and also globally. These cases highlight a number of unanticipated consequences for the host country in signing on to BITs without adequate safeguards. In the sections to follow the International Institute for Sustainable Development's Model International Agreement on Investment for Sustainable Development is compared with the India-Netherlands BITs. In the concluding section, some policy issues have been flagged.

## Understanding Development Concerns in Bilateral Investment Treaties with Special Reference to Dispute Settlement Systems

The core function of a BIT is to create an enabling environment for the inflow of foreign investment by providing certain basic guarantees through a series of rights and obligations between the investor and the state enshrined in the text of the agreement. Whether or not, the investment agreements afford flexibility and policy space for undertaking developmental goals is determined by the *nature* and *scope* of the obligations undertaken in terms of the core substantive provisions of what is or is not permissible under the agreement.[9]

An issue of central importance relates to the very definition of investment as contained in BITs. UNCTAD (2000) notes that the recent trend in International Investment Agreements (IIAs) (an overwhelming proportion of which are BITs) is to have a broad open ended definition of what constitutes investment which may or may not be subject to limitations.[10] Thus, for example, Bilateral Investment Treaty between the Republic of India and the

Kingdom of Netherlands for the promotion and protection of investments lays down the definition of what constitutes 'investment' in Article 1 in an open ended manner.[11] Treaty coverage of all assets included in the definition may not be consistent with the development policy of states at every period in the life of an agreement.[12]

Although, the scope of provisions contained in the various BITS are fairly diverse, the following rights have been seen to arise out of a typical modern BIT:[13]

1. Absolute standards of treatment such as fair and equitable treatment.
2. Freedom from discriminatory measures by providing relative standard of treatment such as National Treatment (NT) or Most Favoured Nation (MFN).
3. Protection against expropriation or nationalization through compensation.
4. Dispute settlement provisions including both state to state and investor to state.

While these treaty provisions cover most sectors unless expressly carved out from application and mostly apply in the post establishment phase, recent trends in US and Japanese BITs have extended these provisions to the pre establishment phase as well.[14]

It is important to take stock of these trends and examine the development concerns arising out of the provisions of BITs especially since the historical nature of BITs is undergoing a change and they are fast becoming a preferred mode of including investment protection measures by developed countries. The substantive guarantees laid down in BITs are leading to a new system of international rights and obligations for the signatories and becoming the fundamental source of international law in the area of foreign investment while displacing customary international law and in some cases even relevant domestic law.[15]

It is sometimes stated that the objective of investment treaties is to foster development. Peterson (2004) examines over 150 treaties entered into by Western governments such as US, Canada and UK to conclude that references to development are 'exceedingly rare' either in the preamble to the treaty or in the treaty's substantive provisions.[16] Even when references are made to economic development there is a linkage assumed between the flow of private capital and economic development. The provisions are tuned to the interests of the foreign investor and do not have clauses towards recognition of government regulation as an element of successful development policy. This 'widespread failure to identify development as an important objective of investment treaties' has important policy implications.[17] Similarly, other provisions relating to existence of Special and differential treatment (S&DT)

by way of relatively less onerous commitments relating to national treatment, carve out clauses for sensitive industries, social sectors, imposition of performance requirements and other developmental obligations are also rare in treaty practice of developed countries such as UK. Peterson observes that overall 'BITs tend to be *highly* reciprocal, narrowly focused on investment protection (rather than development or other policy goals) and garnished with few exceptions. (Emphasis in original)[18]

Chowla (2005) analyses some of the major substantive provisions within BITs to validate the changing nature of BITS over time.[19] Clauses relating to National Treatment (NT), pre-establishment rights, domestic tax exemption, public health exemption, capital movement safeguards and ban on local content requirements have been examined in the study. As far as NT and pre establishment rights are concerned, 50 per cent of the BITs signed before 1990 did not include NT clauses while more recent treaties are likely to include them. While 40 per cent of the treaties signed by Asian countries had NT clauses, African countries had all their treaties with NT clauses. Pre-establishment clauses are not common, though countries such as US, Canada and Japan are likely to have them.[20] All BITS include exemptions to MFN treatment for benefits derived from economic unions or free trade areas.[21] Since patents are covered under the definition of investments, it is important to know whether BITs have public health exemptions. Chowla's examination shows that more recent BITs are more likely to include such protections.[22] As far as capital movement safeguards are concerned certain host countries end up with more safeguards than others indicating the fact that negotiating strength of the respective countries is important for building in safeguards. Similar is the case with performance requirements with poor countries and small economies being unable to sign treaties that enforce performance requirements.[23] Finally, the analysis shows that dispute resolution clause in BITs is almost a universal feature with only five agreements in the sample, and that too before 1981, not including clauses on investor-state arbitration.[24]

A detailed examination of the debates around all the major substantive provisions of BITs is beyond the scope of the paper. In the remaining part of this section, provisions relating to dispute settlement procedures and investment arbitration and some critical issues of development concerns shall be dealt with at some length.

The provisions relating to dispute settlement have been an area of increasing policy concern primarily due to the rise in such cases in the recent years and the substantial financial liability implicit in such clauses. In most BITs, the investor is granted the right to sue the state if governmental actions arise under the pretext of expropriation of the business of the firm. This by itself constitutes an expansion of investor rights as in most cases governments can claim sovereign immunity virtually closing down the legal recourse.

Expropriation has been permitted in cases where it is undertaken for a public purpose, carried out in a non-discriminatory manner following the due process of law and after payment of compensation.[25] The ambit of expropriation has been expanded to include cases of 'indirect expropriation', 'creeping expropriation' or regulatory takings as including measures 'tantamount' or equivalent to expropriation or actions that would substantially impair the value of investments. These terms have been defined in a vague manner leaving the policy makers and the courts with no definitive indication of an assessment of the potential impact of this provision. The arbitration proceedings are not bound by precedents and with limited avenues for appeals. This aspect of BITs has seen the overall caseload expand rather dramatically in recent years. There is an increasing worry that these provisions are prone to misuse as even normal risks of running businesses can be subsumed under the expropriation clause. These provisions have been seen as anti-democratic, as a 'Trojan horse' of investment treaties with the 'secret tribunals being dubbed as a 'private court of capital.[26]

Arbitration has emerged as a preferred method for resolving complex international disputes over options such as the use of force or closed door diplomatic negotiations.[27] Historically, arbitration of investment disputes was not available to individual investors as they had no standing and no direct cause of action against a Sovereign for a violation of international law affecting their investments.[28] The only choice available to investors was to route claims through their home country which filed cases on their behalf at the International Court of Justice. Under this system, it was not easy for claims to be translated into compensation and the only enforcement tool was the enactment of a Security Council Resolution which is not commercially useful in such cases. Alternatively, pursuit of claims in the country of the sovereign against the sovereign was not seen as attractive for the investors.[29]

In order to remedy the situation, investment treaties provided investors with a direct cause of action against a Sovereign for damages and a choice of neutral setting for resolution of their grievances. These shifts were a 'major innovation' and have led to the creation of a private cause of action against Sovereigns and placed the enforcement of public international law rights in the hands of private individuals and corporations.[30] However, though these options have been available since 1960s it is only since the last decade or so that there has been a phenomenal increase in the number of claims brought under diverse investment treaty arbitrations. This trend is seen to be likely to persist in the future.[31]

Investment treaties usually specify the institutions to be used in case of a dispute and the institutions have evolved their own set of rules governing the arbitration process. Thus in the Bilateral Investment Treaty between the Republic of India and the Kingdom of Netherlands for the promotion and protection of investments lays down the provisions relating to disputes between the contracting parties in Article 10 of the treaty.[32] As per different clauses of the Article, if negotiations cannot settle the dispute after six months, either Contracting Party can submit the dispute to arbitration. The arbitration tribunal is to consist of three arbitrators. The arbitrators are to be appointed by each Contracting Party within two months of the receipt of request for arbitration and within two months from them a third arbitrator is to be appointed as the Chairman of the tribunal. If within the periods specified as noted earlier, the necessary appointments have not been made the President of the International Court of Justice is to be invited to make such appointments. The arbitral tribunal shall reach its decision by a majority of votes and such decision shall be final and binding on both Contracting Parties.[33]

The arbitration process is marked by complete lack of transparency in most cases with no public accountability even in cases involving legitimate public interest having significant public impact.[34] Though the rights enshrined in the BITs are reciprocal in nature, it is weighed heavily against the developing countries. Thus for example, an examination of the arbitration cases filed before the ICSID showed that out of 120 cases there were only 2 cases were the plaintiff is a developing country and the defendant a developed country.[35]

The entire procedure including records of meetings, replies, interim relief, evidence gathering, awards, annulment or set aside are governed by strict rules of confidentiality and the process is not transparent.[36] Although, there have been recent movements in favour of incorporating transparency obligations into recent trade agreements and model investment treaties,[37] the overall situation is still shrouded in secrecy. For instance, UNCTAD (2005) notes that concern over transparency still subsists (despite movement towards transparency in some cases) in broader BITS context.[38] It also refers to the fact that increased transparency could be achieved if it was possible to introduce 'relevant modifications to the international arbitral rules that are relied upon by reference in these BITS (first of all UNCITRAL and ICSID rules).' The UNCTAD review further makes mention of the proposed reforms of the ICSID procedure wherein the tribunals would have the authority to accept and consider submissions from third parties and to allow third parties to attend hearings, or even to open them to the public without obtaining the consent of both parties as is currently the case.[39]

Commenting on the nature of the outcomes of investment disputes, Franck notes that while there has been remarkable consistency in some areas such as jurisdictional determinations, there is marked inconsistency as well. Questions have also been raised about the 'legitimacy and reliability of the investment treaty dispute resolution process'.[40] Considering the fact that the dispute resolution process is yet in its infancy, it is perhaps an opportune time to examine what the future holds for investment treaties intertwined as it is with the future of the investment treaty arbitration.[41]

UNCTAD notes instances where the same facts and circumstances can be litigated by different investors in different tribunals even when different results emerge.[42] As a result, investors having shares in the same investment are in a position to initiate multiple arbitrations in the name of an affiliate company under different BITs.[43]

Following Franck, it is seen that inconsistency can arise under three different scenarios:[44]

1. Different tribunals coming to different conclusions about the same standard in the same treaty.
2. Different tribunals organised under different treaties coming to different conclusions about disputes involving the same set of facts, related parties and similar investment rights.
3. Different tribunals organised different investment treaties considering disputes involving a similar commercial situation and similar investment rights but coming to opposite conclusions.

Treaty awards have a significant impact on the future conduct of states in terms of economic development, foreign relations and in the exercise of legislative and regulatory powers.[45] In addition, they increase uncertainty for investors.[46]

Franck has argued for a new framework towards removing the inconsistency of the arbitration process and enhancing the legitimacy of the current investment arbitration approach.[47] She has argued for introducing enhanced textual clarity about the meaning of substantive rights and providing detailed definitions for guidance of arbitrators. Franck also suggests improvements by way of revision of procedural rights in investment treaties and introducing structural safeguards into the text of the treaty's dispute resolution process.[48] Suggestions have also been made for creation of an investment arbitration appellate body which could review awards, correct errors and establish a reliable body of law and for consolidation of similar claims based on the same treaty or same conduct.[49]

Howard Mann et al in their proposal for a Model international agreement on investment for sustainable development, make a number of interesting suggestions towards improvement (henceforth IISD Model Agreement). On the issue of investor/investment-state disputes an important recommendation relates to a dispute between an investor or investment and a host state commencing after domestic remedies are exhausted in relation to the underlying issues pleaded in relation to a breach of the agreement.[50] The IISD Model Agreement also makes a number of other important recommendations relating to issues such as improvement of transparency, building in developmental safeguards and defining the rights and obligations of investors and the host state in a manner conducive to sustainable development. Some of these recommendations have been considered later in the paper.

Another issue of concern relates to the conflict of jurisdictions wherein international dispute settlement processes are initiated despite the existence of a 'domestic forum clause' in the investment contract between the investor and the host country.[51] The ICSID tribunals have held that the 'domestic forum clause' does not restrict invocation of the use of the investor state dispute settlement mechanism of an international investment agreement even though the 'alleged breach of contract on the part of the respondent host country is central to the establishment of a breach of the investment protection obligations in the treaty.[52] The rationale behind the approach is that while domestic forum clauses relate to the breaches of contract only the investor state claim relates to breaches of the treaty itself as a separate international law obligation.[53] This is a potentially a disadvantage to the host country as purely contractual disputes need to be resolved in the appropriate domestic forum and is an area of increasing concern. Such an instance occurred in the Dabhol Power Corporation case in India (referred to later in the paper) where the arbitration proceedings were launched in London during the pendency of the case in the Supreme Court in India. Hearing an appeal in the matter, the Delhi High Court held that the proceedings were oppressive. Despite the fact that the matter was pending before the Supreme Court, the arbitrators were proceeding further without realizing that the decision of the Supreme Court would go into the root of the matter pending before them. The Delhi High Court further held that the defendant be restrained from proceeding further with the arbitral proceedings pending before the arbitral tribunal in London until the pronouncement of the judgement with regard to the jurisdiction of Maharashtra Electricity Regulatory Commission by the Supreme Court.[54]

Finally, the issue of treaty shopping constitutes another area of concern. Foreign investors typically invoke BITs of home countries of convenience that have treaties with host countries where investments have been made.[55] Some of the international investment agreements have a denial of benefits clause which prevents investors who do not have 'substantial business activities' from taking advantage of the agreement. Accordingly, the term 'substantial business activities' can be defined adopting a liberal or strict approach and such misuse can be prevented. However, the fact that many of the BITs do not have this clause suggests that the use of this mechanism was not foreseen clearly by host countries which do not have such clauses.

**Study of BITS in a Comparative Regional Perspective: Case Studies of the Dabhol Power Project in India and Cochabamba Water Privatisation in Bolivia**

*Case Study 1: The Dabhol Power Project, India*

Launched in 1991, the Enron power project in India has emerged as a classic example of how provisions in Bilateral Investment Treaties can be interpreted in unanticipated ways that raise a number of interrelated policy issues and concerns. The Enron case study therefore is instructive in several ways. In this section we shall study the facts of the case relating to its origin and launch and its salient features which are important from the point of view of understanding the litigation around it.

## Origin and Launch of the Power Project

Under the Electricity (Supply) Act of 1948, ownership and regulation of electricity generation was a concurrent responsibility of both the centre and the state. The State Electricity Boards (SEBs) were established in states as per the provisions of the Act as vertically integrated power companies.[56] Despite an extensive network of SEBs by 1990 the country was faced with a severe power shortfall with one of the lowest per capita power generation capacity in the world. There was a thinking that without adequate supply of power virtually no sector of the economy whether agriculture, industry or services could be transformed and put on a high growth path. Following the wide ranging policies of economic reforms and liberalization since July 1991, private participation was permitted in the power sector in India.

It must be remembered that the lending policies of World Bank had an important role to play in influencing the new thinking relating to the power sector. Following India's economics crisis in the first half of the 90s, the World Bank reevaluated its lending policies and decided to stop grant of loans to SEBs that had failed to improve their performance and meet their financial commitments. Over the next three years, the Bank cancelled over $2 billion in non performing loans and refocused its lending strategy to issues relating to the institutional, financial an environmental sustainability of SEBs. The new policy emphasized that lending would be done only to states which agreed to 'unbundle their electricity boards, privatize distribution and facilitate the involvement of private sector in power generation'.[57] Under the power sector reforms programme, eight 'fast track' power projects were proposed to be taken up as negotiated deals through the Memorandum of Understanding route and not through a process of competitive bidding. Thus although the idea of private sector participation was proposed, its operationalisation by

way of arriving at detailed guidelines was not thorough. Though it is well
known that the usual practice is for governments to request competing bids
from several developers, the government chose to close the deal via the MOU
route wherein the bids could be accepted or rejected without any comparative
basis. Under the former stream, the developer with the lowest cost bid as per
the laid down government specifications of the contract wins the deal. As
shall be seen later the deal also attracted fierce criticisms on several other
compelling grounds. Under the negotiated process, the developers and
government arrive at an in principle understanding and after requisite
clearances a Power Purchase agreement (PPA) is signed.

This was the overall setting in which the Enron project took off. With a
proposed capacity of 2015 megawatts (MW) and around $3 billion of
investments, this constituted the largest foreign investment in the country at the
time. The Project constituting of two phases and envisaged establishment of a
total capacity of 2,015 MW at Dabhol on a Build Own and Operate basis
(BOO).[58] Under the proposal, the state governments were required to provide
guarantees to foreign investors, in case the cash strapped State Electricity Boards
(SEBs) failed to pay all outstanding dues. Accordingly, a Memorandum of
Understanding (MOU) was signed with the Government of Maharashtra
(GOM) on June 20 1992 for setting up of a thermal power plan generating 2000
megawatts (MW) of power forming nearly 20 per cent of the installed capacity
in the state. The PPA was signed for a duration of 20 years with the MSEB
having an option of a further extension of 5 or 10 years. The state of
Maharashtra, the second most populous state in the country is an industrial
powerhouse with high levels of industrialization and contributes to nearly one
fourth of the gross value added by the industrial sector in India.[59]

Subsequently, in April 1993, Bechtel Enterprises and General Electric
Company (GE) came together to form Dabhol Power Company (DPC) and
registered it as an Indian Company under the Indian Companies Act, 1956.
(Shareholding pattern of the different constituents were 80%, 10% and 10%
respectively) Additionally, the GOI agreed to sign on a counter guarantee to
the power project restricted to Phase I of the project.[60] Although the PPA was
governed by Indian Laws, the parties agreed to settle any disputes arising
under the agreement by arbitration in London under UNCITRAL
Arbitration Rules.

## Salient Features of the Power Purchase Agreement

The PPA signed between the MSEB and the DPC has been noted by experts
to be the 'most controversial document in the history of power sector in
India'. It was kept away from the public domain and was a closely guarded

secret until political compulsions and widespread criticisms of the deal forced DPC to make it public.[61]

Analysis of the PPA document by some leading power experts in the country revealed the following:[62]

1. Even though the DPC was believed to be liable for heavy penalties, in instances of non performing parameters such as time over-run, capacity short fall and the like, most of these are passed on to the contractors.
2. Internal rate of return (IRR: profitability indicator) was to the tune of 28 per cent (post tax real) equivalent to over 40 per cent flat rate of return in dollar terms. Vanguard Capital, a GOI appointed consultant, recommended that an IRR of 17% to 21 % (posttax, real) was attractive enough for inflow of foreign investment even in high risk contexts.
3. The high capital costs together with the excessive promised rate of return were to result in excess payments of about $ 350–425 million to Enron as a one time payment in 1996 currency.
4. The tariff structure agreed to was very complex. It was backloaded (with an inbuilt rise of four per cent) and dollar denominated as also the Plant Load Factor (PLF). Accordingly, the cost of power was quite high.

Experts noted that the overall cost of the project was excessively high and was considerably padded by Enron in order to generate very high rates of return. Thus for instance, the total cost of the project which was to the tune of $3 billion was five times higher than the cost of the main plant equipment. It has been seen that in indigenously built power projects the cost of the main plant equipment is roughly 60 per cent of the total cost of the project.[63]

Highlighting the one sided nature of the PPA, it was argued that under the terms of the agreement, the GoM and GoI are underwriting all risks of the project while providing an average rate of return of 40 per cent and guaranteeing a 90 per cent off take of power by shutting down cheaper generation and providing other concessions under threat of penalties. Enron for its part was bringing only 10 per cent of the capital with very little liability in comparison. In return, the MSEB would need to shell out Rs. 1200 crore in the very first year of its operation with costs rising every year by four percent on account of capital servicing, foreign exchange rate variation and increased fuel costs.[64] The cost of power as per the terms of the PPA was so high that it was widely considered to be a recipe for financial ruin of MSEB and the GoM who served as guarantors to the project.[65]

In March 1995, when the State Assembly elections were held, BJP-Shiv Sena alliance won the elections thereby replacing the Congress Party government which had led the negotiations to the project. In May 1995, the new government appointed a Cabinet sub-committee chaired by deputy Chief Minister, Mr. Gopinath Munde to investigate the project. In its report, the sub-committee recommended that Phase I of the project be repudiated and Phase II cancelled interalia on ground of lack of transparency in the entire negotiation process, lack of adoption of the competitive bidding process, high costs and high tariffs of the project and the capacity payment agreement under which the MSEB was to pay for the electricity irrespective of whether it was actually being used or not, objections raised by the World Bank[66] towards the project, and on environmental considerations.[67] The PPA was subsequently cancelled by the state government with the Chief Minister, Mr. Manohar Joshi stating that the 'deal is against the interests of Maharashtra. Accepting the deal would indicate an absolute lack of self respect and would amount to betraying the trust of the people'.[68]

In response, the Dabhol Power Company and the project sponsors instituted arbitration claims of damages in excess of $ 300 million in London against the MSEB and the Maharashtra state government.[69] The state of Maharashtra brought in a suit in the Bombay High Court to invalidate the arbitration clause and the guarantee of the MSEB to pay on the ground that both had been secured by illegal means.[70] The US government issued a statement critical of the contract repudiation and cautioned that these developments would have negative consequences for foreign investment in India.[71]

A process of review and renegotiation was then initiated by the state of Maharashtra with the Panel undertaking the exercise and proposing a mutually acceptable renegotiated terms of the Dabhol Project in November 1995.[72] Under the renegotiated terms, a special purpose entity, Maharashtra Power Development Corporation Limited (MPDCL) was created with a 30 percent shareholding transferred from Enron thereby reducing the share of Enron to 50 percent. The PPA was amended and the project put on track by July 1995. Yet again, the controversy refused to die and as criticism continued to mount, the Dabhol project was again shut down in 2001.

The cancellation of the project led to multiple arbitration proceedings at multiple forums. A total of ten arbitration were initiated by stakeholders of the project in London and New York.[73] A total of 16 cases were reportedly filed by the DPC and Indian government each other in and outside India.[74] The arbitration was initiated under clause 8.1 of the shareholders agreement under which disputes between shareholders can be settled under ICC rules in New York State alone, under the exclusive jurisdiction of the New York law.[75] The Mumbai High Court however had restrained both GE and Bechtel for pursuing the arbitration claims. Earlier, an international court had ordered the Union Government to pay Overseas Private Insurance Company (OPIC), a US agency, a total claim of $57 million as per an insurance agreement with

GE and Bechtel.[76] MSEB also issued a contempt of court notice to the DPC in the Mumbai High Court against the Rs 26,000-crore arbitration filed by DPC in a London Court stating that the DPC has violated the Supreme Court's injunction against starting any arbitration proceedings.[77]

In the arbitration case, a suit was filed before Delhi High Court that it should issue an interim injunction to stay the arbitration proceedings before the London arbitral tribunal. Earlier, the Supreme Court had passed an interim order stating that pending its final decision, the arbitral proceedings commenced in London could not proceed. However, despite the fact that the matter was pending before the Supreme Court, the arbitral tribunal continued with the proceedings. The Delhi High Court held that the proceedings were oppressive for the reason that though the matter was pending before the Supreme Court, the arbitrators were proceeding further without realizing that the decision of the Supreme Court would go into the root of the matter pending before them. The Delhi High Court further held that the defendant be restrained from proceeding further with the arbitral proceedings pending before the arbitral tribunal in London until the pronouncement of the judgement with regard to the jurisdiction of Maharashtra Electricity Regulatory Commission by the Supreme Court.[78]

Taking advantage of the BIT between the Government of the Republic of Mauritius and the Government of the Republic of India for the promotion and protection of Investment, GE filed a claim under the treaty. GE and Enron filed the claim through their affiliates Capital India Power Mauritius I and Enron Mauritius Company against MPDCL, MSEB and the state of Maharashtra, leading to an award in excess of US$ 96.7 million pronounced by the International Court of Arbitration of the International Chamber of Commerce.[79] Besides, Offshore Power Production (OPP), a limited liability partnership organised under the laws of Netherlands that owns — through its subsidiary company Enron Mauritius Company (EMC) with a 65% interest in DPC, has filed a notice of claim under the Indo-Netherlands Investment Promotion Treaty.[80]

In December 2005, both Dabhol Power Company and Maharashtra State Electricity Board on Wednesday settled their long-standing disputes on the PPA, with 'consent terms' filed in the Supreme Court ending all legal proceedings in India and abroad in an out of court settlement reached between them.[81] The terms of the agreement are not yet known but the road has been cleared for a revival of the project by a new Joint Venture company, Ratnagiri Gas and Power Private Ltd promoted by the Indian Public Sector Undertakings such as National Thermal Power Corporation and Gas Authority of India Limited.[82] The project has been revived in order to save the reputation of the power elite of the country with a slew of tax concessions and waivers being provided to the joint venture company.[83] It has been estimated by some experts that the burden of subsidy to be borne by what was a defunct project is to the tune of around Rs. 10,000 crores in what has been termed privatization of profits and nationalization of losses.[84]

### Case Study 2: Cochabamba Water Privatisation Case, Bolivia

The Cochabamba water privatization case raises the familiar question of the conflict between contractual obligations of the state towards foreign capital and its regulatory functions of upholding the larger public interest in provision of essential services such as water.

Water has been considered to be the last frontier of privatization around the world.[85] Over 90 percent of the world's water is still supplied by public bodies with 90 percent of the world's investment in water and sewage systems.[86] It has been noted that by the end of 2000, municipalities in at least ninety three countries underwent partial privatization of water or wastewater services including in countries such as China and Cuba.[87] Transnational corporations such as Vivendi Universal and Suez together control over 70 percent of the world's water market.[88]

La Guerra del Agua (Water war), the six month long conflict over water, took place in Cochabamba in Bolivia in late 1999. It was led by the people of Cochabamba post the efforts of the Bolivian government to privatize the city's water system.[89] With seventy percent of its citizens living below the poverty line, hyperinflation of 2500 percent, Bolivia is the poorest nation in South America. In order to stimulate the economy and arrest the economic crises, a series of economic reforms were undertaken by the country in the 1980s which further pushed the economy into recession.[90] A series of deregulation efforts were launched leading to the privatization of the municipal water systems of three of its largest cities, La Paz, Santa Cruz and Cochabamba. The WB loans to facilitate the process were conditional to the reforms of the water sector in the cities of La Paz and Cochabamba. In the latter, water and wastewater systems were run by the municipal water company called Sevicio Municipal de Agua Potable v Acantrillado (SEMAPA). Reportedly, nearly half of the cities residents were not connected to any water system and the quality of water was not up to the mark. In order to augment the water supplies and improve the supplies, construction of a dam, reservoir, tunnel and hydroelectric plants were proposed at costs of more US $390 million. The cash strapped SEMAPA was struggling to meet the needs of water for its citizens as it was operating at a loss of more than $ 2.25 million annually. The Bolivian government accordingly issued a call for tender which attracted only one bid from Agua del Tunari (AdT), a newly formed consortium consisting of International Waters as the primary owner founded by the American firm Bechtel in 1996, Bengoa of Spain and four Bolivian companies.

An agreement was signed on September 3 1999 between the special commission and AdT which was shrouded in secrecy and did not have any inputs from the community or affected groups of people. As the bid did not attract anyone except AdT, the negotiations were lop sided and the government was pushed into a bad bargain wherein the city's water system was leased to AdT for a term of forty years. The company was guaranteed an annual profit of 15–17 percent. The water rates were dollarized and tied to the US Consumer Price Index and water meters were to be set up to monitor the water consumption of both users under the existing SEMAPA system and those who used their own wells. Water laws which permitted use of public waters for irrigation to individuals or groups in place since 1906 were updated to avoid conflict with domestic laws. Law 2029 was passed on Potable Water Services and Sanitary Sewage soon after the contract with AdT was signed, which provided for the state's granting of "exclusive use" rights to the third parties.

AdT started its operations in Cochabamba since November 1, 1999 and post the new water rates taking effect, the price of water shot by as much as 400 percent. This led to a wave of popular protests with people refusing to pay their water bills. After a show of protracted and organised resistance by the people, water rates were rolled back to pre-contract levels. The contract with AdT was rescinded and SEMAPA resumed control of the city's water systems and the controversial water law 2029 was also repealed.

In November 2000, AdT filed for arbitration at the ICSID seeking $25 million from Bolivia as compensation for its lost investment. The claim included expected profits in addition to investment. The ICSID claimed that it had jurisdiction in the matter based on a BIT between Netherlands and Bolivia which was signed in March 1992. AdT was originally registered in the Cayman islands. However, it took advantage of the fact that International Waters, AdT's majority shareholder was registered in the Netherlands. The Bolivian government objected to this interpretation and submitted that the domicile altered in anticipation of potential arbitration but the ICSID tribunal rejected its arguments and proceeded with the arbitration process. The Cochabamba residents filed a petition with ICSID arguing in the main that all submissions in the case should be made public as the outcome would have an immediate and profound impact on them. The request was denied by ICSID since such a request required the express consent of both parties.

In January 2006, the Government of Bolivia and AdT settled their dispute. As per the reports, the claims against Bolivia currently before the ICSID stood withdrawn and compensation was being paid by the Government of Bolivia to AdT for the termination of the concession.[91]

## Comparison of the Netherlands-India BIT with the IISD's Model International Investment Agreement on Investment for Sustainable Development

For purposes of guiding BITs, India has developed a Model BITs text. However, this may or not conform to the actual agreements entered into by India with different countries. Hence in this section a comparison is attempted between the Netherlands-India BIT (henceforth NIBIT) and International Investment for Sustainable Development's (IISD) Model International Agreement.

India's Model Text of Bilateral Investment Promotion Agreement consists of 15 Articles and covers areas such as definition of investments, creation of favourable conditions and of fair and equitable treatment, according NT and MFN status, conditions for expropriation, compensation for losses, repatriation of investment and returns, subrogation clause, clauses relating to disputes between an investor and a Contracting Party, disputes between Contracting Parties, movement of personnel and application of other rules and details relating to duration and termination of the agreement.[92]

Before we turn to the comparison it would be necessary to understand the context in which the IISD's model international agreement text has evolved. IISD argues that the model for current IIAs have been developed over 50 years ago and no longer meet the needs and requirements of the global economy in the twenty first century.[93] It argues that despite the failure of earlier attempts to negotiate binding multilateral rules for international investment such as the Multilateral Agreement on Investment (MAI) earlier, it believes that attempts to forge a new approach that responds to rapid globalization and to the need to promote sustainable development must be made.[94] Accordingly, IISD has undertaken a critical analysis of the weaknesses of the existing agreements and attempted to integrate the concerns of the developing countries in its model text. It seeks to ensure that investor rights and public goods are protected in a legitimate, transparent and accountable manner.

While it is beyond the scope of this paper to get into the details of the model text, select provisions, which are critical from the point of view of putting development at the centre of BITs, would be highlighted. While highlighting the sustainable development functions of investment agreements, the definition of investment has been fairly detailed and seeks to avoid the pitfalls encountered in a raft of arbitration disputes over what constitutes investment and who is an investor. Thus for instance, it has been stated in Article 2 of the model text that certain types of investment would not qualify as 'significant physical presence'.

These have been specified as sales offices without operational facilities, post office box based businesses or internet based business. Also, portfolio investments have not been covered under the agreement. Further, it has enshrined an article specifying the conditions of denial of benefits to those who do not have substantial business activities in the territory of the other party.

This approach stands in sharp contrast to the definition of investments in the NIBIT wherein investments have been defined in a broad and open ended manner without any reference to preclude certain types of investments such as those which do not qualify as 'significant'. Further, there is no denial of benefits clause in the NIBIT.

Under the IISD Model Text, the concept of 'like circumstances' in NT has been made context specific and to be determined on a case by case basis wherein circumstances of an investment to be considered include its impact on the local community, environment and regulatory process applied in relation to a measure of concern. Under NIBIT no such amplification of safeguards has been built into the NT clauses. Similarly, the Model text unlike NIBIT, proposes a number of obligations and duties of investors and investments such as those of pre-establishment impact assessment, anti corruption clauses, post establishment obligations, observance of corporate governance practices which meets internationally acceptable standards of corporate governance for the sector involved, corporate social responsibility provisions in accordance with the developmental plans, priorities of the host state and international goals such as the Millennium Development Goals.

Again, unlike NIBIT, the Model text lists out a number of performance requirements relating to fixing of thresholds for export, achievement of domestic content and sourcing of goods from domestic companies.

Under Article 40 of the Model text, a setting of a dispute settlement body (DSB) has been proposed to manage the dispute settlement processes. The DSB has been proposed to be composed of a Council of the Parties open to all Parties, a panel division and an appellate division. A legal assistance centre, which would function independently of the Secretariat, to assist the developing and least developed countries, has also been proposed. Under Article 45, it is proposed that the investor/investment-state disputes should not commence unless domestic remedies are exhausted in relation to the underlying issues pleased in relation to a breach of the Agreement.

One significant concern relating to the investment arbitration and dispute settlement process relates to the transparency of proceedings. Under Article 46, it has been proposed that all documents relating to a notice of intention to arbitrate, the settlement of any dispute, the initiation of a panel or appeal or the pleadings, evidence or decisions in them shall be made available to the public through an internet site. Further, it lays down that procedural and substantive oral hearings shall be open to the public. Finally, it provides for the receipt of *amicus curiae* (friends of the court) submissions.

It can be seen that the IISD model text is indeed a bold proposal worthy of dialogue and consultation amongst all the stakeholders and takes care of several development concerns which have arisen out of the enforcement of provisions in typical BITs. Based as they are on templates created by developed countries almost half a century back, it is time they are revisited and amended while keeping in view the surfeit of investment arbitrations and their origin in specific provisions of BITs. It seeks to strike an overall balance of the rights of the investor and the host country.

## Conclusion

The literature reviewed in this paper suggests that BITs can present a risk to developmental priorities of developing countries. The need for policy space and flexibility has been seen to be integral to the policy matrix of developing countries since they face greater social and economic needs than their developed counterparts.

Based on perspectives from two case studies: the case of Dabhol Power Corporation in India and the case of the Cochabamba water privatization in Bolivia, we reiterate that developing countries are still in the process of identifying the best mix of policy tools suited to their particular context and levels of development, and BITs can limit their ability to do so.[95]

The brunt of the challenges arising out of the current system of dispute settlement process can be argued to lie disproportionately on the shoulders of the developing countries, given their lack of human resources and financial capability to 'navigate' within this system.[96] Thus, any effort to prevent and manage investor-state dispute settlement process must focus on capacity building and provision of technical assistance in these areas.[97] Following Franck and the model investment text considered earlier, issues of building in relevant safeguards and clearly stating the rights and obligations of the investor/investment and avoiding vague, open ended preambular language in the BITs text is a priority. The importance of revisiting the text of the existing BITs and considering actively to strengthen its provisions from the point of view of development goals and needs cannot perhaps be overemphasized.

## Notes

1. Bilateral Investment Treaties, 1959–2000, UNCTAD, United Nations, New York and Geneva, 2000.
2. Mary Hallward-Driemeier, Do Bilateral Investment Treaties Attract FDI? Only a bit…and they could bite, World Bank, DECRG, June 2003.

3. Mary Hallward-Driemeier, Do Bilateral Investment Treaties Attract FDI? Only a bit...and they could bite, World Bank, DECRG, June 2003.

4. Developments in international investment agreements in 2005 (2006) IIA Monitor No. 2, United Nations, New York and Geneva, 2006.

5. Investor-State Disputes Arising from Investment Treaties: A Review, UNCTAD Series on International Investment Policies for Development, United Nations, New York and Geneva, 2005.

6. Developments in international investment agreements in 2005 (2006) IIA Monitor No. 2, United Nations, New York and Geneva, 2006.

7. Developments in international investment agreements in 2005 (2006) IIA Monitor No. 2, United Nations, New York and Geneva, 2006.

8. Developments in international investment agreements in 2005, IIA Monitor No. 2, UNCTAD, United Nations, New York and Geneva, 2006.

9. Preserving Flexibility in IIAs: The Use of Reservations, UNCTAD Series on International Investment Policies for Development, United Nations, New York and Geneva, 2006.

10. International Investment Agreements: Flexibility for Development, UNCTAD Series on Issues in International Investment Agreements, United Nations, New York and Geneva, 2000.

11. Article 1 in the Text of the Agreement of the Bilateral Investment Treaty between the Republic of India and the Kingdom of Netherlands for the promotion and protection of investments.

12. International Investment Agreements: Flexibility for Development, UNCTAD Series on Issues in International Investment Agreements, United Nations, New York and Geneva, 2000.

13. Luke Eric Peterson, Bilateral Investment Treaties and Development Policy Making, International Institute for Sustainable Development, Canada, 2004.

14. Luke Eric Peterson, Bilateral Investment Treaties and Development Policy Making, International Institute for Sustainable Development, Canada, 2004.

15. Susan D. Franck, The Nature and Enforcement of Investor Rights Under Investment Treaties: Do Investment Treaties Have a Bright Future, U.C. Davis Journal of International Law and Policy, Fall 2005.

16. Luke Eric Peterson, Bilateral Investment Treaties and Development Policy Making, International Institute for Sustainable Development, Canada, 2004.

17. Luke Eric Peterson, Bilateral Investment Treaties and Development Policy Making, International Institute for Sustainable Development, Canada, 2004.

18. Luke Eric Peterson, Bilateral Investment Treaties and Development Policy Making, International Institute for Sustainable Development, Canada, 2004.

19. Peter Chowla, Comparing Naughty BITS: Assessing the Developmental Impact of Variation in Bilateral Investment Treaties, Development Studies Institute, London School of Economics and Political Science, London, 2005.

20. Peter Chowla, Comparing Naughty BITS: Assessing the Developmental Impact of Variation in Bilateral Investment Treaties, Development Studies Institute, London School of Economics and Political Science, London, 2005.

21. Peter Chowla, Comparing Naughty BITS: Assessing the Developmental Impact of Variation in Bilateral Investment Treaties, Development Studies Institute, London School of Economics and Political Science, London, 2005.

22. Peter Chowla, Comparing Naughty BITS: Assessing the Developmental Impact of Variation in Bilateral Investment Treaties, Development Studies Institute, London School of Economics and Political Science, London, 2005.

23. Peter Chowla, Comparing Naughty BITS: Assessing the Developmental Impact of Variation in Bilateral Investment Treaties, Development Studies Institute, London School of Economics and Political Science, London, 2005.

24. Peter Chowla, Comparing Naughty BITS: Assessing the Developmental Impact of Variation in Bilateral Investment Treaties, Development Studies Institute, London School of Economics and Political Science, London, 2005.

25. Mary Hallward-Driemeier, Do Bilateral Investment Treaties Attract FDI? Only a bit…and they could bite, World Bank, DECRG, June 2003.

26. Driemeier (2003).

27. Susan D. Franck, The Legitimacy Crisis in Investment Treaty Arbitration: Privatizing Public International Law through Inconsistent Decisions, Fordham Law Review, Vol. 73, 2005.

28. Susan D. Franck, The Legitimacy Crisis in Investment Treaty Arbitration: Privatizing Public International Law through Inconsistent Decisions, Fordham Law Review, Vol. 73, 2005.

29. Susan D. Franck, The Legitimacy Crisis in Investment Treaty Arbitration: Privatizing Public International Law through Inconsistent Decisions, Fordham Law Review, Vol. 73, 2005.

30. Susan D. Franck, The Legitimacy Crisis in Investment Treaty Arbitration: Privatizing Public International Law through Inconsistent Decisions, Fordham Law Review, Vol. 73, 2005.

31. Susan D. Franck, The Legitimacy Crisis in Investment Treaty Arbitration: Privatizing Public International Law through Inconsistent Decisions, Fordham Law Review, Vol. 73, 2005.

32. Text of the Agreement between the Republic of India and the Kingdom of Netherlands for the promotion and protection of investments.

33. Article 10 (different clauses) of the Text of the Agreement between the Republic of India and the Kingdom of Netherlands for the promotion and protection of investments.

34. Mary Hallward-Driemeier, Do Bilateral Investment Treaties Attract FDI? Only a bit…and they could bite, World Bank, DECRG, June 2003.

35. Mary Hallward-Driemeier, Do Bilateral Investment Treaties Attract FDI? Only a bit…and they could bite, World Bank, DECRG, June 2003.

36. Susan D. Franck, The Legitimacy Crisis in Investment Treaty Arbitration: Privatizing Public International Law through Inconsistent Decisions, Fordham Law Review, Vol. 73, 2005.

37. Susan D. Franck, The Legitimacy Crisis in Investment Treaty Arbitration: Privatizing Public International Law through Inconsistent Decisions, Fordham Law Review, Vol. 73, 2005.

38. Investor-State Disputes Arising from Investment Treaties: A Review, UNCTAD Series on International Investment Policies for Development, United Nations, New York and Geneva, 2005.

39. Investor-State Disputes Arising from Investment Treaties: A Review, UNCTAD Series on International Investment Policies for Development, United Nations, New York and Geneva, 2005.

40. Susan D. Franck, The Nature and Enforcement of Investor Rights Under Investment Treaties: Do Investment Treaties Have a Bright Future, U.C. Davis Journal of International Law and Policy, Fall 2005.

41. Susan D. Franck, The Nature and Enforcement of Investor Rights Under Investment Treaties: Do Investment Treaties Have a Bright Future, U.C. Davis Journal of International Law and Policy, Fall 2005.

42. Investor-State Disputes Arising from Investment Treaties: A Review, UNCTAD Series on International Investment Policies for Development, United Nations, New York and Geneva, 2005.

43. Investor-State Disputes Arising from Investment Treaties: A Review, UNCTAD Series on International Investment Policies for Development, United Nations, New York and Geneva, 2005.

44. Susan D. Franck, The Legitimacy Crisis in Investment Treaty Arbitration: Privatizing Public International Law through Inconsistent Decisions, Fordham Law Review, Vol. 73, 2005.

45. Susan D. Franck, The Nature and Enforcement of Investor Rights Under Investment Treaties: Do Investment Treaties Have a Bright Future, U.C. Davis Journal of International Law and Policy, Fall 2005.

46. See for instance the celebrated Lauder cases, cited in Investor-State Disputes Arising from Investment Treaties: A Review, UNCTAD Series on International Investment Policies for Development, United Nations, New York and Geneva, 2005.

47. Susan D. Franck, The Nature and Enforcement of Investor Rights Under Investment Treaties: Do Investment Treaties Have a Bright Future, U.C. Davis Journal of International Law and Policy, Fall 2005.

48. Susan D. Franck, The Nature and Enforcement of Investor Rights Under Investment Treaties: Do Investment Treaties Have a Bright Future, U.C. Davis Journal of International Law and Policy, Fall 2005.

49. Susan D. Franck, The Nature and Enforcement of Investor Rights Under Investment Treaties: Do Investment Treaties Have a Bright Future, U.C. Davis Journal of International Law and Policy, Fall 2005.

50. Howard Mann, Konrad von Moltke, Luke Eric Peterson, Aason Cosbey, IISD Model International Agreement on Investment for Sustainable Development, International Institute for Sustainable Development, Canada, 2005.

51. Investor-State Disputes Arising from Investment Treaties: A Review, UNCTAD Series on International Investment Policies for Development, United Nations, New York and Geneva, 2005.

52. Investor-State Disputes Arising from Investment Treaties: A Review, UNCTAD Series on International Investment Policies for Development, United Nations, New York and Geneva, 2005.

53. Investor-State Disputes Arising from Investment Treaties: A Review, UNCTAD Series on International Investment Policies for Development, United Nations, New York and Geneva, 2005.

54. Zia Mody and Sushil Jacob, India Interim Injunction, Union of India v. Dabhol Power Co Ltd, Case Comment, International Arbitration Law Review, 2004.

55. Investor-State Disputes Arising from Investment Treaties: A Review, UNCTAD Series on International Investment Policies for Development, United Nations, New York and Geneva, 2005.

56. Details of the Act are available at http://www.msebindia.com/m1/m1_index.shtm Accessed on September 10, 2006.
57. Reforming India's Energy Sector (1978–1999) Precis, World Bank Operations Evaluation Department, Spring 2001, Number 206 available at www.worldbank.org/html/oed Accessed on September 12, 2006.
58. The Enron Story: Controversial Issues and Peoples' Struggles, Subodh Wagle, Prayas, Pune, India, 1997 available at www.prayaspune.org Accessed on September 12, 2006
59. White Paper on Maharashtra's Power Sector Reforms, Industries, Energy and Labour Department, Mumbai, 2002, available at http://www.maharashtra.gov.in/white%20paper%20final%20aug%2027.htm Accessed on September 15, 2006.
60. The Enron Story: Controversial Issues and Peoples' Struggles, Subodh Wagle, Prayas, Pune, India, 1997 available at www.prayaspune.org Accessed on September 12, 2006.
61. The Enron Controversy: Techno-Economic Analysis and Policy Implications by Girish Sant, Shantanu Dixit and Subodh Wagle, Prayas, September, 1995 available at www.prayaspune.org Accessed on September 12, 2006.
62. The Enron Controversy: Techno-Economic Analysis and Policy Implications by Girish Sant, Shantanu Dixit and Subodh Wagle, Prayas, September, 1995 available at www.prayaspune.org Accessed on September 12, 2006.
63. Prabir Purkayastha, The Enron Power Purchase Agreement, Delhi Science Forum, April 2006 available at www.delhiscienceforum.org Accessed on September 15 2006.
64. Prabir Purkayastha, The Enron Power Purchase Agreement, Delhi Science Forum, April 2006 available at www.delhiscienceforum.org Accessed on September 15 2006.
65. Madhav Godbole, EAS Sarma, Aftershocks of Dabhol Power Project, Economic and Political Weekly, August 26, 2006.
66. An evaluation of the Enron project by World Bank carried brought out in April 1993 led to the assessment that the project was unviable, did not satisfy the test of least cost power and is not justified by the power demands of Maharashtra quoted in The Munde Committee, Report of the Cabinet Sub-Committee to Review the Dabhol Power Project, 1995, reproduced in Human Rights Watch Report available on www.hrw.org/reports/1999/enron/enron-b.htm accessed on September 18, 2006.
67. The Munde Committee, Report of the Cabinet Sub-Committee to Review the Dabhol Power Project, 1995, reproduced in Human Rights Watch Report available on www.hrw.org/reports/1999/enron/enron-b.htm accessed on September 18, 2006.
68. Jeswald W. Salacuse, Renegotiating International Business Transactions: The Continuing Struggle of Life against Form, International Lawyer, Winter, 2001.
69. Jeswald W. Salacuse, Renegotiating International Business Transactions: The Continuing Struggle of Life against Form, International Lawyer, Winter, 2001.
70. Jeswald W. Salacuse, Renegotiating International Business Transactions: The Continuing Struggle of Life against Form, International Lawyer, Winter, 2001.
71. Jeswald W. Salacuse, Renegotiating International Business Transactions: The Continuing Struggle of Life against Form, International Lawyer, Winter, 2001.
72. Jeswald W. Salacuse, Renegotiating International Business Transactions: The Continuing Struggle of Life against Form, International Lawyer, Winter, 2001.
73. http://www.thehindubusinessline.com/2003/09/27/stories/2003092702590100.htm
74. http://www.financialexpress.com/fe_full_story.php?content_id=90995
75. http://www.thehindubusinessline.com/2003/09/27/stories/2003092702590100.htm
76. http://www.thehindubusinessline.com/2003/09/27/stories/2003092702590100.htm
77. http://www.thehindubusinessline.com/2004/07/03/stories/2004070302700600.htm

78. Zia Mody and Sushil Jacob, India Interim Injunction, Union of India v. Dabhol Power Co Ltd, Case Comment, International Arbitration Law Review, 2004.
79. International Court of Arbitration of the International Chamber of Commerce, Case No. 12913/MS, Final Award available with the authors.
80. http://www.financialexpress.com/fe_full_story.php?content_id=90995
81. http://www.rediff.com/money/2005/dec/07dpc.htm
82. http://www.rediff.com/money/2005/dec/07dpc.htm
83. Madhav Godbole, EAS Sarma, Aftershocks of Dabhol Power Project, Economic and Political Weekly, August 26, 2006.   ·
84. Madhav Godbole, EAS Sarma, Aftershocks of Dabhol Power Project, Economic and Political Weekly, August 26, 2006.
85. Violeta Petrova, At the Frontiers of the Rush for Blue Gold: Water Privatization and the Human Right to Water, Brooklyn Journal of International Law, 2006.
86. Violeta Petrova, At the Frontiers of the Rush for Blue Gold: Water Privatization and the Human Right to Water, Brooklyn Journal of International Law, 2006.
87. Violeta Petrova, At the Frontiers of the Rush for Blue Gold: Water Privatization and the Human Right to Water, Brooklyn Journal of International Law, 2006.
88. Timothy O' Neill, Water and Freedom: The Privatisation of Water and Its Implications for Democracy and Human Rights in the Developing World, Colorado Journal of International Environmental Law and Policy, Spring 2006.
89. Timothy O' Neill, Water and Freedom: The Privatisation of Water and Its Implications for Democracy and Human Rights in the Developing World, Colorado Journal of International Environmental Law and Policy, Spring 2006.
90. The basic facts of the case as described in this part of the write up have been derived from the article of Timothy O' Neill, Water and Freedom: The Privatisation of Water and Its Implications for Democracy and Human Rights in the Developing World, Colorado Journal of International Environmental Law and Policy, Spring 2006.
91. http://www.bechtel.com/newsarticles/487.asp Accessed on October 12, 2006.
92. Text of the Model Bilateral Investment Promotion Agreement is on file with the authors
93. IISD Model International Agreement on Investment for Sustainable Development, available at www.iisd.org
94. IISD Model International Agreement on Investment for Sustainable Development, available at www.iisd.org
95. Preserving Flexibility in IIAs: The Use of Reservations, UNCTAD Series on International Investment Policies for Development, United Nations, New York and Geneva, 2006.
96. Investor-State Disputes Arising from Investment Treaties: A Review, UNCTAD Series on International Investment Policies for Development, United Nations, New York and Geneva, 2005.
97. Investor-State Disputes Arising from Investment Treaties: A Review, UNCTAD Series on International Investment Policies for Development, United Nations, New York and Geneva, 2005.

# Annexure I

## Table 1: International Investment Agreement Concluded by Regions in 2005, and Cumulative

| Region | BITs | | DTTs | | Other II As | |
|---|---|---|---|---|---|---|
| | Year 2005 | Cumulative | Year 2005 | Cumulative | Year 2005 | Cumulative |
| Asia and Oceania | 31 | 1,003 | 36 | 968 | 12 | 89 |
| Latin America and Caribbean | 13 | 464 | 9 | 322 | 5 | 62 |
| Africa | 21 | 660 | 17 | 436 | 2 | 34 |
| SEE&CIS | 15 | 671 | 27 | 576 | 0 | 34 |
| **Memorandum** | | | | | | |
| Developed countries | 45 | 1,511 | 38 | 2,111 | 7 | 127 |
| Developing countries | 60 | 1,878 | 53 | 1,604 | 14 | 185 |
| South-South | 20 | 644 | 25 | 399 | 7 | 86 |
| Least developed countries | 16 | 399 | 5 | 184 | 2 | 35[a/] |

*Note*: The above figures reflect multiple counting (e.g. BITs concluded between countries from Asia and Africa are included in the list *both* regions). The net total of each category of II As is therefore lower than the sum of the above figures.

a/  This number includes agreements concluded by regional groups that have one or more LDC members.

*Source:* UNCTAD.

## Table 2: Top 10 FDI Sources for India and BITs

| Rank (Based on Cumulative Flows from August 1991 to July 2006 | Amount in US$ Million | Country | Does India have a BIT |
|---|---|---|---|
| 1 | 12290 | Mauritius | Yes |
| 2 | 5302 | US | No |
| 3 | 2153 | Japan | No |
| 4 | 2071 | Netherlands | Yes |
| 5 | 2058 | UK | Yes |
| 6 | 1610 | Germany | Yes |
| 7 | 1483 | Singapore | Yes |
| 8 | 815 | France | Yes |
| 9 | 771 | South Korea | Yes |
| 10 | 654 | Switzerland | Yes |

*Source*: Based on data from Department of Industrial Policy & Promotion, Government of India.

Figure 1:  Number of BITs Concluded (1995–05), year by year and Cumulative

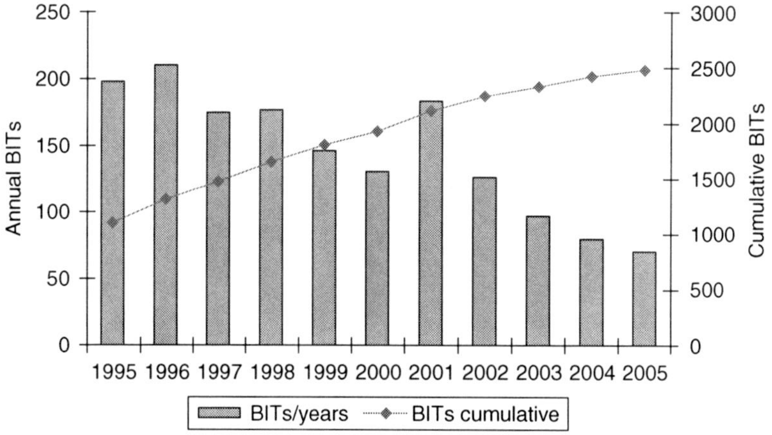

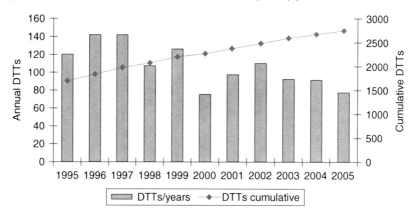

*Source*: UNCTAD 2006.

Figure 2:  Number of DTTs Concluded, (1995–05) year by year and Cumulative

*Source*: UNCTAD 2006.

Chart 1: Geographical Distribution of BITs as of July 2004

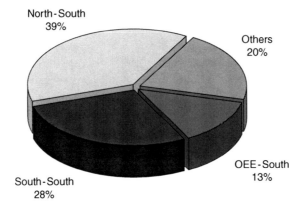

*Source*: UNCTAD 2006.

Chart 2: Distribution of PTIAs as of July 2004 (excluding BITs and DTTs)

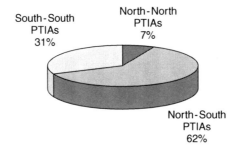

*Source*: UNCTAD 2006.